Urbanisation in China:

TOWN AND COUNTRY IN A DEVELOPING ECONOMY
1949–2000 AD

R. J. R. KIRKBY

CROOM HELM
London & Sydney

© 1985 R. J. R. Kirkby
Croom Helm Ltd, Provident House, Burrell Row,
Beckenham, Kent BR3 1AT
Croom Helm Australia Pty Ltd, First Floor,
139 King Street, Sydney, NSW 2001, Australia

British Library Cataloguing in Publication Data

Kirkby, R. J. R.
    Urbanisation in China: town and country
    in a developing economy 1949–2000 AD
    1. Urbanization — China — History —
    20th century
    I. Title
    307.7'6'0951   HT147.C48

ISBN 0-7099-1548-9

Photoset in English Times by Pat and Anne Murphy,
10 Bracken Way, Walkford, Christchurch, Dorset, England

Printed and bound in Great Britain
by Billing & Sons Limited, Worcester.

CONTENTS

FIGURES

TABLES

Tables

To
Zhou Nanshan and Li Yongshan

PREFACE

It was only a little over a decade ago that the crisis of urbanism — both in the advanced nations of the West and in the developing world — became a prominent concern of politicians, planners and academic geographers. To a minority, the general malaise seemed incurable within the given framework. The spatial problems of the cities were seen to be embedded in the broader structure of capitalist society. In the 1930s, the remarkable transformations of the Soviet Union had provided the shining model for the disillusioned; in the 1970s, the self-advertisements of Cultural Revolution China offered an alternative even more entrancing. Much of our fascination with peasant societies derives from a pro-rural sentiment which has survived (or, perhaps, is kept alive by) two centuries of industrial urbanism. Innate susceptibility to oriental mysteries — fuelled by the revolutionary rhetoric of Maoism and provoked by China's very inaccessibility — made the 'Chinese model' all the more attractive.

For urbanists the great appeal was that China claimed a rapid industrialisation without a parallel growth of the urban population, let alone the familiar pathologies of 'over-urbanisation'. Cultural Revolution travellers' tales confirmed that the Chinese cities were not ringed by shanty areas, that the colonies of the urban poor were absent, and that the ambience of the great metropolises was gentle and village-like. It was to witness all this that I first visited China in 1973; not satisfied with the regimen of political tourism — for there was no escape from it in those days — I decided that the way to find out about the Chinese road to urbanisation was to stay longer. From 1975 to 1977 I lived in Nanjing, and from 1978 to 1980 in the capital of Shandong Province — Jinan.

I was soon to discover that to the overwhelming majority of Chinese, the experience of building a revolutionary society had in no way dimmed the bright lights of the city. Indeed, in many respects the progressive policies of the Chinese government (in particular a stable urban wage economy) had *increased* their magnetism. Yet despite the obvious material and cultural differential between town and country, the flood from the villages was manifestly absent. If the rural people's communes had not eradicated at source the causes of 'push' from the land, the day-to-day experience of living in China left me in doubt that it was not revolutionary zeal which accounted for this lack of mass migrations. The actual reasons are analysed in chapter 2.

In recent years, the gathering of consistent and comparable economic and social statistics has taken on a new importance in China. Their publication has enormously aided our understanding of contemporary issues. But students of Chinese urban development have not shared in the new bonanza of data. The persistence of eccentric and impossible urban statistics has been a major stimulus for the present study. The result is a time-series for aggregate urban population provided in chapter 4 — which could only be pieced together by first establishing what 'urban' means with respect to modern China (chapter 3). The bare statistics show that far from industrialising without urbanising, post-1949 China has seen urban growth at a rate and on a scale unprecedented in world history. But equally unprecedented has been the great decanting of city populations — a drastic remedy peculiar to China's polity. A feature of the post-Mao era has been renewed urban growth on the grand scale: the wheel has gone full circle.

An aspect of the Chinese development process which has had considerable appeal abroad is its supposed avoidance of 'inequitable' concentration of urban populations. Chapter 5 evaluates the distributional aspects of urban growth, both in terms of its spatial disposition and its vertical concentration, and questions whether abstract notions of spatial egalitarianism are adequate as an explanation of major patterns of resource allocation. China has proclaimed a socialist revolution, but that does not free her from many of the constraints which surround the development process in a poor nation.

The central point of debate amongst China's urbanists today concerns the viability of a future urbanisation pattern founded on small settlements. The preference of many planners for such a strategy arises because of the severe congestion of the existing cities. The broad reasons for that congestion — which has arisen despite an artificial reduction in urban population in the 1960s and early 1970s — are discussed with reference to the key issue of urban housing policy (chapter 6).

Chapter 7 describes the sweeping changes in China's countryside which arise from an official determination to make the shift from a basically subsistence farming to a system of highly-productive agriculture. The consequences for the not-too-distant future will be that several hundred million people fewer will be required by tradition rural pursuits. The great question is where to accommodate this burgeoning non-agricultural population without over-burdening the urban sector, and without incurring the high economic costs associated with small-town industrialism. This conundrum, and the recent emergence of quite differing views on the subject, are discussed in chapter 8.

It may be felt that any serious study of China's urbanisation demands copious international comparisons. I do not share the view that China is an island; indeed, many of the fundamental issues confronting China are common to all the so-called developing countries. But the sheer size of the task of detailing China's urbanisation process has meant that it will be left to others to make the appropriate comparisons.

This book would not have been written without the encouragement of Michael Safier of University College London, and the support in the initial stages of the Overseas Development Administration, the British Academy and the Social Science Research Council. And it could not have proceeded had it not been for the cooperation of many people in China — in Nanjing and Shandong Universities, in the Ministry for Urban-Rural Construction and Environmental Protection, and in the Chinese Academy of Social Sciences. In particular, I should like to thank Mr. An Yongyu, Mme Xia Zonggan and Mr. Jin Jingyuan of the Ministry, Professors Song Jiatai and Cui Gonghao of Nanjing University Geography Department, and Professor Ma Xia and Mr. Gu Jirui of the Academy. John Dolfin of the Universities Service Centre (HK) also deserves my thanks, as do Nick Jeffrey and other of my colleagues at the Architectural Association Planning School in London. Finally, I should never have got through the tedium of writing a book without the electronic assistance of WordStar, and I am grateful to Ankie Hoogvelt for her advice on writing in the computer age.

China: Provincial Divisions and Capitals

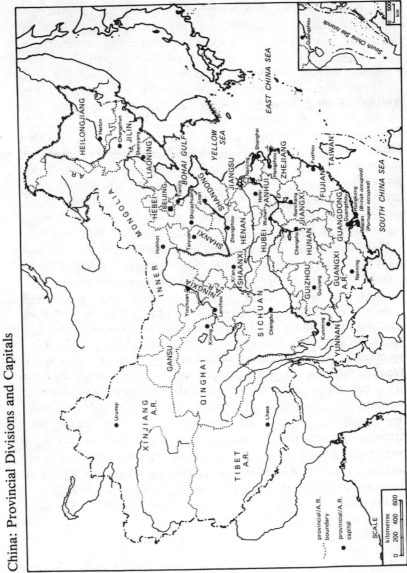

1 CHINA AND ANTI-URBANISM

Anti-urbanism in Marx and Engels

We are not provided with a blueprint for the socialist society of the future. But in so far as they addressed the question at all, it is customarily assumed that the prescription of Marx and Engels was for a strongly urban-centred economy. Take, for instance, these comments of an authority on Soviet housing:

> No Jeffersonian suspicion on the city and its evil ways existed in Marxist thought to hamper the Soviet leadership's . . . drive to the cities. The life of the future, the life of communism, is to be centered in the modern, highly organized city.[1]

A broader survey of the classic writings of Marxism shows this interpretation to be mistaken. In the early works, the new bourgeois class is applauded for its role in pushing forward history by creating a proletariat concentrated in large cities. When the *Manifesto of the Communist Party* speaks of the 'idiocy of rural life', the meaning seems unmistakable.[2] Yet in *The German Ideology* written a few years earlier, Marx and Engels had made their position on de-urbanism rather clearer. The antagonism between town and country must surely be abolished, but it cannot be prematurely wished away. Indeed, in the immediate future, the further attenuation of the capitalist mode of production will cause the urban-rural rift to deepen. It is in this sense that there should be rejoicing at the growth of an industrial labour force, and, incidentally, at the demise of the culturally-isolated and ignorant peasantry. Every step towards a heightening of the urban-rural gap is also a step towards its eventual abolition.

This perspective is developed further in the late writings of Engels. In his *Housing Question* of 1872–3, Engels demands 'as uniform a distribution as possible of the population over the whole country', and as a result, soon finds he has to defend himself against charges of utopianism. These emanate from a surprising quarter — those very social reformers who were more usually the

1

butt of the scientific socialists' accusations of naïvete. Tellingly, Engels' critics ridicule his extreme de-urbanism on the grounds that it is not the physical distinction between city and countryside which is crucial, but rather, the exploitative relationship between the two. In his vigorous but rather hollow defence, Engels now even finds a good word for Fourier and Owen, whom earlier he had habitually dismissed as mere idealists.[3]

The belief that nothing less is required than the physical eradication of the urban-rural differential is restated in *Anti-Dühring* (1876–8). An even spread of industry throughout a national territory, achieved through the application of an economic plan, 'has become a direct necessity of industrial production itself'. Engels goes on:

> The abolition of the separation of town and country is therefore not utopian . . . It is true that in the huge towns civilisation has bequeathed us a heritage which it will take much time and trouble to get rid of. *But it must and will be got rid of, however protracted a process it may be.*[4] (Emphasis added.)

Engels' anti-urbanist position of forty years before had been very different from that of the utopian socialists, who hoped their rural-based experiments would take root within the interstices of capitalism and gradually displace it. Yet by the 1870s, Engels' belief was that European capitalism had reached its apogee, and had therefore pushed forward the urban-rural distinction to its ultimate extreme. The extremely dynamic development of capitalism in these four decades had, ironically, brought his and the utopian socialists' views on the town and country question roughly into line.

It might be wondered why there has been no physical abolition of the cities in the first post-capitalist society, the Soviet Union. This is an important question, for it also bears on the possibilities of de-urbanisation in socialist China. In the 1920s, the de-urbanist position was certainly a lively issue in the grand debates on the future of Soviet society. By 1931, along with other 'lifestyle' issues, it had been eliminated as part of the anarcho-Trotskyist plot; the march of industrial urbanism was not to be hindered by any effete objections of the bourgeois intelligentsia.[5]

It is important to bear in mind that Marx and Engels were adamantly opposed to premature efforts to build a collectivist socialist society. They believed that this grand project could only safely be embarked on where capitalist development had pushed the technological level of production to its highest level, where the transforming forces of capitalism had penetrated to every nook and cranny of the society. They certainly did not envisage the possibility of revolution in a backward economy such as Russia's rapidly taking on an anti-capitalist character.

In the Soviet Union, then, history dictated that many of the tasks which, in the Marxist schema, capitalism was scheduled to perform, had now to take their course under an intrinsically anti-capitalist (and nominally socialist) regime. Thus the pushing forward of production in the Soviet Union of the 1920s and 1930s, and the increasing pace of urbanisation and proletarianisation brought about through the state's intervention in the economy, might be regarded as an equivalent stage to the process of capitalist development in late-nineteenth-century Britain upon which Marx and Engels based their initially pro-urban model.

That is, the condition of enhanced contradiction between town and country which held within it the seeds of a de-urbanised future had been far distant in the still largely agrarian society of late Czarism. If the agenda of capitalism was to be completed only under a nascent planned economy, one might still expect the de-urbanist programme to have made a belated appearance in the Soviet Union. But subsequent positions on the city and countryside question hold no hint that the powerfully-pursued strategy of massive urban industrialisation was regarded as a temporary stage, a mere stepping-stone to a de-urbanised society. For example, it is typical that in his visionary account of the socialist future written in the 1960s, Alexei Gutnov proposes 'world-wide urbanisation' and condems all notions of restoring the habits and the appearance of the countryside in the city as mere 'bourgeois naturalism'. Thus, planned proliferation of cities becomes the end in itself rather than a means towards their eventual dissolution.[6] After the debates of the 1920s had been buried, then, Soviet polemicists performed a complete, but never yet acknowledged, revision of the original Marxist notions on the town and country question in socialist society.

China's Anti-urban Image

That socialist China is wedded to a broad anti-urban strategy has long been received wisdom.[7] This would seem to be a most natural state of affairs, for China is not only an ancient agrarian society, but in the century of foreign incursion which began with the first Opium War and ended with the US intervention in support of the Guomindang, the cities became the repositories of alien corruption and vice. In supposedly opting for an anti-urban development strategy, it is suggested that the CPC chose to ignore both the classic Marxist prescriptions, and their faithful adoption by the great guide and Elder Brother, the Soviet Union. As we have seen in the previous discussion, the confusions are thus compounded.

So anti-urbanism, or — if preferred — pro-ruralism, is normally seen to be central to Maoist revolutionary tenets, and a guiding force in the CPC's choice of development strategy once it achieved power. Let us briefly rehearse some of the arguments which are marshalled in support of the anti-urban thesis. First, there are those which rest on matters relating to the origins of the Chinese revolution.

The most frequently encountered common-sense explanation for post-1949 China's supposed anti-urbanism lies in the means to state power taken by the Chinese Communist Party. The Bolsheviks came to centre-stage through a series of urban insurrections dependent on the muscle of the industrial proletariat. Not surprising, then, that Soviet development policies would thereafter show an urban bias, bringing spectacular urban-industrial expansion alongside a relative stagnation of agriculture. By contrast, the Chinese Communists owed their national ascendancy to a rural-based struggle resting on the massed ranks of the peasantry. After 1949, the argument goes, it was therefore only natural that the Party would show a leaning towards the peasantry and a sympathy towards rural problems.

Then there are the lines of reasoning which draw a close association between personal backgrounds and the overall direction of the Chinese revolution. We are reminded that on the eve of the Liberation, over 90 per cent of all Party members were of peasant origin. And most important, the single most influential personality of the Chinese revolution, Mao Zedong, hailed from peasant stock. We hear of Mao's 'attachment to the soil', his life-long preference for peasant simplicity and earthiness, his respect for their hard-working and honest spirit. Flowing from these rustic traits is his instinctive mistrust of Soviet (read 'city-centred') notions of how to build a socialist society — notions which emphasise modern technology, the need for a prior development of the (urban) productive forces, an acceptance of a fair degree of (usually urban-based) bureaucratic planning routines, and so on.

Secondly, there are those assertions of anti-urbanism which rest on the empirical evidence provided by various strands of post-1949 development policy. The Maoist reaction to urban elitism and technological determinism, we are given to understand, was the Great Leap Forward with its wholesale abandonment of urban-centred planning strategies. Instead, the key to communism was to be reliance on the spontaneous enthusiasm of the masses in city and countryside, and, most vitally, the magic mechanism of the rural people's communes. The Great Leap Forward set the stage for a whole number of policies favouring the countryside and penalising the cities, these encapsulated in the strategic slogan of the early 1960s — 'agriculture the base, industry the leading sector'.

The anti-urban direction of the Chinese revolution appeared to be brought to a higher pitch with the onset of the Cultural Revolution. On the one hand, there was the enormous attention given to the promotion of a self-reliant agriculture and on the other, the excision of tens of millions of urban educated from the cities in an effort, ostensibly, to dissipate the new and threatening forces of urban-based elitism while at the same time spreading modern skills more evenly throughout the land.

Pro-ruralism also seemed to be writ large in the enormous weight accorded to self-reliant agricultural development in the propaganda messages of the day. In particular, there was the powerful promotion of the Dazhai Brigade as a national model. Despite the considerable attention given to industry, it was the farms rather than the factories that dominated the self-advertisements of Cultural Revolution China.

In the realm of spatial planning, anti-urbanism was apparently underlined in the prominence given to the physical model of the Daqing oilfield. Here, the normal agglomerative tendencies of vigorous industrial development were being strongly resisted, and in their place was promoted a dispersed pattern of settlement and industrial location. This pattern was claimed by the Chinese to be the negation of urban bias, and as such was the spatial expression of the general egalitarian spirit of the Cultural Revolution.

These, then, are just some of the many issues which seemed to overwhelmingly confirm that the Chinese road to socialism was an anti-urban road. We shall re-examine them shortly.

Anti-urbanism and the Chinese Revolution in Perspective

Native Anti-urbanism

It cannot be denied that, although the relationship between town and country in traditional Chinese society is sometimes described as 'symbiotic', there was cause for a certain anti-urban sentiment on the part of the majority of China's population, the peasants.[8] Incipient anti-urbanism was born of the fact that the urban-based merchant and artisan classes occupied a lesser status, and were thus 'less virtuous' than the peasantry in general and the scholar-gentry in particular. Such feelings were greatly stimulated by the arrival in the early 1840s of foreign intruders on Chinese soil. Having established a military and commercial beachhead in Canton, the British with their art of divide-and-rule were able to collaborate with the merchants of the Co-Hong to good advantage. When the peasant bands rose up against the invading forces at Sanyuanli it was Canton's Chinese merchants, indeed its citizenry in general, who shared their wrath. As Wakeman notes:

> for the Cantonese, the figure of the 'traitor', the *han-chien*, coagulated all of the anti-urban, anti-merchantile and anti-foreign sentiments. The purism, the 'righteousness', of the rural gentry came to be shared by the peasantry.[9]

The Treaty of Nanjing (1842) was but the first of a long chapter of humiliations heaped on the Chinese nation by foreigners. If anti-urbanism had become a discernible trait in the China of the 1840s, a further half-century and more of military defeat, and the rude designation of ancient Chinese cities as foreigners' 'Treaty Ports' was to bring it to a much greater pass. It can, therefore, be assumed to have been an important ingredient in the formation of consciousness amongst the politically-aware youth of Mao Zedong's generation. And the mood was to extend beyond the righteous peasantry: in the creeds of the students' political study circles active in Beijing and Shanghai from 1917 to 1920 it formed a prominent feature. Taking their cue from newly translated Tolstoy and the Populists in general, leading left-wing thinkers such as Li Dazhao urged China's youth to abandon the tainted cities, and spend their energies in helping the wholesome peasants in their struggle to throw off the shackles of feudal ignorance.

In examining the direction of the Chinese Communist Party in power, we are bound to take account of the attitudes of the individuals (and especially the prominent figures) who formed it. There is every reason to believe that Mao Zedong himself was infected by the anti-foreign and anti-city climate of early-twentieth-century China. We know that Li Dazhao, the espouser of nationalist-populist theories, was an important influence on the youthful Mao. Even before his Beijing period, while still a student in Changsha, Mao had cultivated a deep-rooted disdain for the soft and flabby ways of the towns. According to his own account, this expressed itself in an ascetic rejection of city comforts and a penchant for forced marches through the countryside, for racing up mountains with his band of braves, and leaping into freezing wells.[10] Later, the struggles of the Party having begun in earnest, Mao's particular emphasis on the role of the peasantry in the revolutionary process came to the fore. His analyses of the rural class question undertaken in 1926 and 1927 were to be seminal works.[11]

A Peasant Party, A Peasant Revolution?

The question here is whether the anti-urban climate in which Mao and many of his comrades were socialised and politicised became a determining force in both the selection of the revolutionary battlefield and, later, when nationwide power had been won, in the choice of development policies. In the late 1920s, the CPC under Mao's influence had begun to grasp the interlinkages of the revolutionary process in China, of which the peasant struggle was a vital strand. But no leader, least of all Mao, was heard to demand that the Party's programme should be limited to the social transformation of the villages, or the establishment of a simple rural collectivism in isolation from the great cities.

For years the Communists were confined to remote rural base areas. In the Yanan period, foreign observers were tempted to portray the Party as having settled for some idyllic rural stasis.[12] This was a serious misreading: while the traditional cultivation and cottage industries of the revolutionary base areas would have more than satisfied the dreams of any nineteenth-century Russian populist, to the Communists they were no more than a pragmatic response to an enforced rural exile. Despite its populist imagery (commonly seen, for example, in the appeals to 'the Chinese people' rather than to specific classes), the rural-based Party under Mao never lost sight of its ultimate objective. This, as we shall see, was urban-based industrialisation, initially at least in the image of the Soviet Union.

Now we shall return to the idea that the Chinese and Russian revolutions had entirely dissimilar ambitions because of their different origins. First, we should not lose sight of the fact that the Chinese Communist movement did not abandon its city bases out of choice, but was forced from them at the point of a bayonet. From the moment they lost the cities, the Communists harboured ambitions to return.[13] But throughout the almost two decades of rural exile, a constant struggle had to be waged against the adventurist urge to stage an urban come-back which might prove to be premature and very costly. The genius of Mao's patient guerilla tactics was to ensure that the eventual return to the cities was not short-lived.

While it is over-deterministic to suggest that each phase of the Chinese revolution was a logical and planned precursor of the next, the analysis provided by Kau Ying-Mao is useful in evaluating 'peasant party, peasant revolution' interpretations of the CPC's long road to power. The road describes a cycle. In its first phase (1919 to 1927) it was unambiguously urban-based. From 1928 to 1945 the Communist movement had little choice but to be centred on the rural hinterland. The third phase, 1946 to 1949, saw a step-by-step return to the urban centres — through set-piece battles and the activation of underground Party workers in the cities. Finally, the revolutionary process was consummated in the great shift — in Mao's words — of its 'centre of gravity'.[14] So the process of the revolution began in the cities, and its momentum was eventually to bring it back. Once the Chinese revolution's gravitational centre had shifted to the cities, the overwhelmingly dominant concerns became urban/industrial, and the cyclical pattern changed to a linearity.

It will be recalled that the other argument centring on origins and roots of the Chinese revolution concerned the predominantly peasant composition of the CPC on the eve of national power. Would this not determine a pro-rural weighting in subsequent developments? In the first phase of its life, the Party had depended for its support on the urban workers. One study shows that in 1926, 66 per cent of the membership was classified as urban working class; the tragedy of 1927, and the terrible hardships of the Jiangxi base and the Long March (when over two-thirds of the original participants perished), meant that by November 1939 a mere 3 per cent of the membership was now of the urban proletariat. Nevertheless, the composition of the hierarchical Party was far from homogeneous. At the top of the pyramid, almost all of the seventy most influential individuals (those who at some stage had sat on the Party Central Committee before 1949) were either of urban origin, or of mixed urban/rural background. Like Mao, many had been born into peasant families but had gained their education and their formative experiences in the county towns and provincial capitals. Further down, 75 per cent of those classed as middle-level cadres, and just 5 per cent of grass-roots or village-level Party officials, had urban or rural/urban antecedents.[15]

Again, these facts are not offered with the purpose of con-clusively proving that the antecedents of its dominant personalities necessarily predisposed the CPC either to rural- or to urban-biased policies. The aim here is simply to challenge the common-sense interpretation which holds that the Party was made up mainly of peasants, and, ipso facto, the thrust of post-1949 policies was pro-countryside. One thing is quite clear, however: the orientation of the Chinese Communists on the eve of national victory was power-fully towards embracing the cities. In his speech at Pingshan County, Mao's admonitions hinted of the now scarcely containable urge within his forces to turn their backs on the village muck-heap.[16] He warned of the temptations and insidious corruptions of urban life, the 'sugar-coated bullets' which might threaten the very heart of the revolution. But in cities such as Canton shortly after-wards it was just as Mao had feared: 'They [the former guerilla fighters] were vulnerable to the pleasures of the city: food, women, drink and gambling', remarks Ezra Vogel. In the new urban setting of the revolution, 'guerilla mentality' was now an embarrassing hindrance.[17]

It is not suggested here that, had the upper echelons of the Party been occupied by persons of an exclusively rural background, its orientation regarding the city/countryside question would have been a foregone conclusion. A tendency to idealise agrarian societies has clouded our vision: for the average Chinese farmer, nature is a deeply hostile force, to be romanticised only by the comfortable poet and painter. Long association with village migrants to the cities of China has convinced this writer of a strong direct relationship between the earthiness of an individual's rural antecedents and the firmness of his attachment to the city and its ways. Early Populist and Marxist pleas for a de-urbanised future were a reaction to urban-industrialism and the profound disruption and squalor which it brought to nineteenth-century Europe.

Modern-day attachment to the same vision is kept alive in the West by the crumbling of the Victorian cities and, when projected elsewhere, by guilt at Third World urban squalor. Naturalism of the contemporary Western variety springs from a profound disturbance at the manifestations of industrial society. The imputation of anti-urbanism as the key to development processes in Communist China suggests a well-articulated native critique of industrialism. But the emergence of such a critique cannot be expected under conditions of agrarian backwardness, and has therefore yet to be seen in China.

Is Anti-urbanism Possible in China?

If we cannot allow that the CPC embodies a broad philosophy of anti-urbanism, is there not, nevertheless, a restricted sense in which the term is applicable to China's development strategy? I refer to the limitation, and at times the reduction, of China's urban population. Let us recall for a moment the most active phases of mass sending-down of city dwellers to the villages and small towns: the 'back to the villages' (*huixiang*) movement of the early 1960s resulted in the ejection of over twenty million people, and the 1966 to 1976 Cultural Revolution period saw the removal from the towns and cities of huge numbers of youth, of political officials and of the intelligentsia.

During these times, the de-urbanising impulse was in fact only one aspect of the whole. The *huixiang* was a drastic step necessitated by a sudden mass inflow of roughly equal proportions during the Great Leap Forward of just a couple of years before. The great sending-downs of the Cultural Revolution were almost matched in overall numbers by a simultaneous recruitment of peasants to the urban labour market. Most important to the present argument, this see-sawing is reflected in the overall figures for urban growth in the PRC. As is shown in detail in chapter 4, aggregate urban population has expanded almost three-fold in the thirty odd years since 1949. Even in its most confined definition, therefore, anti-urbanism seems an unwarranted description.

The Imperative of Accumulation. If we are to abandon the grand explanation of 'anti-urbanism' because it does not stand up empirically, or because in its broader sense it is plainly metaphysical, how can the thrust behind Communist China's undoubted transformation be understood? Unlike most developing nations past or present, industrialisation and economic development in China is mediated through conscious planning decisions. Or more-or-less conscious ones. In so far as 'less' applies here, it is partly because of ineptness in manipulating the highly complex process of planning an economy (and especially one as enormous as China's), but more because externalities impose their own agenda for planning. That is to say, the major priorities of the Chinese economy are determined by factors which are not immediately apparent.

At this stage, let us consider the nature of the Chinese state. Today the Communist Party is about 40 million strong, but only a few thousands of the senior members are directly and indirectly involved in the formulation of strategic decisions at the national level. In some areas such as foreign policy, there are only a handful of decision-makers. The top leaders of the CPC speak and act in the name of the broader rank and file. The Party as a whole substitutes itself for the people of China. Such is the nature of mass democracy in China today. But at the same time, the bureaucracy's objective function is not mainly to satisfy its own consumption needs, and still less is it to represent the interests of the defeated landlord and capitalist classes. Its independent purpose, and that of the Chinese state with which it is in a sense synonymous, is accumulation at the national level.

Accumulation can provide the wherewithal for deferred consumption, but at any given point in time the demands of each seem opposed. China's leaders have, undeniably, been personally concerned to better the lot of the people, and particularly of the most oppressed groups who backed them on their road to power. But the Party arrived at that power in a country racked by the severest impediments of backwardness. And because of native Confucianism and the influence of the Soviet model, it brought to its new tasks an authoritarian approach to the question of how power should be dispensed.

Thus, in its role as arbiter of the national economy, it has consistently tended to opt for a division of the national cake which grants as much to accumulation as the inchoate popular demands for consumption will tolerate. At the same time, in order to increase its room for manoeuvre, it has always pressed for an expansion of the surplus, an enlargement of the cake. Depending on the particular faction in the ascendancy, this has sometimes been attempted through moral exhortation, sometimes by naked material incentive, sometimes by political bludgeoning and fear, and occasionally by simply sending in the army. In the *Critique of the Gotha Programme*, Marx warned of the obstacles to progress in a socialist society that would be presented by its 'birthmarks'. In a backward society, forced into a premature anti-capitalist collectivism and surrounded by antipathetic forces, we can speak not of birthmarks but of congenital deformities.[18]

Obviously China, in common with other poor countries, has to cope with the economic pressures of an inimical world order. Though China's international trade is still miniscule in terms of the domestic economy, every time she steps into the marketplace, whether selling labour-intensive products or buying wheat and high technology, the cards are stacked against her. Only more advanced technical levels of production — sector by sector and item by item — can erode this structural exploitation. This factor is consciously registered by China's leaders and it provides a potent pressure for accumulation.

To add insult to injury, the dominant world capitalist economy works in more insidious ways to influence the priorities of national planning. Such are the global interlinkages and flows of information today that even in a comparatively enclosed nation such as China, popular perception of consumption needs is defined not by local/historical benchmarks but by the prevailing levels in the most industrially advanced nations. In as much as China's bureaucracy has to meet demands for improved living conditions, the agenda of planning is again partly determined by the capitalist world. The Party's instinctive response to such pressures is to strengthen the nation's economy through greater accumulation.

A most important source of the accumulation impulse lies in the general nation-building imperative. In 1949, the new regime's major preoccupation was to unify the country and to mark out and consolidate its boundaries. This was no simple matter, for even the traditionally cohesive heartland of Han China had been fragmented by warlordism, civil war and invasion. Firm incorporation of the vast regions of the periphery demanded an even greater effort.

Aggravating these difficulties of domestic cohesion has been a consistent threat from without. This appeared early on with the US-led attempt to roll back the Chinese revolution via the Korean peninsula and the Straits of Taiwan. The late 1950s saw a resurgence of the military pressure from the Americans and the

Guomindang in the south-east and south-west. Then came the troubles in Tibet and the border war with India. Throughout the 1960s, the increasing US presence in Indochina was viewed by Beijing as yet another spear aimed at the Chinese revolution. At the end of the decade came the serious skirmishes on the Sino-Soviet frontier which propelled the Chinese into an accommodation with Washington over the heads of their Vietnamese allies. Only in the late 1970s did the immediate pressure on China begin to diminish, and this can be said despite the persistence of the Taiwan problem, the volatility of the situation on the Vietnam and Laos borders after the 1979 conflict, and the continuing pressure from the Soviet forces massed around half of China, from Afghanistan to eastern Siberia.

The effort to assert and then preserve its national integrity has thus occupied a central place in overall Chinese policy. The tasks of national revolutions in Europe and the Americas — to stake out and defend territorial claims against all-comers, and to unify lands administratively and economically — have fallen to the Chinese Communist revolution in the twentieth century. And so long as there remain alienated territories (Taiwan, Hong Kong and, less prominently, Macao), the historic role of the Communist Party will be unfulfilled. Extraordinarily rapid industrialisation has been the means adopted by the CPC in pursuit and defence of its nation-building tasks.

It is such preoccupations as these that lie at the root of China's accumulation process. The broad objectives, moreover, are clearly stated by the Chinese leadership — in the past in such ambitions as overtaking Britain in steel production (this has not been difficult in recent years), and in the present period in building China into a 'strong' and 'modern' state by the year 2000. While agriculture and other aspects of economic life are always accorded some recognition in the stated planning programmes, the key consideration has remained the needs of industry. *The Chinese revolution has above all been an industrial revolution.*

This broad judgment is clearly supported by the bare bones of the newly-available data on agriculture and industry. Though at least four-fifths of the population have all along since 1949 been directly dependent on farming, in each of the five-year planning periods the industrial sectors have received from five to six times as much state investment as has agriculture. The consequences are forcefully illustrated: with industrial and agricultural output value each indexed at 100 in 1952, the rise by 1982 had been to just over 300 for the latter and to more than 2,100 for the former.[19]

Agriculture's Role. The agricultural sector's chief rationale in the grand design has been to service industry by providing both a surplus product and a ready source of labour. And at times its role has been that of a dumping-ground for the unrequired urban population. The countryside has acted as a reservoir and a cushion for the industrialisation process.

The Party's constant headache has been to ensure an adequate agricultural surplus. It has set about this not so much by central investments in agriculture as by reorganisation of production, by close supervision over the productive activities and consumption of the peasants, and by pressing for locally-financed capital construction. The 1950s witnessed a step-by-step collectivisation of agriculture which ended in 1958 with the establishment of the people's communes. The purpose was not merely socialist political rectitude. As in the Soviet Union of the early 1930s, collectivisation was intended to guarantee an adequate food surplus for the spiralling non-agricultural population, and the raw materials needed for industry. In recent years has come the painful recognition that collectivisation had become over-rigid, and as such basically counter-productive. The post-Mao retreat from the people's communes is a daring attempt to increase peasant well-being and, more importantly, to secure the agricultural surplus so desperately required by a new era of industrial advance.

Urban Production Versus Urban Consumption. Spatial configurations of economic activities and settlement are, naturally, a function of China's industrial-centred priorities. It is the industrialisation imperative that has shaped China's urbanisation, not abstract notions such as anti-urbanism. The primacy of urban production has never, in fact, been absent from the official messages. On the eve of Liberation the future role of cities had been clearly stated: henceforth they were to be transformed from slothful and effete 'consumer cities' (*xiaofei chengshi*) into tough and purposeful 'producer cities' (*shengchan chengshi*). No traveller to the People's Republic in the Mao years could avoid the endless repetition of this formula. The fetishisation of production was writ large — in the brief introductions of tour guides, in the slogans which festooned factory workshops, and in the moral tales of 'hard struggle and plain living'.

After decades of war and neglect, the Communist victory had found the cities in a parlous physical state. While a great deal of remedial effort was expended on urban problems in the early 1950s, the relentless industrial-urban growth of the first decade of the People's Republic brought ever-greater pressures on the fabric of the cities. In the villages, housing, transport to work, fuel and water supply, are all matters for the individual household. The Maoists could never quite accept that in the urban areas, these things now had to be provided by the state.

The Party was not opposed to the cities as cities. But its deepest instincts set it solidly against the demand for ever-greater *non-productive* urban expenditures (in housing, roads, public transport facilities, drains, electricity supply, shops, and so on) occasioned by industrial growth. One way out was to use the urban population more efficiently: while in the early 1950s, the labour participation rate averaged around 15 per cent, today it is around 60 per cent, a very high ratio indeed considering the youthful age structure.[20] Another way out, stressed in the current period, is to increase the technological structure of production.

It is not surprising that the prevailing productionism also meant an official shunning of those groupings which made no *tangible* contribution to urban output. Hence, it was always the brain workers (the intelligentsia and the pen-pushing funtionaries), as well as the potentially-unemployed youth, who became the prime targets in any urban manageability campaign. If they could not prove their worth in the cities, then they were sent off to the countryside.

Daqing Revisited. Let us return briefly to the example of Daqing. In the 1960s and 1970s, Daqing was, of course, the great model for China's industry. But it was also pressed upon the reluctant spatial planners, and in turn presented by foreign admirers of the Cultural Revolution as the living proof of China's unique 'agropolitan' development strategy. Their enthusiasm is excusable, as the Chinese descriptions made Daqing appealing on both the practical and the ideological levels. To quote one writer in the then *Peking Review*:

The conventional way of developing a big mine or oilfield under capitalism is to build a city right there or a distance away . . .

When Taching [Daqing] was being opened up in 1960, some people bound by capitalist and revisionist conventions wanted to build a 'petroleum city' 30 kilometres away. But Taching broke away from this traditional concept . . . Chairman Mao pointed out [that] 'big enterprises should engage in agriculture, trade, education and military training as well as industry'.

Furthermore, fortuitous support of the Daqing model was supplied by the Marxist classics:

The revolutionary teachers of the proletariat long ago pointed to the need to eliminate the differences between town and country and between worker and peasant in communist society. Marx and Engels in the *Manifesto of the Communist Party* called for 'combination of agriculture with manufacturing industries, gradual abolition of the distinction between town and country'.[21]

In reality, the greatest virtue of Daqing was that it provided industrialisation on the cheap. The main burden of housing and feeding the oilfield's population was thrust on to the backs of the workers and their families. Not only had they to move to the hostile environment of Heilongjiang, but once there they were obliged to grow their own food, and provide themselves with rough houses of tamped earth.

Meanwhile, the problems of congestion and neglect in the great cities were becoming ever more pronounced. Though the pretence of its great value had to be maintained, it was clear that the Daqing model had nothing to offer them except the old exhortations to produce more and consume less.

Obviously it is in the nature of things that an oilfield built on virgin territory will in its early days display a dispersed pattern of settlement. By 1983, Daqing was dominated by a single great metropolis of 760,000 persons.[22] The chimerical nature of Daqing-style anti-urbanism is now plain to all.

Limitation of Urban Size: Its Pro-Industrial Purpose. Earlier, we considered a minimal definition of anti-urbanism — the limitation of urban growth. When this has occurred, it has not been for the sake of abstract revolutionary principle, but because of a keen understanding that over-inflation of the cities would threaten the great objective of optimum industrial growth. The threat loomed in two main ways: firstly, mass migrations from the villages would deprive agriculture of its labour force, with catastrophic results during the labour-intensive periods of planting and harvesting. Secondly, the growth of urban population without corresponding expansion in the available food surplus, and in expenditures on the urban fabric and essential services, would present a political threat. The CPC had had long experience of management in the rural milieu, and had developed a certain mastery of the class and production situations. In these and in the arts of war, in which it was initially ignorant, its struggles had made it an 'insider' (*neihang*). But in the cities, with their potentially competing social groupings and unfamiliar forces of production and exchange, it felt itself to be *waihang* — an outsider. In the new, urban arena the Party was thus far less confident, far more aware of the need for caution and for the maintenance of civil stability; it feared the emergence of social dissatisfactions which might easily challenge its new mandate. The imperative of industrialisation meant minimal investments in non-productive urban infrastructure, and thus the only safe recourse was to restrict migratory flows to the cities and periodically — when the imbalance between demand and supply became manifest — to shift people out to the villages.

The Party has, then, sought to protect its historic mission of industrialisation by guaranteeing urban manageability. It has also perceived another, more cataclysmic threat to its purpose. Back in 1960, Mao announced: 'We must disperse the residents of the big cities to the rural areas and construct numerous small cities, for under the conditions of atomic war this would be comparatively beneficial.'[23] While such perceptions were less significant in determining location in the 1960s, by the early 1970s the expectation of attack by the Soviet Union had brought the active policies of *shan san dong* (literally, 'dispersal to the mountains and caves'). Many productive and research units were uprooted from their eastern, and particularly north-eastern, locations and transferred wholesale to the interior provinces (Sichuan was a favourite destination — see Appendix Table A5.8). A shroud of secrecy will probably continue to hang over these events; it is unlikely, though, that they affected more than a few million people — a drop in the Chinese ocean. While foreign observers were aware of these relocational policies, they accepted the explanation that their aim was aid to the interior, prevention of unfair concentration of resources, and so on. Providing the most congenial — and convenient — answer is an old Chinese tradition. Generally considered, the purpose of constraining urban concentration in China has been to *enhance*, rather than to curtail, the role of the cities as loci of production.

Anti-urbanism and False Consciousness. It would seem that certain anti-urban sentiments have contributed to our evaluation of China's development process as anti-urban. Sometimes these seemed to be justified by the attitudes discovered amongst ordinary Chinese. For example, in China today, a subjective disdain for the cities (and especially for the former Treaty Ports) is apparent. Take Shandong's sober captial of Jinan and the province's main port, Qingdao. Jinan people consider their Qingdao cousins to be fast-talking, pleasure-seeking, wheeler-dealing, and generally 'too fashionable'. In the late 1970s, Qingdao students at the provincial university in Jinan felt constrained to guard against any indiscretion which would expose them to local displeasure. Particularly obvious was their tendency to dress down, to cultivate a peasant look. The same amusing behaviour was evident in Nanjing's Shanghainese residents. But this 'anti-urbanism' is shallow and contradictory. Given the chance, few Jinanese would turn down the opportunity to move to brazen Qingdao. What is seen here is not so much anti-urbanism as inverted snobbery.[24] Certainly, the Chinese themselves never articulate such residual suspicions of big city life in terms of anti-urbanism. We have come by various loose definitions of the concept as it has been applied to China. It is significant that none of them elicits any recognition in China itself.

Finally, perhaps the most important factor behind the anti-urban scenario has been our own Western susceptibility to agrarian utopias and oriental fantasy. The ambience of the Chinese city — the apparently gentle pace of life, the throngs of bicycles, the village-like lanes and vegetable patches — in short, the absence of many of the familiar urban attributes of Europe and America — all contribute towards an anti-urban illusion to which Westerners seem predisposed. If the Chinese are united in one thing, it is in a shared consciousness of struggle against the ravages of nature; it is an irony that we should choose to project on to such a people our own naive rusticism.

Notes

Explanations of the abbreviations used will be found in the Glossary.

1. A. J. DiMiao Jr., *Soviet Urban Housing: Problems and Policies* (Praeger, New York, 1974), p. 43.
2. K. Marx and F. Engels, 'Manifesto of the Communist Party', *Selected Works* (Foreign Languages Publishing House, Moscow, 1958), vol. 1, p. 38.
3. F. Engels, *The Housing Question*, first published as three articles in 1872 (Progress Publishers, Moscow, 1954), pp. 87–97.
4. F. Engels, *Anti-Duhring 1876–78* (Foreign Languages Publishing House, Moscow, 1954), pp. 411–12.
5. For a number of different evaluations of the debate in the Soviet Union, see El Lissitzky, *Russia — An Architecture for World Revolution* (first published in Vienna in 1930; English edition — Lund Humphries, London, 1970).
6. A. Gutnov *et al.*, *The Ideal Communist City* (first published in Moscow in 1966; English edition — George Braziller, New York, 1970), pp. 1–5.
7. The 'anti-urban' thesis is to be found, for instance, in: C. P. Cell, 'Deurbanization in China: The Urban-Rural Contradiction', *Bulletin, Concerned Asian Scholars*, vol. 11, no. 1 (1979), pp. 62–72; L. J. C. Ma, 'Anti-Urbanism in China', *Proceedings of the Association of American Geographers*, vol. 8 (1976), pp. 114–18; C. L. Salter, 'Chinese Experiments in Urban Space: The Quest for an Agropolitan China', *Habitat*, vol. 1, no. 1 (1976), pp. 19–35; M. B. Farina, 'Urbanization, deurbanization and class struggle in China 1949–79', *International Journal of Urban and Regional Research*, vol. IV (December 1980), pp. 487–501; R. Murphey, 'Chinese Urbanisation under Mao', *Urbanization and Counter-Urbanization*, vol. 11 (1976), pp. 311–28.
8. For an analysis of the characteristics of the Chinese city in history, see R. Murphey, 'The City as a Centre of Change: Western Europe and China', *Annals of the Association of American Geographers*, vol. 44 (1954), pp. 349–62.
9. F. Wakeman Jr., *Strangers at the Gate: Social Disorder in South China 1839–1861* (University of California Press, Berkeley, 1966), p. 51.
10. For further insights into the formation of Mao's thought, see: M. Meisner, *Li Ta-chao and the Origins of Chinese Marxism*, (Harvard University Press, Cambridge, Mass., 1967); S. R. Schram, *The Political Thought of Mao Tse-tung*, 6th edn (Praeger Publishers, New York, 1976), pp. 28–34; also, the interviews with Mao Zedong in Edgar Snow's classic, *Red Star over China* (numerous editions in Pelican).
11. Mao Tse-tung, 'Report on an Investigation of the Peasant Movement in Hunan', in *Selected Works of Mao Tse-tung*, Volume I (Foreign Languages Press, Peking, 1965), pp. 23–59.
12. For instance, M. Gayn, 'Mao Tse-tung Reassessed' in F. Schurmann and O. Schell (eds), *China Readings — 3: Communist China* (Penguin, Harmondsworth, 1968), pp. 91–107.
13. The ensuing framework is that of Y-M. Kau, 'Urban and Rural Strategies in the Chinese Communist Revolution' in J. W. Lewis (ed.), *Peasant Rebellion and Communist Revolution in Asia* (Stanford University Press, Stanford, 1974) pp. 253–70.
14. Mao Tse-tung, 'Report to the Second Plenary Session of the Seventh Central Committee of the Communist Party of China' in *Selected Works of Mao Tse-tung*, Volume IV (Foreign Languages Press, Peking, 1961), p. 363.

15. Y-M. Kau in Wilson, *Peasant Rebellion and Communist Revolution in Asia*, pp. 265–6.

16. Mao Tse-tung in *Selected Works of Mao Tse-tung*, Volume IV, p. 374.

17. E. Vogel, *Canton under Communism: Programs and Politics in a Provincial Capital, 1949–1968* (Harvard University Press, Cambridge, Mass., 1969), pp. 59–60.

18. Karl Marx, *Critique of the Gotha Programme*, written in 1875 (English edition: Foreign Languages Press, Peking, 1972), p. 15.

19. TJNJ 1983, pp. 17, 324–5; the industrial investments mentioned here include, of course, some sectors which directly benefit agriculture — farm machinery, fertilisers, etc. These agricultural investment figures are listed as 'agriculture, forestry, water conservancy and meteorological work'.

20. Kang Yonghe, RKYJ, no. 1 (1982), pp. 17–18.

21. Chiang Shan-hao, 'Taching [Daqing] Impressions (IV): Combining Urban and Rural Life', *Peking Review*, no. 27 (27 May 1977), p. 24.

22. Ding Yaolin, 'Daqing Oilfield Today', *Beijing Review*, no. 13, (28 March 1983), pp. 23–5.

23. Cited by E. Friedman, 'On Maoist Conceptualizations of the Capitalist World System', *China Quarterly*, no. 80 (December 1979), note 35, p. 826 (from the unofficial editions of Mao's speeches and writings published in the Cultural Revolution and known as *Mao Zedong sixiang wansui*).

24. Observed by the author while working in Nanjing and Jinan in the 1970s.

2 MEASURES TO RESTRAIN URBAN GROWTH

Long before the advent of the Communist Party rule in China, Mao had explained his own views on the role of migration in the socialist economy of the future:

> The peasants are the future industrial workers of China and tens of millions of them will go to the cities. For if China wants to construct large-scale, indigenous industry and to build a great number of large modern cities, then she will have to undergo a long process of transformation in which the rural population become residents of the cities.[1]

Such a scenario came naturally, for had not the 'Elder Brother' of the Soviet Union experienced precisely such a shift in the urban-rural population balance during the first years of planned industrialisation? Indeed, far from restricting migration to the cities during the First Five Year Plan, the Soviet authorities had actively encouraged it.

After twenty years of exile from the cities, the Communists made no secret of the fact that they viewed their new tasks of urban management with some trepidation. They now had to learn to cope not only with commerce, banking, and factory production, but, more disconcertingly, with the potentially competing groupings of a complex social order. The Communist Party was determined to deal with these challenges in its own way, and on its own terms. To maintain political hegemony of the cities it was essential to ensure that their inhabitants were housed, clothed, employed and — most importantly — fed. Urban manageability was seen as the precondition for fulfilment of the strategic task of the new age — the transformation of 'consumer cities' into 'producer cities'.[2] It was in pursuit of this pragmatic purpose that China was obliged, from the mid-1950s on, to introduce strong measures to restrain urban population growth.

The necessity for the introduction of stern state controls over individual mobility and domicile arose out of the fundamental rift between urban and rural living standards, and the 'migratory gradient' which is its natural consequence. Ironically, the town/ country division of Chinese society has been aggravated, ossified even, by the wage and welfare standards which the regime early on bestowed on the urban-industrial sector. This is not to deny that the CPC has put a great deal of effort into lifting the siege of the cities by eliminating the basis of the urban/rural differential at source. Witness the campaigns to bring mass literacy and mass culture to the villages, to provide the safety net of the 'five guarantees' for the rural disadvantaged, and to establish a basic collective medical system in the countryside. Yet the statistical evidence now confirms what the rare outside observer could see with his own eyes — throughout the Mao period, the great gap between town and country persisted. Indeed, in some parts of the country it probably grew wider in the twenty years after 1958.[3]

The formal adoption of a centrally-planned collectivist economic strategy (augmented by a state monopoly over foreign trade) is the necessary condition for setting a poor nation on the road to socialism, but it cannot guarantee instant socialist remedies. China in 1949 was overwhelmingly an agrarian society; for all the talk of 'eliminating the three great differentials',[4] industrial expansion was bound in its initial phase to be chiefly financed by the rural producers. The burden on the countryside was made all the greater by certain conscious policy decisions: first, largely as a response to the external threat presented by the Western powers, the CPC decreed a very rapid pace of industrial growth. Secondly, it set urban living standards (and particularly grain consumption) at relatively high levels. Third, for most of the period between 1958 (the birth of the rural communes) and 1978, it prevented the peasantry from supplementing their income through traditional handicrafts, small-scale livestock rearing, and petty trading. The rationalisation for this was presented in ideological terms, but the underlying reason was the state's obsessive concern to restrict peasant energies to grain and cash-crop production which would benefit the non-agricultural sector.

Thus the migratory gradient from countryside to city has been a fundamental characteristic of China's incipient industrialisation under the Communists. Indeed, since 1949 there have only been three brief interludes during which this gradient has somewhat levelled out. The first of these was at the time of the Land Reform movement of the late 1940s and early 1950s, when small numbers of people with rural connections returned to the villages to take their share of the land confiscated from the landlords and rich peasants. The second instance was in the early 1960s, when urban citizens with rural backgrounds considered that the temporarily-liberalised regime in agriculture offered better opportunities than the urban way of life. The third (and longest-sustained) phase is that of the present, and it arises directly from the radical changes in rural policy brought in by the post-Maoist regime of Deng Xiaoping, Zhao Ziyang and Hu Yaobang. In 1979 came the dramatic increase in purchase prices of agricultural goods; arguably, at a single stroke this did more to narrow the urban-rural gap than had twenty years of the people's communes. Equally important has been the virtual abandonment of collective agricultural production and remuneration, in favour of the 'contract system' of farming. A corollary has been the enormous diversification of rural employment opportunities. Both these radical reforms have, since 1979, brought a swift increase in rural income, and the statistics show that though there is great unevenness between regions, year by year the overall urban-rural consumption gap is fast narrowing. A sure sign of the changing balance is the increasing number of rural Chinese who, in the mid-1980s, no longer yearn for the chance to head for the nearest city.[5]

For almost all of the period between 1949 and 1979, therefore, the impulse for rural-to-urban migration was intense. Given the Party's preoccupation with urban manageability, the official response has had to be equally powerful. Hence the emergence in the 1950s of a complex of measures designed not merely to prevent migration to the urban areas, but also — whenever an imbalance between the demand and the supply of jobs, housing and grain threatened — to decant the existing urban population from city to countryside and from eastern metropolis to hinterland township.

Already by 1952, the provisional organs of the new Chinese state began to sound the alarm over the scale of the drift to the urban areas. A memorandum of the Central-South Military and Administrative Commission warned: 'After the rural autumn harvest, a slack period has set in, and a large number of peasants are bound to move blindly to the cities, thereby increasing the number of unemployed'.[6] The industrial expansion demanded by the First Five Year Plan sucked in hundreds of thousands of peasant recruits each year. But the Communists had set themselves the task of turning 'consumer cities' into productive engines of the new socialist order. The first step had proved difficult enough — the finding of jobs for some four million urban unemployed in the period immediately after 1949. Now the flood from the villages threatened the very rationale of China's new socialist urbanism. The mass deportations of newly-arrived peasants ordered by many large cities in these early days were felt to be too uncoordinated and limited a solution. The pressing problem of the 'blind influx of the rural population' (*nongcun renkou mangmu wailiu*) began to receive increased official attention, and between 1953 and 1958 was addressed by a number of ever-sterner directives issued by central state organs.[7]

In 1955, good harvests and the success of the deportation programme in various large cities were sufficient to allay some of the earlier fears. But the flood to the cities soon gathered pace once again, the *People's Daily* reporting in February 1957 that the municipalities were carrying a 'floating population' of over two million.[8] Of particular concern to the authorities was the perceived imbalance between the employed and the dependant population. A survey of 1957 showed how, for fifteen large cities, productive employment had increased by an average of 28 per cent between 1953 and 1956, service industry employment by 5 per cent, and the dependant population by a huge 70 per cent. The latter category had come to constitute 60 per cent of the combined population of the cities in question.[9]

By 1957, the problem of 'blind influx' into China's cities finally brought the intervention of the highest bodies of Party and state, with the Central Committee and the State Council issuing a joint directive exhorting tighter controls over migrants.[10] In January 1958, the National People's Congress passed more specific regulations intended to put a stop to unauthorised population movements.[11]

The Party had, therefore, soon moved from its initial position of passivity regarding peasant movement to the cities to a system of formal controls over personal mobility and domicile. These controls have not always to be entirely watertight, though their flagrant disregard in late 1958 (during the Great Leap) was never to be repeated. But they can, nevertheless, be regarded as key instruments in planning human resource allocation in the industrialising economy. They lie at the root of China's peculiar pattern of urban growth, and the ability to repress or — as in the early 1960s — reverse the urbanisation process. We shall now move on to examine the particulars of China's urban growth restraint system, these broadly dividing into two groups — measures to prevent migration into the urban areas on the one hand, and those designed to decant existing urban populations on the other.

Passive Measures to Restrict the Growth of Urban Population — Migration Controls

Population and Employment Registration

Article 10 of the 1958 law issued by China's parliament, the National People's Congress, declared that each household should have a 'permanent registration booklet' (*hukou bu*).[12] The registration system divided the entire population between those with 'urban residence' (*chengshi hukou*) and those having 'rural residence' (*nongcun hukou*). The purpose was not merely to monitor population movements, but to anchor people to their native places, and — in particular — to prevent unauthorised movement from the countryside to the city. One of the most important functions of the civil police authorities has been to supervise population movements and maintain the household registration records, special 'registration police' being located in every urban neighbourhood.

Temporary residence in the urban areas is possible without a change in registration, but only with the sanction of the local officers. It is granted to those who are visiting relatives (especially to elderly peasants who often spend prolonged periods with their urban children), to contract workers, and to persons on official missions away from home who have the necessary 'letter of introduction' (*jieshao xin*) from their parent unit. Registration police are aided in their task by a local network of unpaid functionaries who report on strangers in the neighbourhood and on various comings and goings. Everyone is expected to keep their residence document close at hand.

The residence system is buttressed by registration of employment. Every employed person is issued with a small red booklet containing his or her photograph and personal details, as well as the name of the employing unit (the all-important *danwei*). This is the 'work identity document' (*gongzuo zheng*). Regulations which evolved in the 1950s, and were finalised in 1958, stated that a would-be migrant to the cities could only depart from the village with a police permit. In theory, this could only be issued on the production of an invitation from an urban labour bureau, an educational institution, or from an urban public security organ.

The Rationing System

Since the 1950s, a rationing system has been applied which at various points has encompassed almost all foodstuffs, other consumables and consumer durables. The complexities of this equitable but tedious system, ever-changing and ever-varied between cities and regions, would on their own provide the subject for a major study. Suffice it to say that the rationed allocation of two essential items, edible oil and grain, has been the major instrument in physically preventing prolonged illicit residence in the towns and cities.

The all-important rationing of foodgrains dates from August 1955, when the State Council issued its 'Provisional regulations for the supply of fixed quantities of grain in the cities.[13] Standards laid down by the central authorities determine monthly quotas for every section of the non-agricultural population. Those in heavy manual occupations (for example, in mining and the metallurgical industries) may be allowed up to 25 kg of rice, wheat flour or other foodgrains. Sedentary work qualifies for much lower rations, teachers and officials getting around 15 kg monthly, and children less according to age. The administration of the grain rationing system varies from province to province, but in all cases it is dependant on the individual's possession of the urban household registration documents, grain being purchased monthly at the neighbourhood grain shop to which the family is assigned by the registration police. The mix of allocated grains depends on the state of the harvest nationally, on regional tradition, and in cases of migrants from distant places (where special pleading is possible) on the grain of his or her place of origin.

It should be borne in mind that throughout almost all the period since 1949, the overall grain surplus available for distribution to the non-agricultural population has been extremely limited. Furthermore, in the rare circumstances in which the peasantry have had personal grain surpluses, they have not been permitted to dispose of them by sale to the urban population. Grain rationing has proved, therefore, an extremely potent instrument of control over migration. Its value to the state is directly reflected in the fluctuating value of the grain ration tickets (*liangpiao*) on the black market: after the disastrous period of starvation of 1960 and 1961, for instance, the street value of a one-*jin* ration ticket ('worth' around 15 Chinese cents at the time) was over three *yuan*.[14]

Impact and Ramifications of Passive Controls: Some Observations

Throughout the 1950s, the effectiveness of registration and rationing measures proved uneven. With the activities of illicit brokers, an informal labour market continued to circumvent the official processes of the labour bureaux. 'Black' labour could be used as a poorly-paid and flexible reserve. The considerable numbers of peasant migrants who took up unregistered self-employment in the cities, relying on their families back in the villages for grain, were also difficult to control in the absence of strong neighbourhood monitoring of illegal residence. Gradually, however, the system of controls became more effective; despite the onslaught of millions of peasant migrants in the short period of the Great Leap Forward (1958–9), by the early 1960s it had become sufficiently powerful to provide the administrative means of deportations on an unprecedented scale.

The early years of the Cultural Revolution saw a spectacular collapse of most established norms, and for a short time the regulations governing population movement were ignored by millions of young people roaming the country in the great 'exchange of revolutionary experience'. But by 1968, the army had been called in, and a semblance of public order restored. The ferocious political campaigns which marked the remaining years of the Cultural Revolution produced a climate which was powerfully inimical to all forms of social deviance.[15]

Once again, in 1974, the residence and rationing regulations began to be flouted on a large scale. Hundreds of thousands of young people filtered back to their home cities, preferring to live on their wits in familiar surroundings than to endure further a rural exile. The families to whom they returned were able to supplement official food rations by purchases on the black market.[16] The free peasant market in grain and other produce was still officially outlawed as a dangerous vestige of capitalism. Yet in most cities from 1974 onwards, the peasant traders made an irregular appearance. In certain back streets of Nanjing, for example, it was usually possible to get hold of a variety of vegetables, even a chicken or a little rice. From time to time the local militia would launch a clean-up campaign, scouring the streets for hawkers, loading them on trucks and dumping them in some remote corner of the countryside. A week or a month later — depending very much on the overall political temperature — they would be back again.

During the late 1960s and early 1970s, recruitment of rural labour by urban units continued at a high rate, for demand could not be met from urban school-leavers who were mostly sent out of the cities. Indeed, between 1966 and 1976, the city labour bureaux authorised the transfer of 14 million peasants, not far off the 17 million 'sent-down' youth of the same period.[17] But unlike in the days of the First Five Year Plan, by the 1960s the rule was to recruit single people (predominantly young males) and permit them alone to effect a change in residence registration. Until the late 1970s, another route to urban employment and residence favoured by single males was a spell in the armed forces: demobilisation usually meant a good city post.[18] Of course, the practice of rural youth leaving for a period of work in the nearby town was hardly an invention of the Communists. Long before 1949, young men had customarily gone off to the nearby town to work for a period in the craft industries and workshops of the day. Far from being able to abandon this form of urban recruitment — as had been mooted in the early days after Liberation — soon it came to be regarded as indispensable to the urban economy. The advantages were many-fold. There was less pressure on housing, as accommodation for single employees is normally provided by their work-units in stark and densely-packed dormitories. The needs of urban production could be met, yet the unwanted extra pressures on the urban fabric caused by a dependant population could be completely avoided.[19] And, most importantly, the central state authorities were not faced with a much-increased burden of urban grain supply. On the rural side there were also advantages: during the frenetic harvesting and planting seasons, those dependants left behind — female peasants, old people and children — could be fully utilised. And the maintenance of close property relations in the countryside offered a safety net in the event of any strain on the urban economy which required the shedding of industrial labour.

China's labour recruitment policies may have proved economi-cally advantageous, but they have separated families and heightened social distinctions between town and country. Factory hands who come from the nearby countryside can return for a few hours each week: the exodus of bicycles, their carriers draped with brightly covered bed-quilts, is to be seen in any city on a Saturday afternoon. But for the millions whose origins are further afield, the lonesome city existence is punctuated by home visits only once or twice yearly. And during the Mao era at least, separation from family was an ordeal with no prospect of end. If a marriage match had been made in the village, so it was; divorce was almost impossible to secure, and extra-marital relationships taboo. As one former university colleague (separated for twenty years from his illiterate peasant bride) frequently lamented, his arranged marriage and enforced separation through the household registration system made him a victim both of the feudal past and the present realities of New China.

Even the single male without any marriage contract in his native place would not find it easy to marry out of the village. Many urban families would not countenance the stigma of a match so close to the soil. It is remarkable that such prejudice is common even amongst those who are themselves first-generation urban dwellers. In the mid-1970s, when this writer was resident in Jiangsu, marriage between the rigid categories of 'worker' and 'peasant' was rare enough. On the extraordinary occasion, however, when a girl from an 'intellectual' family background married an ordinary peasant lad, it was cause for a whole series of glowing articles in the provincial newspaper. It is a fact that of the tens of millions of rusticated youth — the 'new peasants' of the Cultural Revolution — the number who actually married into the peasantry was miniscule.[20]

One case closely observed in 1976 in a provincial unversity is worth recalling, for it illustrates not merely the human costs of the states's monopoly over domicile, but also the accentuation of the rural-urban divide which the *hukou* system has tended to bring. Day after day, the whole university community was privy to a tirade of denunciation against its leaders, presented in a series of wall-posters pasted up on the main gates by a fiery young peasant woman.[21] The essence was that her betrothed — now a university student — had realised that contrary to earlier expectations, he was not going to be sent back to the village after graduation. Wherever the state assigned him (most likely in a city), it would be certain that his supposed future wife would not be allowed to accompany him. Therefore, he had decided to break off the relationship rather than risk a lifetime of family separation. A basic feature of post-1949 organisation is the power over individuals vested in the Party leaders of work-units, and this *in loco parentis* relationship is all the stronger in educational institutions. By accusing the university authorities of abetting the student's decision (thereby helping to produce 'bourgeois intellectuals' who turned their back on their rural antecedents) the young woman had hoped to force them to impose an outcome favourable to her. She was not successful.

None the less, despite all the difficulties entailed in the single-person recruitment policies (for example, the spartan barrack-room existence), and despite, too, the economic exploitation implicit in the system (cheap and unpleasant canteen food, lack of medical care for spouse and offspring, and so on), in the pre-1979 period at least there was never any shortage of willing candidates. This is a telling measure of the huge gap between city and countryside which twenty years of the people's communes did little to narrow. No peasant family could afford to forego the economic advantage which a member in the urban wage economy offered. In certain times and places it could still — even in the 1970s — mean the difference between impoverished survival in the village and being driven to a wandering beggary.[22]

Post-1978 Developments. In the period after 1978, the measures to control urban growth by restricting migration began to lose a great deal of their sharpness. The reasons were several, but foremost amongst them has been a growing rural prosperity arising directly from the decision to abolish the collective system of rural work and remuneration.[23] The quest for urban household registration becomes increasingly irrelevant where labour in the village (whether it be in agriculture, sidelines, or services) is more financially rewarding. On the other hand, some aspects of the reformed rural system have encouraged the unauthorised drift into the urban areas. In particular, as part of the effort to diversify rural employment, ever-greater numbers of rural artisans and labourers have been allowed to go off in search of jobs in the construction trades. Indeed, the enormous urban housing programme of the post-1978 period would not have been possible without extensive employment of peasant contract labour. By the beginning of 1984, there were over 4 million peasant builders working away from their home areas. Many have gone great distances, with skilled Jiangsu workers now contributing to major urban projects as far afield as Karamai in Xinjiang and Shenzhen in Guangdong. Having completed their contracted period, these people are supposed to leave the cities, but a large proportion manage to stay on through illicit contracts with state units, or in various forms of casual employment.[24]

The opportunities for female peasants in the cities are fewer, though in the early 1980s the growth of private domestic service in the households of higher cadres and the intelligentsia became a further avenue for unregistered and, hence, illegal urban residence. A much larger group of female peasants — and their children — have entered the cities since 1979 for other reasons. They are the spouses of men recruited at an earlier stage into urban employment. Take, for example, the case of a middle-aged woman known personally to this writer. Unusually literate and resourceful, she had left her village and brought her three children to the provincial capital, where her husband had long been employed as a clerk. The move brought considerable initial inconvenience, not least being that of accommodation, for the family of five had no alternative but to crowd into the single room allocated by the husband's unit. An important objective was to secure a good education for their children, who through the quiet intervention of an influential official, were soon enrolled in a good school in the neghbourhood. The husband's work-unit was willing to turn a blind eye — perhaps because his wife had lost no time in making herself useful as a domestic help to some of the unit leaders. In the meantime, unsuccessful representations were made to the local public security bureau in order to obtain the transfers of household registration from rural to urban *hukou*. Eventually, more steady employment came up, and the woman and around forty others in a similar position were taken on by the unit's printing shop. Official enumeration of 'extra-plan' recruitment from the villages by urban units is attempted, the nationwide figure for 1981 being 4 million.[25] But such statistics probably greatly understate the true situation, for it is to the advantage of the units involved to keep quiet about their inflated payrolls.

Since 1978, the private peasant market for foodstuffs in the urban areas has been ever-growing, and this innovation provides the basic wherewithal for large-scale illegal residence. Urban existence outside the rationing system used to be a precarious business. In the mid-1980s, however, the vast range of rural produce — grain included — now available on almost every street corner deprives the system of its surest penalty of hunger. In addition, the private peasant markets in the urban areas are responsible for swelling the illegal population in a more direct way. Huge numbers of peasants are involved in street trading, and keeping track of their movements (to prevent them from becoming *de facto* addition to the urban community) presents the registration police with a major difficulty. The new fluidity of China's population is added to by the sudden fashion for tourism, and by the legitimation in 1983 of what was preciously condemned as 'speculation' (*dao ba*) — the purchase by individuals and units of commodities where they are cheap, and their disposal where they are at a premium.

The post-1978 policies have, therefore, caused a severe erosion of the two major pillars of the migration-restraint apparatus — the rationing of grain and other foodstuffs, and the employment and residence registration regulations. Rises in rural living standards notwithstanding, the result has been a massive increase in the illicit urban population, part of which is settled and part floating between city and village. Since the countryside has the ability to feed this increment in the non-agricultural population, it might be expected that the authorities would now take a relaxed view of the new situation. This they did until 1984, when once again official concern began to be registered regarding the threat to urban social order and general manageability.[26] In May 1984, new measures were announced to tighten up residence regulations and reassert official supervision over the movement of population. The State Council decreed that all citizens over 16 would soon be issued special identity cards, these taking precedence over the existing employment documents and household registration booklets.[27]

Active Measures to Restrict the Growth of Urban Population — Sending-down Policies

The measures preventing unplanned migration to the cities have been complemented by others designed to remove substantial numbers of their existing inhabitants. The decanting of the urban population — down the urban hierarchy and ultimately to the villages — is collectively referred to as *xia fang* — 'sending-down'. The periodic campaigns to remove urban citizens have served a number of particular ends. But they are held together by a common thread — the necessity for the Party to maintain a stable and manageable urban polity in a situation of severely constrained central investments in the non-productive urban fabric and insufficiences in grain supply. The official sensitivity to the imbalance of demand and supply on the urban front has been especially marked in the sphere of employment.

A vital consideration has been the assertion of Party hegemony in the cities. Transfer of officials, of large sections of the intelligentsia, and of huge numbers of potentially-malcontent youth has been with this end in view. Other, lesser, purposes have also been served. The despatch of millions of young urbanites to the remote border regions of Xinjiang, Tibet, Yunnan, Heilongjiang and Inner Mongolia has been regarded as essential to the great task of nation-building. The migrants have brought their skills to the development process, but more crucially in the eyes of the central authorities, their very physical presence has bolstered the sparse local populations of the sensitive border provinces. The patriotic and security aspects of planned transfers have been repeatedly emphasised in recent times in an effort to quell the clamour to return to the eastern cities: Han immigrants are seen as a vital factor in the control and stabilisation of local minority populations whose attachment to Chinese citizenship might not always be entirely firm.

In some cases, it is straightforward economic objectives which have been paramount. In the 1950s, for example, thousands of urban personnel were sent off to the deserts of Gansu to open up the Yumen oilfield. A similar migration occurred in the 1960s, this time in order to develop the famous Daqing field in the wastes of Heilongjiang. On the agricultural front, transfers to state farms in the North-east since the 1950s have been primarily aimed at bringing virgin territory into extensive production of cereals.

Those various sending-down movements lacking an explicitly punitive motivation have been accompanied by strident campaigns emphasising the lofty spirit of the participants, the warmth of their reception in the distant town or village, and the pride of relatives left behind. Such appeals to patriotism (registered more as a demand for unquestioning obedience to the Party) have not been framed solely in a mood of pragmatic cynicism. Take, for example, the massive expulsion of youth from the cities after Mao's 1968 call. The factional divisions of the Cultural Revolution apart, senior Party leaders were doubtless genuine in their desire that the long struggle before 1949 should not now be brought to nothing for lack of 'revolutionary successors'. The pinnacles of power were occupied by men for whom the years of rural exile and adversity were, above all, the virtuous years. As old men might, they saw hard labour at the grass roots as the surest means of instilling revolutionary consciousness in the new generation. It was to be prescribed, too, for those amongst their contemporaries who had succumbed to the 'sugar-coated bullets' of the post-Liberation good life. The nation-building, socialistic and egalitarian aspects of sending-down movements have, thus, been those highlighted by official propaganda (and, in turn, seized upon by Western enthusiasts of the 'Chinese road'). In general, however, such aspects are no more than the convenient ideological spin-off of a strategy designed to achieve aims of a far more prosaic nature. While this may not have been clear to the foreign admirers of the sending-down process, it was transparent to the millions of Chinese who were its victims.[28] We shall now outline the various sending-down programmes by examining the different urban groups involved.

Peasant Migrants

In the years of warlordism, civil strife and foreign invasion which occupied the first half of the twentieth century, China had become a nation of ever-shifting populations. In many instances, urban dwellers fled to the countryside to wait out the occupation of the cities by hostile forces. But the greatest upheavals were of the peasantry, whose economic basis had been torn asunder by rampant landlordism, war devastation, and — to an extent — by the undermining of traditional markets. Under such conditions, they were easy prey to the ever-present threat of flood, drought and disease. By the end of the 1940s, with the great majority of the farming population dispossessed of their property, the remedial impact of the Communist Party's land reform can hardly be over-estimated.

For the great majority of China's peasantry, land reform put an end to the constant threat of a wandering destitution. None the less, the Communists' ascendancy to power could not entirely guarantee against calamity — either natural or man-made — though when it did occur, the scale of rural dispossession was now hardly comparable to that of past years. Since 1949, therefore, the periodic upsurges in peasant itinerancy have primarily affected the rural townships, where the official response has generally been passive non-intervention. When there has been an upsurge in unsolicited peasant entries into the cities, however, arising from these localised and short-term impulses (and of course, from the underlying differential between town and country), the response has been increasingly active.

In the early years, city officials had adopted a benign approach to the unwanted migrants from the villages — loosely referred to as *youmin* ('vagrants') in the official accounts. In 1949, for instance the authorities in Shanghai had provided them with large discounts on railway tickets as an inducement to return home. Some peasants were given cash grants to enable them to resettle in their home areas and start small businesses.[29] Relief schemes to support unemployed peasants were introduced in a faltering manner in Shanghai and elsewhere. But the establishment of the mutual aid teams in the rural areas, localised pressure on land and (in 1954) extensive flooding in East China, brought influxes of peasants which demanded stronger measures. Former villagers were rounded up and shipped out *en masse* to the surrounding countryside. In April 1955 alone, Shanghai expelled 43,000 peasants, many of them despatched to northern Jiangsu where the Huai River Labour Corps had been established to combat flooding and reclaim land.[30] Good harvests in 1955, and the promise of a better rural existence provided by the setting up of the higher-level advanced producer cooperatives, encouraged the spontaneous return of large numbers to their former villages. Shanghai alone was able to claim an expulsion of half a million peasants in that year.[31]

The tide of migration from the villages again turned in 1958, when the official regulations controlling employment and household registration were temporarily abandoned. As a response to the powerful 'pull' of frenetic industrialisation of the Great Leap Forward, as many as 20 million rural dwellers flocked to the cities in late 1958 and early 1959. As is described in chapter 4, by the early 1960s this was to lead to the 'back to the village' (*huixiang*) campaign of mass deportations of comparable numbers.[32] The political and economic retrenchment of the 1963–5 period brought more liberal rural policies, which in the short term were favourable to the re-absorption of population in the villages. By 1966, urban China had been overtaken by the chaos of the Cultural Revolution, and until its conclusion a decade later both the pull of the urban areas and the push from the land were markedly diminished. On the one hand, the faction fighting and insecurity of the cities inhibited casual movement from the countryside — the old adage 'in times of trouble, stay in the village' had never seemed more appropriate. On the other hand, the political campaigning brought some unexpected bonuses to farmers: the rural bureaucracy, preoccupied with the power struggle and cast loose from the constraints of higher authority, were inclined to neglect their often-stifling supervisory functions over rural production. In many country areas, the peasants took full advantage, and in some parts of Shandong, for example, daily earnings were raised by as much as 50 per cent in the course of 1967.[33]

In the latter part of the Cultural Revolution (that is from the 9th Party Congress of 1969 to the death of Mao in 1976), rural incomes were generally depressed despite some excellent harvests (for example, 1970) and the relief of population pressures due to increased recruitment of peasants by urban labour bureaux. The reasons for this lay in the ceaseless and diversionary political campaigning, the stop-go policies regarding private peasant enterprise, and the increased rate of grain purchases which resulted from constant pressures on the peasants to overfulfil state supply quotes. The scale of illicit peasant migrations to the cities which this situation occasioned, and the scale of expulsions which were consequent, will never be known. As far as the contemporary official line on these matters was concerned, peasant itinerancy was unequivocally a thing of the past.

In recent Chinese history, the worst years as far as political instability, economic stagnation and natural calamity are concerned were 1975 and 1976. Yet, being in a position to observe conditions in many large cities during this period, the present writer came across almost no sign of urban vagrancy. In China of the Cultural Revolution, however, the empirical observation of foreigners was often the least reliable guide to reality. In this case it was contradicted by copious anecdotal evidence of a continuing peasant itinerancy. At a time of growing foreign tourism, the public security authorities were masterly in hiding problems from the outside world. It was public knowledge amongst Chinese, for example, that before the bi-annual international trade fair in Guangzhou, the streets were swept of peasant vagabonds. In fact, in every city open to foreigners, a special agency known as the 'reception centre' (*shourongsuo*) was charged with the responsibility of rounding up itinerants, and shipping them back to the countryside — in many cases to labour colonies. From the evidence on the ground, it must be assumed that the *shourongsuo* went about their duties with great efficiency.

Some, at least, of the traditional causes of large-scale rural destitution and itinerancy did remain, whatever the public front of an incontrovertibly 'excellent' situation in the countryside. In the early 1970s, for instance, Anhui Province was regularly affected by failed harvests caused by flood and drought, and was a continuous source of peasant itinerants. Here it was commonplace for commune authorities to issue certificates entitling villagers to leave in search of relief, and many would wander as far south as Guangdong. On a more dramatic scale, the summer of 1975 saw widespread flooding of four counties in Henan province, caused by a breach in dykes and reservoirs connected to the Yellow River. Four counties were inundated, huge numbers of peasants lost their lives, and thousands wandered to the local towns and cities to beg. (These events were not known to the outside world.[34])

Some indication of the true situation as regards peasant vagrancy in the cities came in the years immediately following the Cultural Revolution. It was the experience of this writer that in 1979, for example, as many beggars from the countryside could be counted in a ten-minute wander in the downtown district of any provincial capital as in two years during the later Cultural Revolution. The explanation was not that there were more itinerants than previously (indeed, there almost certainly fewer), but rather that city officials had lost the will to deal with them with the ruthlessness of the past.

Urban Youth

The sending-down of young people, since the 1960s referred to as 'educated youth going to the mountains and country areas' (*zhishi qingnian shang shan xia xiang*), first came to prominence in the mid-1950s. Its underlying spirit had been no stranger to the Chinese Communist movement: in the 1930s and 1940s, thousands of young city-dwellers had trekked to the interior to join the battle against the Japanese.

Six years after the Liberation, Mao addressed himself to the problem of urban youth employment and the question of 'training revolutionary successors'. 'All people who have had some education,' he wrote, 'ought to be very happy to work in the countryside if they get the chance. In our vast rural areas there is plenty of room for them to develop their talents to the full.'[35] As well as the patriotic and character-forming benefits of going off to the villages, the cities would be relieved of population pressures, the cultural and economic levels of interior regions would be raised, a greater grain surplus produced to aid industrialisation, and China's 'unbalanced' population distribution would be corrected.[36] Even in the 1980s, with the release of much data relating to China in the 1950s, there is still a gap as far as the overall impact of sending-down is concerned. The scale of youth transfers can only be guessed from the fragmentary data of contemporary newspaper accounts. By the end of 1957, for instance, two million school-leavers had gone off to the villages, and between one-half and two-thirds were sent to the new reclamation projects and state farms in the far-flung frontier regions of the North-east, Inner Mongolia and Xinjiang.[37] In 1958, the National People's Congress and the Party Central Committee repeated the admonition to the nation's youth to turn their backs on the cities,[38] but it was only after the 'three bad years' (1959–61) that the campaign of youth rustication was properly re-activated. This was the time of the great 'back to the village' (*huixiang*) movement, when the government determined to get rid of the around 20 million people who had flocked to the urban areas during the Great Leap Forward. In 1963, the Party launched the Socialist Education Movement, aimed at re-establishing a tighter control over the countryside.[39] Millions of young people were obliged to leave for the villages on temporary assignments, and many of those with poor academic records were told that they would be staying permanently.[40] One youth paper claimed in 1964 that the cumulative total of youth deportees since the first campaigns of the 1950s stood at a staggering 40 millions, though this may have included those only sent out for short periods.[41]

The first two years of the Cultural Revolution provided China's youth with an unprecedented opportunity to travel the country. It is estimated that around 20 million school and university students were on the move in 1966 and 1967, and half of them managed to get to Beijing for the huge rallies presided over by Mao Zedong.[42] Many who had been banished to the countryside in the previous years now took advantage of the general chaos and worked their way back to their home towns; in 1967, the Central Committee issued no less than three directives urging them to return to their rural jobs.[43]

But the most severe application of the *shang shan xia xiang* policy was yet to come. In 1968, the earlier admonitions to youth were refurbished by Mao Zedong with the appropriate class content, giving rise to one of the most slavishly repeated saying of the whole Cultural Revolution: 'It is necessary for young people to go to the countryside to be re-educated by the poor and lower-middle peasants.'[44] Over the next eight years, around 17 million young people 'heeded the great call', responding in the great majority of cases with an initial enthusiasm which was almost always soured by the first few months of rural existence. By then, of course, it was too late. As with all of the great campaigns, implementation varied from locality to locality. But even those provinces where the leadership were inclined to resist the more extreme trends of the Cultural Revolution were not averse to the youth policies, for they promised to relieve the hard-pressed cities of potential trouble-makers, not to mention the intractable problems of housing and employment. This was the case in Jiangsu of the early 1970s. Other provinces, such as Shandong, were obliged to moderate their sending-down programmes on account of very high rural population densities, and the consequent difficulties which the absorption of youth in the villages presented. Not unexpectedly, it was Shanghai that truly excelled in excising its youth: with an urban population at the end of the Cultural Revolution which stood at around 5.5 million, the city managed to export 1.29 million young people between 1968 and 1976.[45]

Shortly after Hua Guofeng's masterly coup of late 1976, the new Chairman's image-builders gave strenuous publicity to an event designed to show the nation that Maoist orthodoxy was to be maintained. Hua — so went the story — arrived incognito at a meeting at his daughter's middle school, called to persuade parents and their offspring to submit to the sending-down experience. But the humble Chairman's altruistic proclamation in support of his own child's rural exile cut little ice with city people exhausted by the false bravado of years of propaganda. Under the pressure of unprecedented mass protests of rusticated youth in Yunnan and Xinjiang, by the end of the 1970s *shang shan xia xiang* policies were quietly shelved. Indeed, such were the political pressures on the post-Hua regime that after 1978 the mass movement of young people was not merely stopped but put into swift reverse; by 1983, the majority of those sent out (in the Cultural Revolution, at least) had returned to their native towns and cities.

Cadres

The phalanxes of peasant cadres who had 'joined the revolution' before 1949 anticipated that the fruits of its eventual victory would be the urban good life. But the early years of the new regime proved that for many, the transition from guerilla fighting in the hills to the humdrum of city administration would be a difficult one.[46] When, in the mid-1950s, it was decided to target various urban groups for expulsion from the cities, it was hardly surprising that the lower ranks of urban officialdom were included. Of course, the notion that functionaries should go down to the grass roots and take a share in rural labour was nothing new in a Party which had long resorted to the maximum use of its forces in the struggle for food production. The symbolic aspects of the Nanniwan tradition were also important.[47]

Shortly after the Liberation, huge numbers of the newly-instated urban administrators had been required to pack their bags and head back for the villages in order to supervise an orderly land reform. Once again, on the eve of the First Five Year Plan (1953–7), many urban cadres were despatched to the countryside to explain and 'support' the new programme. Such assignments were not unwelcomed by minor officials, for they allowed a more active assertion of authority — and, more critically, they were of finite duration. The open-ended expulsions from the cities, first introduced in 1955 and occurring at various junctures thereafter, were a different matter entirely. The 'downward transfer of officials' (*ganbu xia fang*) swiftly came to be regarded by all concerned as little more than a concealed form of punishment. It is no coincidence that the major waves of *xia fang* have taken place in the midst of fierce political campaigns; not only do such campaigns — through their purgative qualities — throw up a layer of political victims and scapegoats, but they also induce the tense climate in which compliance to the demands of a greater authority is a matter of necessity. For instance, the most successful cadre *xia fang* in the city of Shanghai followed on the Party purges of Spring 1955; on the national level, the major downward transfer of cadres of 1957 coincided with the great 'anti-rightist' crusade.

At the 8th Party Congress held in 1956, bureaucracy and over-staffing were identified as major dangers to the new socialist order, and sending down of surplus personnel was proposed as a major remedy. Thereafter, official pronouncements on cadre *xia fang* became more forthright. As an editorial in the *People's Daily* of October 1957 explained:

Beijing municipality has recently sent out, and will continue to send, large groups of cadres to participate in manual labour in the countryside and to work at basic levels . . . The sending down of cadres to the labour front is a means of preventing cadres from becoming idle in the state organs, and of raising efficiency in work . . . The Party and government organs at all levels in the entire country, from the centre to the county level, should send down cadres.[48]

By February, the success of the movement was evident, with 1.3 million officials sent out to the smaller townships and villages.[49] By no means all found themselves labouring in the fields, for *xia fang* embraced a wider meaning. For example, while the majority of cadres removed from Guangzhou in the first wave of 1955 were sent to open up the jungles of Hainan Island, the far greater number sent down in 1957 and 1958 included many who were simply required to continue in their role as administrators but at a lower level of the urban hierarchy.[50] Officials in provincial organs would be transferred downward from the capital city to minor municipalities or county towns. County cadres might be required to go down to the *xiang* (township) level, and so on.

According to Schurmann, cadre *xia fang* continued even during the Great Leap Forward, when the general movement of population was overwhelmingly in the other direction. Urban managers were regarded as superfluous at a time when the spontaneous enthusiasm of the masses was to be the springboard for the leap into communism. It was not until 1961 that most returned to their offices.[51]

In 1961 and 1962, thousands of urban factories closed down and their personnel urged to return to their native villages (the *huixiang* campaign). Along with millions of young people, and ex-peasants who had entered the cities in the Great Leap, redundant officials were expected to leave for the countryside. Most had, of course, to be prised from their urban niches; but this was the time of extreme hunger in the land — the 'three bad years' (1959–61) — and many cadres realised that their superior skills and authority would probably ensure survival in the villages.[52] Whatever the case, even as early as the winter of 1960–1, enormous numbers of officials were reported to have been removed to the countryside. Seven coastal provinces alone were able to claim the sending-down of half a million.[53] The Socialist Education Movement also occasioned the large-scale removal of urban cadres to the countryside, but they were there in an investigatory and supervisory role, and few had to stay more than a year or so.

It was the Cultural Revolution which brought cadre *xia fang* to a completely new level. Whereas the movements of the 1950s and early 1960s had encompassed pragmatic aims — thinning out the bureaucratic apparatus, and reducing urban populations — now the purpose was more clearly political. Complete layers of the urban bureaucracy were conveniently removed to the farms, where they were expected to 'learn from the poor and lower-middle peasants' and expunge revisionist thinking through hard toil. The severity of the regime to which they were subjected was generally in direct relationship to their previous rank in society. Run-of-the-mill officials were merely expected to show a correct attitude to the working people and to perform labour (*laodong*) alongside them. After 1968, the business of 're-educating' the urban bureaucracy was streamlined through the establishment of the 'May 7th cadre schools' (*wuqi ganxiao*). These institutions were often established in areas of marginal land, their inmates coming from a particular ministry, urban bureau or work-unit. Conditions in the cadre schools varied over place and time, but on the whole they did not impose too rigorous a regime; cultivation of one's 'world view' rather than of the soil was the rule, though one's ideological purification came all the quicker if one was willing to make a show of hard labour. For the ordinary cases, stints in countryside were of fixed length — six months, a year or perhaps even two years. Though many cadres regarded their time away from home as an inconvenience, it did allow them to escape the heat of the ever-present struggle in the cities.

The less fortunate fell into a more open-ended rural exile. In particular, those officials castigated as firm adherents of revisionism were sent to army-supervised farms to be 'reformed through labour' (*laogai*). After the Cultural Revolution, many of them managed to have their names cleared and get back to the cities. Yet the numbers removed since the 1950s had accumulated to vast proportions. For example, in 1978 alone, 100,000 former officials and members of the intelligentsia who had been condemned as 'anti-rightists' two decades before were suddenly allowed back to their home towns. (Those still of working age were expected to be taken in by their former work-units.[54]) Amongst the middle- and high-ranking cadres of the post-Hua Guofeng regime, few have not been caught up in the great cadre *xia fang* movements. But they are the lucky ones. Untold millions more have never been allowed to return to the cities, not so much for reasons of political malice, but more because of the sheer impracticality of re-absorbing them into an already swollen urban-based bureaucracy.[55] Since 1978, a reduction in officialdom has been repeatedly demanded by China's reforming leaders. There has been some simplification of the central government (the abolition and merging of ministries and retirement of ministers). But it is at the middle and lower levels of the bureaucracy that the overstaffing remains most severe in the mid-1980s. It is not impossible that the situation will deteriorate to the point when drastic action — in the form of wholesale sendings-down — will again be imposed.

Skilled Labour

The great cities of eastern China have, over the years, despatched untold numbers of skilled workers and technicians to other parts. Foremost amongst the exporters of labour have been Shanghai and Tianjin. Between 1950 and 1956 alone, Shanghai contributed over a quarter of a million personnel to strengthen existing enterprises or establish new ones. They went to the electrical, machine tools, rubber and auto sectors; agronomists from Shanghai even went out to Qinghai to establish a dairy-farming unit for the capital, Xining.[56] Shanghai technical personnel can be found in all corners of the land — in every university and research institute, in every large factory's complement of engineers. Indeed, in the three decades from 1953, the city exported 1.3 million workers and technicians (this figure excluding their families).[57]

The export of skills has frequently been under the aegis of inter-unit or inter-provincial production agreements. Shanghai and Tianjin, with their vast appetites for industrial raw materials and foodstuffs, have offered technical aid as a means of guaranteeing supplies. For example, the Ma'anshan iron and steel complex (Magang) in eastern Anhui owed its rapid development in the 1960s to Shanghai, and in return furnishes its mother city with much of its product. To this day, many of the technical staff at Magang keep on their residences in Shanghai and spend as much time there as possible. Shanghai companies have, in some cases, assured their supplies by maintaining ownership of distant plants which they have assisted in the construction of — establishing a kind of extra-territoriality.[58] As will be described in chapter 8, the scale of such inter-provincial arrangements was accelerated in the early 1980s, though many of the technical personnel were only transferred now for temporary stints.

Sending-down and Dispersal of Enterprises and Their Staff

Four interrelated purposes lie behind the dismantling of whole units in the coastal provinces and their removal to hinterland sites (*qiye xia fang*). The first is economic — arising from the needs both of originating cities and the target regions of the interior. Production technologies and personnel surplus to the requirements of the large cities have been shifted to the smaller towns, with or without the establishment of satellitic relationships. The second purpose has been to relieve sheer physical congestion of the large eastern cities. The third has been ideological — and has involved mainly academic and research institutions. The fourth, and most important aim of such transfers has been military-strategic.

China had won its Liberation from the Guomindang, but they and their backers were not content to accept defeat. The early 1950s was a time when Taiwan and the Western powers had high hopes of rolling back the Chinese revolution by military means. To the new masters of urban China, this expanded state of siege suggested old remedies. Over the two decades of guerilla warfare which had brought the Communists to power in 1949, a key tactic had been the strategic retreat. Where the Communist forces went, their limited industrial equipment followed, to be reassembled and put to work until the next move. In 1949, the Mayor of Shanghai, Chen Yi, had this in mind when he announced: 'We must evacuate the population of the city systematically and transfer factories to the interior wherever possible.'[59] But it was during the latter part of the Cultural Revolution that the most widespread application of the strategic policies were implemented. Despite the raging Indo-Chinese conflict, again seen by Beijing as ultimately aimed at China, the chief external threat to the Chinese revolution was regarded as the Soviet Union. After the bitter skirmishes on the north-eastern border of 1969, the old notion of the 'three lines' (*san xian*) was given new life, and the policies of 'dispersal to the mountains and caves' (*shan san dong*) brought into active play. Untold numbers of strategic plants and scientific research institutions were shifted lock, stock and barrel to the 'second line' of the interior provinces. Sichuan Province was a favoured destination, particularly for units from the vulnerable north-eastern provinces of Jilin and Liaoning.

Strategic units such as the Institute of Space Physics were also evacuated from Beijing. And before the Cultural Revolution, there were eight key educational establishments in the capital which were known as the 'eight big colleges' (*ba da xueyuan*). By the end of the Cultural Revolution, only three remained in their old locations. In the early 1970s, most departments of Shandong University (Jinan) were transported to the safer rural site at Qufu to the south, and billeted on the campus of the teachers' training college in the county seat. Transfers such as this suited political as well as security objectives, for they removed the potentially tiresome intelligentsia from the cities and landed them in the bosom of the peasantry, their supposed 're-educators'. The 'learn from the Chaoyang Agricultural College' movement of 1976 was the signal for another energetic round of dispersal of educational institutions, though this time the purpose was more overtly ideological than military-strategic.

By the end of the decade, most of the educational institutions despatched to the hinterland during the early 1970s had been restored to their original sites. The return was relatively simple, for rarely had college campuses been completely turned over to other uses. Not so for most of the factories sent down — with new land in the cities increasingly scarce, their premises had often been put to other uses, and transfer was deemed permanent.

Criminal Elements

In the People's Republic, the dividing line between criminality and unorthodox political conduct has proved to be very thin. Apart from those cadres and members of the educated classes in effect criminalised by political campaigns (from the time of the 1957 'anti-rightist' campaign onwards), millions of Chinese citizens have been consigned to rural labour camps for more clear-cut sins against society. Not all, of course, have been of urban origin.

The penal camps divided into two main groups. In the 1950s, the government had issued various vague pronouncements specifying that certain categories of miscreant should be subjected to 're-education through labour' (*laodong jiaoyang*). Included were citizens considered to be counter-revolutionaries yet not convicted on any specific charge, those guilty of minor infringements such as larceny, and even people who had refused to accept work assignments.[60] Before 1966 at least, 're-education through labour' sentences were supposed to be for around three years. In practice, however, large numbers sent to re-education camps in the remoter provinces of the interior were obliged to settle down nearby once their formal sentences had been discharged. Even those who had left a large eastern city to take up a work assignment in the interior found it extremely difficult to return; the ex-inmates of penal camps found it well-nigh impossible.

Much more serious was to be sentenced to a prison farm for 'reform through labour' (*laodong gaizao*). While the regulations of the mid-1950s emphasised the importance of rehabilitation, Mao's own utterances on the subject and the testimony of ex-prisoners suggest that 'labour' is the main feature. *laogai* — as it is known — was to 'prevent counter-revolutionaries serving a sentence from eating without working'.[61] Few Western nations have a prison population exceeding 0.1 per cent of their total populations. Shanghai alone is said to have around thirty various penal institutions. But the truth is that, as regards the numbers incarcerated in the nation as a whole, there is no basis for hazarding an estimate.

Sending-down Policies: Some Observations

Those who have been prevented from moving from village to city have, naturally, viewed the array of constraints on migration with antipathy. Most existing inhabitants of the urban areas have, however, welcomed measures which hold back the rural tide. As for the programmes of sending down, they have evoked a hostility that is almost universal. Peasants hard-pressed for land and food have resented the influx of strangers, and being cast in the role of 'educators' of the urban interlopers has been scant compensation. Minority peoples in the border areas have seen the large-scale resettlement of Hans from the eastern cities and villages as an intrusion on their land and customs. And, of course, the direct victims of sending-down have quickly come to regard their lot as a form of internal exile. This seems to be the view even in the minority of cases where transfer has not been accompanied by any reduction in living standards.

For the majority, of course, sending-down has not brought improved material conditions. This has aroused bitterness, but popular resentment of *xia fang* flows equally from the sense of being wrenched from one's family and friends, from one's native area. More so perhaps than in any peasant nation, long traditions of localism founded on dialect, on social custom and cuisine, have imbued the Chinese with an extraordinary attachment to native place.[62] A literary gem of the Cultural Revolution illustrates the intensity of local attachments: in one of the few volumes of lighter reading permitted at that time, the author (Mao's batman) describes the following situation: having braved countless miseries in the course of the Long March, the southern armies were confronted by an obstacle that at first seemed insuperable. At this particular point in the saga, rice-cultivating China had been finally left behind, and the armies found themselves in the unfamiliar territory of millet and maize. No one knew how to deal with these strange grains, and the ranks were thrown into disorientation and confusion. It was only the timely culinary advice of Chairman Mao himself that saved the day.[63]

A profound parochialism was displayed even by the supposedly fearless and 'revolutionary' ex-Red Guards who filled the universities in the mid-1970s. It was painfully clear, for instance, that what the graduating classes feared most was assignment to jobs in the interior. The sure way to avoid being sent off to some place far from home was to proclaim early on obedience to the directions of the Party and volunteer (through publicly-displayed 'letters of pledge') for a posting to Tibet or Xinjiang. But even those given comfortable jobs in Beijing were to voice the old villager's complaint: 'the water does not taste good there'.[64]

China is a country where 'home' is very definitely always 'best', and the resistance to sending-down has, therefore, been enormous. The recourse for many has been to attempt to avoid being despatched in the first place (through connections with high-ranking officials or special pleading, exaggeration of physical infirmity, and so on). Amongst the adult population, open opposition to being sent down has been only a rare occurrence. An instance is the case of a scientific research institute located in Changchun, in 1973 ordered to divide into two parts in line with the strategic *shan san dong* policy. Half of the 4,000-strong workforce were packed off, along with their equipment, to a county town in Sichuan several thousand kilometres distant. One hundred or so brave souls valued their attachment to their home ground highly enough to refuse to move. For the next four years they were deprived of their salaries, urban household registration and — therefore — rations; many were reduced to begging in the countryside. Ten years later, those who had made the transfer to Sichuan were no happier, despite the better weather, the far superior food supply, excellent housing, and (from 1983 on) a special supplement to their salaries of five *yuan* a month, quaintly termed an 'entering the mountains subsidy' (*jinshanfei*). Away from one's native place 'water and soil are discommodious,' (*shui, tu bu fu*) as the ancient saying goes.

Resistance amongst the sent-down youth has been more common, and occasionally very fierce. It is no accident that most of the 17 million young people expelled from the towns and cities during the Cultural Revolution have now returned.[65] Those obliged to stay have engaged in campaigns of civil disobedience rarely seen in the People's Republic, most notable amongst them being the strike of 50,000 Shanghai and Beijing youth in the beautiful but inaccessible area of Yunnan Privince known as Xishuangbanna.[66]

Since the late 1970s, the government has been eager to make restitution to officals, 'intellectuals' and even ordinary workers whose families had been broken up in the 1960s and 1970s. Hundreds of thousands of spouses have been reunited after separations of up to twenty years, but the problem remains extensive, especially in the great cities such as Shanghai.[67]

Conclusions

Before its ascendancy to power the Communist Party had anticipated a swiftly urbanising New China. The rapid stabilisation of urban life after 1949, combined with the persisting uncertainties of rural existence, gave the cities a magnetic glow. The waves of peasant migration stimulated by the First Five Year Plan were soon perceived as a threat not only to the productive role of the cities, but to the very existence of Communist power. The response was a variety of measures to prevent migration and to decant existing urban populations. These divide broadly into *passive* measures — preventing uncontrolled movement into the urban areas — and *active* measures designed to rid the cities of large numbers of unwanted, and sometimes undesirable, inhabitants.

The overall effectiveness of the passive controls can only be judged obliquely: before they were brought into play (the early to mid-1950s) and on the occasions when they have been relaxed (the Great Leap Forward, the late 1970s), the cities have spontaneously drawn in millions from the rural areas. It must be assumed, therefore, that under the same political and economic conditions in city and country, had the restraints been absent altogether urban China would have been simply inundated by peasant migrants.

The policies designed to transfer people down the urban pyramid have not, in the long term, proved as effective as the government might have hoped. Yet despite the eventual return of huge numbers, many millions have been permanently excised from the larger cities. At crucial junctures in the history of the People's

Republic (notably, the early 1960s when mass starvation loomed, and in the latter part of the Cultural Revolution when China's youth threatened to get out of hand) the regime has used mass deportations to its great advantage. From the standpoint of the authorities, therefore, sending-down can be regarded as a measured success.

A higher rate of urbanisation might have been supported, of course, had the government been willing to devote more resources to agriculture (especially grain production), to non-productive urban capital projects, as well as to labour-absorbing light industry. But the *raison d'etre* of the cities — so far at least as the Maoist side of the Party was concerned — was as repositories of industrial production. Investments in urban housing, schools, roads, sewerage systems and the like, were to be kept to the absolute minimum. The growth of the urban-industrial workforce was, therefore, to be as far as possible fed by the existing urban population — by sharply raising the labour participation rate.

As we shall see in chapter 4, the overall effect of China's controls over personal mobility is that, over the first three decades, net immigration accounted for only around 30 per cent of all urban growth. Yet despite the controls, fluidity between town and country has been enormous; many middle-aged urban dwellers of today started out life in the countryside before 1949, moved to the towns in the 1950s, perhaps were shifted out again in 1957, returned in 1958, were forced back to the village once again in the early 1960s, only to return in the late 1970s. For a large part of China's current urban population, the past thirty years has been one grand game of snakes and ladders.

It has often been asserted by those who deplore the urban excrescences which are the common feature of capitalist urbanisation that the 'developing nations' can learn from China's experience. This would seem a fatuous suggestion, for the Chinese government has only been able to implement its restrictive measures because of a thorough-going rural land reform. History has proved that such a precondition is unlikely in the twentieth century outside the context of a general overturning of feudal and capitalist relations in society.

The present evaluation of China's urban growth restraint model has dwelt on the human costs, all too often overlooked by outside experts who have seen fit to assume that what is good for the Chinese authorities is also good for the individual. In the case of the Chinese model, the happiness of society at large has been at the expense of real people — and tens of millions of them at that. Nevertheless, the adoption of measures to control personal mobility has obviated the alternative mass miseries epitomised by the shanty-town existence — unemployment, hunger and disease.

Notes

1. Mao Tse-tung, 'On Coalition Government' in *Selected Works of Mao Tse-tung*, Volume III, (Foreign Languages Press, Peking, 1965), p. 250.
2. Mao Tse-tung, 'Report to the Second Plenary Session', p. 365.
3. This was the firm view of many peasants to whom the author spoke in the late 1970s; in East' China, certain areas such as southern and northern Shandong, northern Jiangsu, and most of Anhui gained reputations for worse rural conditions than average. The glowing foreign accounts of rural life, which were the rule during the period until 1976, were based solely on the conditions in the model units in better-off regions. The Chinese authorities were masterful at hiding the true state of the countryside from the outside world.
4. Between 'mental and manual labour', 'city and countryside', and 'worker and peasant'; this formulation was borrowed from Stalin. See, for example, J. V. Stalin, *Economic Problems of Socialism in the USSR* (English edn: Foreign Languages Press, Peking, 1972), pp. 24–9.
5. Chinese publications regularly carry details of the narrowing urban-rural consumption gap in the post-1979 period. See, for example, 'Peasant are faring better', BR, no. 20 (16 May 1983), pp. 9–10: here a sample survey of the State Statistical Bureau finds that, between 1978 and 1982, rural consumption increased by 67.4 per cent, and urban consumption by 38.3 per cent (in real terms). A personal observation here: after eight years of regular, and sometimes prolonged, periods in the Chinese countryside (1975–83) the present writer only in 1982 began to come across villagers who no longer harboured a desire to leave agriculture. The positive transformation of rural fortunes which this signifies seems set to continue well into the late 1980s.
6. Reported in *Changjiang ribao* (Wuhan), 21 October 1952 (GCPP, no. 0863, pp. 260–1).
7. The first of these came from the Administrative Council (*Zhengwuyuan*) in early 1953 and was reported in RMRB, 18 April 1953 (GCPP, no. 0863, pp. 260–1). The deepening apprehension regarding urban unemployment and localised rural manpower shortages caused by mass emigrations prompted further instructions in March 1954, this time from the Ministry of the Interior and Labour (RMRB, 15 March 1954).
8. RMRB, 27 February 1957.
9. 'Can the Dormitory Shortage be Solved Quickly: Anshan', *Xinhua banyuekan*, no. 7 (1957); see also C. Howe, 'The Supply and Administration of Urban Housing in Mainland China: The case of Shanghai', *China Quarterly*, no. 33 (1968), p. 93.
10. 'Directive for checking the blind outflow of the rural populations', RMRB, 9 December 1957 (GCPP, no. 0863, pp. 260–1).
11. New China News Agency, 9 January 1958, cited by L. Orleans, 'The Recent Growth of China's Urban Population', *Geographical Review*, vol. 49 (1959), p. 53.

Orleans' article is a rich source of information on population movements and official responses during the 1950s.

12. Ibid., p. 53.

13. GCPP, no. 0743, p. 226; the directive was issued 25 August 1955, and originally reported in the *Renmin shouce (People's Handbook)*, Peking, 1956, p. 490.

14. Private communication.

15. For example, the following campaigns of the late 1960s and early 1970s: 'Cleansing of the class ranks', 'One strike, three antis', 'May 16th', 'Criticise Lin Biao and Confucius', not to mention the 'Water Margin' and other anti-Deng Xiaoping campaigns of 1975 and 1976.

16. The illegal returnees from the countryside made a living by ticket-touting outside the downtown cinemas, and by other 'anti-social' activities. In 1975, their appearance (long hair, bell-bottomed trousers of dark dakron) cut them out from the normal street crowd.

17. Feng Lanrui *et al.*, ZGSK, no. 6 (1981).

18. For example, driving (official cars, buses, trucks) in the city — very much one of the elite professions for the working class; in the 1970s and earlier, the exclusive source of civilian drivers was the People's Liberation Army.

19. In the early 1950s, new urban housing construction took 9 square metres per person of 'living space' as its standard (at a time when the average was just over 4 square metres). New dormitory accommodation for single workers was at a standard of only 2.2 square metres.

20. For instance, of the 17 million youth sent out of the urban areas between 1966 and 1976, only 900,000 married and settled down permanently. See the speech given by Chen Yonggui at a conference on youth assignments, reported in XHDR, 15 December 1978.

21. This occurred at Nanjing University. The 'human interest' story that emerged proved a welcome diversion from the customary heavy political campaigning conducted through *dazibao* (wall posters). This was a time when even anti-mosquito campaigns were taboo: such issues were said to be a diversion from the class struggle.

22. It was well known, for example, that in parts of Anhui, the impoverished peasantry were regularly granted official leave by their commune cadres, and told to go off to beg.

23. It is *de rigeur* in China of the mid-1980s to attribute all the new prosperity to the decisions of the 3rd Plenary Session of the 11th Party Central Committee, held in December 1978.

24. TKP, 12 April 1984.

25. Ma Qingyu, CSGH, no. 2 (1983), p. 131.

26. Take, for example, the interviews with Shanghai Public Security officials made by Keith Parsons ('Too Many People', BBC World Service, 20.30 GMT, 26 May 1984).

27. 'Chinese Citizens to Have ID Cards', *Beijing Review*, no. 22 (28 May 1984), p. 10. At the end of 1983, 'household service work' organisations were set up in Beijing and elsewhere, as part of the official effort to regularise the informal labour market which had been developed by female peasants in the cities illegally. See 'Household Chores Done by Company', *Beijing Review*, no. 25 (18 June 1984), p. 12.

28. The author can only offer his personal observations in support of this statement. Having discussed sending-down with literally hundreds of Chinese who, from the 1950s to the 1970s, had been the targets of rustication movements, he has yet to meet an individual who was not opposed to it.

29. L. T. White III, 'The Chinese Model of Urbanization: Population and Capital

Aspects', unpublished paper prepared for the Annual Meeting of the American Political Science Association, Chicago (September 1976), p. 6. This is an excellent account of sending-down in Shanghai.

30. Ibid., p. 6.
31. GMRB, 29 December 1955, cited in Orleans, 'The Recent Growth of China's Urban Population', p. 52.
32. The *huixiang* campaign was launched at the April 1962 session of the National People's Congress. See F. Schurmann, *Ideology and Organization in Communist China*, 2nd edn (University of California Press, Berkeley, 1968), p. 400.
33. For example, in the Weifang area of Shandong Province — information from private communication.
34. The author personally witnessed the flooding in Henan, and some of the devastation it caused.
35. GCPP, no. 1936, pp. 551–2; information orginally from *Nongcun de shehuizhuyi gao chao* (People's Publishers, Beijing, 1956), p. 378.
36. See H. Y. Tien, 'The Demographic Significance of Organized Population Transfer in Communist China', *Demography*, vol. 1 (1964), p. 223.
37. GMRB, 22 September 1957.
38. GCPP, no. 1936, p. 552. The 8th plenary session of the 8th Party Central Committee directed that 'agriculture was the foundation' of the economy, and it should be supported in all ways possible.
39. The Socialist Education Movement was inaugurated in late 1962, and came to an end two years later. It was primarily aimed at rural cadres. The campaign was initially referred to as the 'Four Clean-ups' (*si qing*); see Schurmann, *Ideology and Organization*, p. 509.
40. Ibid., pp. 587–8.
41. ZGQB, 25 January 1964, cited in GCPP, no. 1936, p. 552.
42. F. Schurmann, *Ideology and Organization*, p. 590.
43. GCPP, no. 1936, p. 552.
44. Editorial in RMRB, 22 December 1968; my 'worker-peasant-soldier' (*gong nong bing*) students of the mid-1970s repeated this formula endlessly.
45. P. Elvory and W. R. Lavely, 'Rustication, Demographic Change and Development in Shanghai', *Asian Survey*, vol. XVII, no. 5 (May 1976), p. 445.
46. E. Vogel, *Canton under Communism: Programs and Politics in a Provincial Capital, 1949–1968* (Harvard University Press, Cambridge, Mass., 1969), pp. 59–60.
47. Nanniwan — a village near Yan'an where Party officials demonstrated their willingness to help the struggle for self-reliant agricultural production during the Anti-Japanese War.
48. Editorial in RMRB, 6 October 1957, cited in GCPP, no. 0371, pp. 112–13.
49. L. J. C. Ma, 'Anti-Urbanism in China', *Proceedings of the Association of American Geographers*, vol. 8 (1976), p. 117.
50. Vogel, *Canton under Communism*, pp. 216, 226.
51. Schurmann, *Ideology and Organization*, pp. 296–7, 465.
52. For instance, I am acquainted with a case of a now-elderly rural production brigade official who, like so many northern peasant cadres, joined up with the Communists during the closing stages of the Civil War (1945–9) and was demobilised in one of the Yangzi cities. In the mid-1950s, he had engineered a transfer to Shanghai, but when times got hard in the early 1960s, he decided to return to his ancestral village where he had maintained a home. By 1963 the food crisis had eased, and he tried unsuccessfully to get back his position. As the brigade acquired some simple farming equipment, however, the rural life became more rewarding: he was the only person around with any rudimentary mechanical knowledge. Soon he felt it would be preferable to stay in the village, and refused subsequent offers of urban posts.

53. *China News*, 5 January 1961, cited by Cell, 'Deurbanization in China: The Urban-Rural Contradiction', p. 68.

54. Interview, Beijing planning officials, August 1979.

55. In early 1979, tens of thousands of such people — ragged and embittered — came to Beijing and demonstrated repeatedly outside the Party residences at Zhongnanhai. These unusual events were witnessed by many foreigners, including the present writer.

56. White, 'The Chinese Model of Urbanization: Population and Capital Aspects', p. 15.

57. *China Daily*, 25 April 1982, p. 4; of the 1.3 million, 950,000 were sent out between 1953 and 1963, and 200,000 between 1963 and 1981. The article expresses official concern at the possibility that even a small proportion of these people will choose to retire in Shanghai (as they were originally promised they might do).

58. The arrangements between Shanghai and other interior places were manipulated to the advantage of the eastern metropolis during the Cultural Revolution. This caused much bitterness amongst the six provinces supplying the city with most of its foodstuffs and raw materials. Immediately after the fall of the 'Gang of Four' in late 1976, there were rumours that the six provinces would place an embargo on future shipments to Shanghai. Peng Chong, Party Secretary of Jiangsu during the preceding period (and an arch-opponent of the 'gang') was transferred to Shanghai to prevent this happening.

59. Cited by J. Salaff, 'The Urban Communes and Anti-City Experiments in Communist China', *China Quarterly*, no. 27 (1967), pp. 83–4.

60. 'Decision concerning the question of re-education through labour', issued 3 August 1958 (GCPP, no. 0678c, p. 210).

61. 'Regulations for reform through labour', RMRB, 7 September 1954/GCPP, no. 0678, p. 209).

62. The signs of localism are everywhere to be seen in China; college students from the same province or county form their own exclusive circles, outsiders coming into a small community are shunned even into the next generation, migrants to other areas are unable to speak the local dialect even after decades, etc., etc.

63. I only recall that the book was entitled 'On the Long March with Chairman Mao'.

64. Personal observations at Nanjing University, 1975–7.

65. Interview with personnel of the then newly-formed Ministry of Urban-Rural Construction and the Environment (*Chengxiang jianshe huanjing baohu bu*), June 1982.

66. Witnessed by this writer on a visit to Xishuangbanna in February 1979. A shocked central government eventually quelled the strikers by using a mixture of carrot and stick. Leaders were arrested and jailed, while the rank and file were taken out of the villages and put to work in the county towns and commune townships.

67. XHDR, 20 December 1980; also, *Guardian*, 12 April 1982, reported that 100,000 couples had been reunited, including 60 per cent of all scientists separated from the 1960s on.

3 THE DEFINITION OF URBAN POPULATION IN THE PEOPLE'S REPUBLIC OF CHINA

A major difficulty confronting any study of urbanisation is the definition of what constitutes urbanness. Thus, as prelude to the quantification of China's urban population between 1949 and 1982 (chapter 4), the present chapter considers the Chinese data and the functional attributes of the urban system in the People's Republic. The analysis demands an examination of the minutiae of Chinese urban categories and shifting criteria. These cannot be easily omitted or appended, though the general reader may well be satisfied to pick up the threads towards the end of the chapter, at the beginning of the section entitled 'A Summary of China's Urban Criteria'. Here, three urban definitions are outlined and the problems of overall urban definition are illustrated by a close examination of the morphology of a Chinese city.

Sources of Information on the Chinese Urban System

First some general remarks concerning the availability of data on post-1949 China. During the years of the First Five Year Plan (1953–7) — looked on by many Chinese today as a golden era in the life of the People's Republic — Beijing was more than eager to advertise its sparkling achievements to the world. Moreover, the many specialist journals on the economy and society, indeed on the methods of compilation and interpretation of social statistics, indicated a keen recognition of the need for accurate and copious accounting in a planned economy. The relative openness regarding statistical disclosures can be seen in the publication of a celebratory volume on the first decade of Communist Party rule entitled *Ten Great Years*.[1] Thereafter, China's international position was to change in a vital respect: the Soviet Union was no longer considered the trusted ally and guide, but was seen as an increasing threat to national integrity. In the 1960s, China's growing isolation in an almost totally hostile world led to an embargo on the disclosure of meaningful aggregate economic and social statistics, an embargo which was to last until the late 1970s. There is much debate amongst students of China as to whether the Chinese authorities themselves were, during the Cultural Revolution years (1966–76), party to reliable information at a time when central and local bureaucracies were all but disbanded, and routine data gathering rendered impossible.

During the two decades of severe data drought, foreign observers of China sought their own means of assessing global economic levels and trends. The least reliable picture of what was happening in Cultural Revolution China came from the foreign enthusiasts who were all too ready to generalise from the limited number of model communes, factories or neighbourhood committees which the regime was happy to publicise.[2] A more accurate assessment was provided by the Western intelligence agencies and by those academic sinologists whose stance was dispassionate (and, apparently at least, un-ideological).[3]

The post-Hua Guofeng regime, brought, by the end of the 1970s, a restoration of the central state statistical apparatus, and a growing confidence in Beijing regarding China's international position. Copious national economic information began to appear in the press and in foreign language publications such as *Beijing Review*; after a lapse of two decades, 1980 saw the open publication of major statistical compendia. First came the *Encyclopaedic Yearbook of China* (1980), followed by the *Economic Yearbook of China*, and the detailed *Statistical Yearbook of China* published in 1982, and greatly expanded and improved in its second edition published in 1983.[4] Such sources, which tend to provide only the barest statistical series, are greatly complemented by the newspapers and the scholarly journals which have become officially available to the foreign reader. Of the journals, many have been revived following suspension at the outset of the Cultural Revolution. Yet more were new on the scene, a great number being published by specialists in university departments. Particularly remarkable has been the flowering of journals in the social sciences — a field which had been taboo under the Mao regime. Of the dozens of titles available in the 1980s, an important few address the subject of the present book.[5] The rapid appearance of these extraordinarily rich source materials has meant new problems for the researcher. One such is represented by official efforts to reconstruct the lost materials from the past — an exercise which is welcome in essence but nevertheless problematic when enthusiasm for a complete historical series stretching back through the statistically barren years of the Cultural Revolution gets the better of the compilers. The gaps of the most chaotic years — notably the time around the Great Leap Forward and the height of the Cultural Revolution — are often too tempting, and are made good through the crudest methods of extrapolation. Chinese statisticians abhor a vacuum.[6]

The newly-available historical data on China's global population at least have the merit of internal consistency. This is, unfortunately, not the case with the information regarding urban population. Far from bringing welcome enlightenment, each successive disclosure of urban data has served to further confuse and confound. This is true of all the various yearbooks available since 1980; it is remarkable that even successive issues of the same publication have been unable to embrace common criteria of China's urbanness.

Given the paucity of urban population data over the 1960s and 1970s, unrelieved in the 1980s by the offerings of the various yearbooks, it was anticipated that the 1982 census would finally clear up past mysteries. A particular expectation of this writer was that the census would lay the basis for the enumeration of China's future urban population in a period of dynamic change and development. With the publication of the first aggregate returns it was clear that the 1982 census had incorporated a definition of urbanness entirely inconsistent with any previous urban series.[7] As will be described in this chapter, their relationship to earlier series can only be understood by a complete revision of all previous criteria of urbanness used by Chinese officialdom. Again, no proper account of changed criteria is offered by the census makers, and we are left to a labyrinthine process of deduction.

These difficulties of definition have dogged domestic as well as foreign students of China's urbanism. In the early 1980s, differing government bodies persisted in using their own urban compilations.[8] Even the central ministries charged with overall supervision of urban development and planning were without a clear basis for estimating urban population.[9]

The Foreign Estimates of China's Urban Population

The absence of a plausible basis for determining the size of China's urban population has led some Chinese specialists to rely on foreign estimates. A major analysis of China's urbanisation conducted in 1982 beat an unashamed retreat from the slough of official data, and is written entirely around various United Nations figures.[10] In 1970, for example, when China's actual urban population was slightly over 100 million, the UN figure accepted without comment in this Chinese study was 166.71 million.[11] Yet another Chinese writer accepts without comment an unattributed World Bank figure of 240 million for 1980.[12] If the resident Chinese experts are incapable of agreement on even basic definitions, what hope is there for the foreign researcher?

Not surprisingly, amongst the foreign analysts there has been considerable disagreement regarding China's aggregate urban size. This is evident even in the UN data — some agencies, for instance, putting the 1970 figure at 160 million, and others pitching it at almost 220 million.[13] There is slightly more agreement amongst the non-UN sources: for the same year, Leo Orleans gives 120–130 million, Theodore Shabad 130–150, Chen Cheng-siang 160, and Chang Sen-dou 125 million.[14] As a condition of China's recent admission to the World Bank, Beijing was required to open its books to scrutiny. The series of reports which resulted make fascinating reading; yet an obvious failing lies in the quality of the urban population data. Their garbled nature attests once again to the confusion amongst China's own experts in this area.[15] In short, it is the complete absence of any coherent analysis of urban statistics — both within China and amongst the Western specialists — which has provided the impetus for the present study.

A Note on National Urbanisation Data

An examination of the national urban data available for international comparison might lead one to the conclusion that the assessment of China's urban size is a matter of no more than academic interest. Take, for example, the material in the UN *Demographic Yearbook*.[16] The range of definitions of urbanness incorporated here is extremely broad. Table 3.1 sets out the maximum and minimum sizes of urban place within each of the seven standard regions. With such huge variations in the criteria used to assess national urban population statistics, does it matter that China has failed to establish its own clear standards of urbanness? The basis for useful international comparisons may indeed be fragile, but in most cases, consistently-applied criteria at least permit an analysis of each nation's urbanisation characteristics. This is not so for China, where almost no attempt has been made to maintain a consistent definition of urbanness.

Table 3.1: Urban Criteria — Some International Variations

	INCLUSION AS URBAN	
	Minimum (persons)	Maximum
Africa	500 (South Africa)	10,000 (Senegal)
N. America	1,000 (Canada)	2,500 (Mexico)
S. America	c.500 (Peru)	2,500 (Venezuela)
Asia	2,000 (Israel)	50,000 (Japan)
Europe	200 (Norway)	10,000 (Spain)
Oceania	500 (Papua N.G.)	1,000 (New Zealand)
USSR	n.a.	n.a.

Note: The table presents merely the crude numerical thresholds. In almost all cases these are subject to conditions. For example, the Republic of South Africa allows a smaller minimum figure providing there are one hundred or more white residents. Many national standards of minimum settlement size to be included as an urban place stipulate that a certain proportion of residents should be non-agricultural. In the USSR standards vary between Republics.
Source: UN, *Demographic Year Book 1981*, pp. 203–75.

China's Functional Approach to the Urban–Rural Question

Given the key role of state direction in the development process of the past three decades, China's central planners have required some yardstick by which to distinguish between the urban and rural populations. The possession of urban population data is essential to the physical planning of cities; China, however, has until recently shown little ambition in this direction. Of far greater importance to the central ministries has been the division of the entire population into *agricultural* and *non-agricultural* persons. As we have seen, post-1949 Chinese development policies have for the most part been premised upon a keen awareness of the link between the size of the mobilisable agricultural surplus and the pace of industrial growth. Not for nothing was the slogan 'agriculture the base, industry the leading sector' coined in the early 1960s.[17] The Chinese Communist Party's authority is — in the eyes of both rulers and people — legitimised not so much by progress towards the nebulous and illusive goal of communism, but by rather more prosaic measures. The most basic of these is the ability to guarantee the people grain.

Table 3.2: Urban/rural and Agricultural/non-agricultural Population, 1949 and 1980

	Rural		Urban		Non-agricultural		Agricultural	
	No.	%	No.	%	No.	%	No.	%
1949	484.02	89.4	57.65	10.6	93.00	17.4	447.26	82.6
1980	853.05	86.4	134.00	13.6	160.89	16.3	826.16	83.7

Note: The urban total shown for 1980 is the official figure, defined as the non-agricultural population of all designated towns and municipalities (*chengzhen feinongye renkou*). With the addition of the non-registered urban residents, aggregate urban total for 1980 comes to over 140 million (see chapter 4). Population figures are in millions.
Source: Zhu Zhuo, RKYJ, No. 3 (1980), p. 12; Ma Qingyu, JJDL no. 2 (1983), p. 126.

For the great majority of China's population — the rural dwellers — the state plays only a tangental role in ensuring grain supply. Except where there has been some untoward event which has meant a severe shortfall in the local harvest, the central state only impinges on rural grain consumption in so far as it has the ability to set broad quotas for sales to its granaries and the level of agricultural tax. The grain removed from the producers by these two means is the surplus available for redistribution: some goes to processing industries, a small proportion is exported in order to finance the importation of other and cheaper varieties of grain. But the vast bulk of this 'commodity grain' (*shangpin liang*) is used to feed China's great non-agricultural population.

The key constraints on the rate of planned conversion of occupations to the non-agricultural sector — in broad terms on the pace of industrialisation — are the levels of output and commodification of grain. Throughout the period since 1949, the latter has stood at between 15 and 20 per cent of all grain production.[18] As we have seen, it is the scarcity of surplus grain which has been the major preoccupation of China's leaders since 1949, and the division of the population into 'agricultural' (basically self-supplying of grain) and 'non-agricultural' (basically depending upon the state for grain) has been of far greater practical issue than any abstract definition of urban and rural. Table 3.2 shows the distinction between the urban and the non-agricultural figures for 1949 and 1980. While non-agricultural population is higher than the urban population category in both 1949 and 1980, the relative difference between these two measures declined from 1:0.61 to 1:0.83. That is, over the years there has been more rapid growth in aggregate urban population than in non-agricultural population. This is indicated also by the relative decline of non-agricultural population as a part of China's total population (down from 17.4 to 16.3 per cent) alongside a 3 to 4 per cent increase in the share of urban population. This demonstrates that over the years the towns and cities have become more urban-like in their population composition. More significant here, with the expansion of grain output roughly keeping pace with total population growth, the figures highlight the failure of the Chinese development process in freeing itself from the constraints of low agricultural productivity and the extremely limited agricultural surplus which results.

The Administrative Framework of China's Urbanism

The Horizontal System

The organisational framework bearing on China's urban development is complex, for there exist two intertwining sets of urban hierarchies, each with its own rationale. Firstly, there are those towns and cities which play a role in the administrative field system. These are the capital cities of the various regional divisions, ranging from Beijing at the centre through to the provincial and prefectural seats, and the county towns. Still lower on the scale, and — as is explained elsewhere in the present chapter — not to be reckoned in a formal sense as urban places, are the seats of the rural people's communes (many of which became centres of the newly-restored *xiang* or 'township' administrations[19]) and the communes' brigade and team villages. These settlements, lying as they do within a concentric spatial hierarchy, can be thought of for the present purpose as forming a *horizontal* system.

The numbers at each level of this horizontal system of seats in the administrative field system at the end of 1982 were as follows:[20]

1	national capital (Beijing)
29	provincial (*sheng*)/autonomous region (*zizhiqu*) capitals
210	prefectural (*zhengqu* or *diqu*) or prefectural-equivalent capitals
2,133	county (*xian*) or county-equivalent seats
c. 53,000	rural people's commune (*renmin gongshe*)

headquarters
c. 5,000,000   villages, many of which were sites of production
brigades (*shengchan dadui*) and production teams
(*shengchan xiaodui*)

The Vertical System

Many of the settlements of the horizontal system also figure in a
second hierarchical order which can be termed the *vertical* system
of cities. This vertical ordering itself divides into two layers — the
'designated municipalities' (*she shi*) at the top and the more
numerous 'designated towns' at the lower echelon. Provincial
governments and the State Council have the right to grant
municipal charters to cities of a certain size or significance.[21]
Municipalities (*shi*) divide into three tiers, the highest of which is
formed by the three major metropolises — Beijing, Tianjin and
Shanghai. In keeping with the Chinese attachment to hierarchy, the
three separate levels of *shi* are defined in relation to the two tiers in
the horizontal system to which they are firstly subordinate and
secondly equal. That is, the three metropolitan centres are 'directly
governed' (*zhixia shi*) by the central government. As such, they are
equivalent in status to the 26 major administrative divisions (21
provinces and 5 autonomous regions).

Next, there are those important cities, including all the provincial
seats, which are described as being directly under the provincial
governments, and, therefore, equal to the prefectural tiers. At the
end of 1982 there were 109 such places, which we can term second-
order *shi*. Almost all these second-order municipalities have been
promoted at some stage in their development from third-order
status. This is the lowest rung of the vertical hierarchy of
municipalities, described as sub-prefectural or county-equivalent.
At 1982-end there were 133 third-order *shi*.[22]

The towns (*zhen*) form the lower echelon of the vertical hierarchy
of chartered urban places. Of the 2,000-odd county seats, all but
around 400 are formally designated as such. In addition there are
several hundred places which are not county seats but nevertheless
are sufficiently important to merit incorporation as *zhen*. Town
status is formally granted by county authorities, though it seems
likely that superior levels of government must concur. At the end of
1982 there were 2,819 *zhen*.[23]

The Chinese City Region

A major problem in evaluating urban size in contemporary China lies in the fact that many of the larger municipalities incorporate substantial rural tracts. We are frequently told, for instance that with a population of almost 12 million, Shanghai is one of the world's largest cities. In fact, Shanghai's core size in mid-1982 was just 6.32 million and even if we add to this the inhabitants of its chief satellite towns, the total urban size was not 7 million.[24] Of the three classes of municipality, it is the first-order *shi* — Beijing, Tianjin and Shanghai — and the 109 second order *shi* (1982-end) which present the chief complicating factors for our evaluation of urbanness.[25] The following figures illustrate the scale of the inflation of China's urban population through inclusion of the farming populations in municipal figures: at the end of 1981, the then 229 *shi* had a combined total population (*zong chengshi renkou*) of 138.7 millions. As it happens, this was very slightly more than China's offical aggregate urban population (a figure which included at that time over 3,000 more non-municipal settlements). Of the 138.7 total, no less than 45.04 million (32.4 per cent) was actually registered agricultural population. The more truly urban total for the 229 municipalities (denoted by the phrase 'municipal non-agricultural population total' — *chengshi feinongye zong renkou*) stood at only 93.78 million. Of China's then official urban total in the same urban definition, this was just 67.6 per cent. The remaining 30-odd per cent was, of course, contributed by the non-agricultural population in the several thousand smaller places.[26]

Apart from the 3 great metropoli, of Beijing, Tianjin and Shanghai, it is the second-order municipalities (those under the direct control of the provinces and equal in status to counties) which have had the right to annex large agricultural territories — indeed, whole counties. The city-region concept will now be examined in detail.

Lines of Command

The city-region arrangement answers an essential need which arises more from the peculiarities of the Chinese bureaucratic system than from the considered requirements of urban spatial planning. China would claim a centrally planned economy — and correctly, if what is implied is that the law of value has been displaced as the chief determinant of production, distribution and the flow of resources. Yet planning is a relative concept. Post-1949 China's economic planning system has at times been more centralised and command-style, at times more loose and open to local manipulation. But the formal devolution of controls (for instance, that of 1957 when many centrally-run enterprises were handed over to the provinces) has never fundamentally challenged the vertical nature of decision-making. The Communist Party has been keenly aware that the communication of central commands cannot be straightforward. Apart from the sheer size and physical divisions of China, there are strong traditions of local autonomy, of clannishness. Doubtless the strength of the vertical (*tiao tiao*) as opposed to the horizontal (*kuai kuai*) under the Communists has much to do with fears of local factionalism and its threat to their hegemony.

Ironically, the vertically-biased order often seems to foster the very localism, the 'independent kingdoms', the 'unit-itis' (*benweizhuyi*) which it is supposed to suppress. Absence of co-ordination in economic plans and duplication of effort are routine features of the system. It is in the interest of the individual work-unit — the *danwei* — to maximise its power and manoeuvrability within the limits laid down by the vertical hierarchy. Often the unit's local responsibilities — its horizontal base — can thus become so broad that it threatens both the vertical constraints and competing adjacent units in the same horizontal sphere. At the local level this means poor coordination in the local economy and all the wasteful dysfunctions which follow.[27] A typical case is described in the Chinese press: 'A certain thermal power plant cannot use the coal from a mine just outside its walls because the plant and the mine fall under different administrations.' In another city, industrial oxygen is produced by thirty different units, and because of over-production due to vertical planning, 80 million cubic metres are released into the atmosphere each year.[28]

Formal administrative control is thus a vital precondition for planning at the local level, and it is in recognition of this that China's major cities have extended their boundaries tens, and sometimes hundreds, of kilometres beyond their urban cores. Yet even where nominal controls exist, there can be serious problems of command and a lack of common purpose. Take the case of a county administration in a *xian* under the direct authority of a provincial capital city. The county authorities and the provincial university had for years been engaged in a major land dispute.

Because the university was a keypoint (*zhongdian*) institution coming directly under the control of the central education ministry rather than the city or provincial authorities, it was unable to enlist local government support for its just case. Finally the county authorities accepted a material reward from the university too handsome to refuse, and the matter was settled.[29]

What such situations demonstrate is that despite the centralised authoritarism of the Chinese regime, and the sense of discipline and uniformity which might be imagined to hold sway, much local room for manoeuvre remains. The interstices in the system which make this possible arise from over-verticality, something which the territorial aggrandisement of municipalities is aimed directly at overcoming. Lofty rationalisations about 'narrowing the urban–rural gap', or eradicating the 'three great differentials' are merely the convenient ideological glaze. The Chinese are fond of saying 'leadership is all', and what is meant is not so much inspiration at the top as an unambiguous chain of command from top to base.

The Process of Municipal Promotion and Territorial Annexation

Consider a new and rapidly expanding mining venture located in a primarily agricultural region. Very soon the imported workforce can no longer rely on informal arrangements with local rural collectives (or, since 1979, on the private peasant market) for supplies of non-staple foodstuffs. The need for a firmer and more regular basis of supply is indicated, and the enterprise management contracts with nearby rural units for deliveries of 'subsidiary foodstuffs' — vegetables, pork, poultry, eggs, fish, and so on. Further industrial growth might then bring matters to a point beyond which the local communes can no longer meet increased demand without infringing on the delivery requirements imposed upon them by those state agencies responsible for purchase of rural food surpluses. The emerging conflict of interests could then be resolved by administrative means, especially if the rapidly expanding project were situated in an existing settlement in the system of seats and designated urban settlements (that is to say, in a county town or a place that had *zhen* status). The 'owners' of the new mining district (let us say, for example, a central ministry) might then solicit the support of the provincial government in their petitioning of the State Council for administrative upgrading. The purpose would be the designation of a new municipality of third-order (or county-equivalent) status.[30]

Now the burgeoning demand for agricultural products would be satisfied on a more regular and assured basis, the new municipality's needs being incorporated into the state's regional calculations of food purchases. Additionally, the statutes setting out the incorporation of the *shi* would, most probably, have laid down that certain tracts of agricultural territory should be extracted from the surrounding county. Neither complete rural counties (which are a status equivalent to the new urban centre) nor large areas of non-*xian* land can be administered by a third-order municipality. But almost all such places incorporate some rural land which can be used directly to supplement their supply of non-staple foodstuffs. This may be farmed under the customary rural units — in the pre-1979 years communes and their brigades and teams — but the new measure of direct control (usually simply termed 'ownership' in China) is crucial to ensuring that the municipality and its key enterprises have first call on the farm products it requires.

Yet more urban/industrial expansion may eventually prompt the provincial government to upgrade the municipality from third- to second-order status. Such promotion would bring various advantages, not least amongst them the possibility of acquiring further land for construction projects, and for guaranteeing additional supplies of foodstuffs and agricultural raw materials now required by a growing light industry. With the approval of the province, and, perhaps, despite the wishes of the prefectural and county authorities concerned, the second-order *shi* may assert the right to annex one or more counties.

The legistative basis for this annexation was laid down in a directive of 1959:

> For the purpose of coping with rapid development of the socialist construction of our country, especially since last year's Great Leap Forward in industrial and agricultural production and the establishment of People's Communes in the rural areas, for the purpose of promoting mutual support between industry and agriculture, and facilitating the assignment of manpower, it has been resolved that independent municipalities and relatively larger municipalities may have jurisdiction over counties and autonomous counties.[31]

A transferred *xian* will retain its territorial and nominal integrity but may well lose whatever degree of sovereignty it has managed to eke out from its former prefectural superiors. Under certain circumstances, the new municipality might be satisfied to excise extensive tracts of agricultural land from the surrounding counties without actually annexing them *in toto* — a common *shi* configuration in the 1970s.[32] These, then, are the steps to municipal status which many a small rural township has followed, the key purposes being establishment of formal controls over local resources.

Annexation for Specific Purposes

Purposes other than simply securing control over food supplies have lain behind some municipal expansions. Again, they are of a practical nature, designed not to eradicate the urban–rural divide so much as to serve the specific interests of the core *shi*. For example, Hangzhou (capital of Zhejiang) embraces a vast rural territory of no less than seven rural counties. The apparent purposes of its westward thrust was to incorporate the hydro-electric installations of Xin'anjiang. The objective of Beijing's further northward extension in the early 1960s was direct control of several large reservoirs. The heavy-industrial and armaments centre of Chongqing took territories almost 100 kilometres to the south of the city-proper in order to ensure supplies of non-ferrous ores. Lhasa in Tibet administers the very largest *xian* tract, extending 650 kilometres from east to west and encompassing a record eleven counties. The extent of Lhasa's hinterland arises from the lack of competing administrative units, and the traditional networks of supply of rural produce to the city.

   Municipal annexations have occurred in waves. One such accompanied the Great Leap Forward (1958–9) and reflected the political premium on self-contained development. The ideology of 'self-reliance' was to become a central feature of Cultural Revolution economics, and it was to bring a further round of territorial expansion by the *shi*. Regardless of local conditions, city fathers were pressed into following the models of self-reliant municipal rectitude offered by Shenyang and Shanghai. Their virtue was that they had not merely become self-sufficient in vegetables and other non-staples, but were able to grow most of the grain they required. From the central state's standpoint, this was a vital consideration, for much of China's need to import grain was seen to arise from the large cities' neglect of cereals cultivation. It was at this time that in Liaoning Province, a bastion of the Maoist left, the process of takeover of counties was brought to an extreme, so that by 1976 only two normal prefectures and subsidiary *xian* remained in the province.

Further south, the city of Nanjing[33] mechanically applied the lessons of Shanghai, which with ten rich and fertile rural counties attached had a good basis for self-reliant agricultural production. The obsessional call to 'take grain as the key link' meant that in the early 1970s, fine vegetable lands around the city were indiscriminately turned over to rice and wheat. In order to increase the area under grain, Nanjing had to annex further territory. In 1974, Luhe *xian* to the north of the Yangzi was brought under its direct administration. Despite this measure, which at a stroke added several hundred more square kilometres to the city's dimensions, the goal of self-sufficiency remained elusive. Yet its pursuit was the cause of considerable disruption in the city's supply of non-staples. In 1975, for the first time since the early 1960s, rationing of vegetables and meat was imposed on the citizens of Nanjing. A chief cause for genuine rejoicing at the arrest of the 'Gang of Four' in late 1976 was the expectation that food supplies would now return to normal.

Variations in Annexation Patterns

Since the early 1980s, both the pace of municipal annexation and its underlying causes have changed. Previously, the first and second-order *shi* had adopted three distinct forms of expansion:

Firstly, the direct incorporation of whole counties by cities. In 1979, only 45 per cent of the then 104 second-order municipalities had exercised their right to attach counties, ranging from one to eleven in number.

Secondly, 46 per cent of all second-order *shi* had taken within their boundaries some small non-*xian* agricultural districts. In this respect their morphology was usually little different to that of the over one hundred third-order municipalities.

Thirdly, the taking over of large non-*xian* rural tracts, including within them numerous townships: of all the second-order cities, just 9 per cent had adopted this means. The municipalities concerned were almost all settlements founded on spatially-dispersed industrial activities — typically mineral extraction.[34]

Examples of the third configuration are Huainan, Datong, Jixi,

Tangshan, Benxi, Fushun, Pingxiang, Jingdezhen, Zibo and Zaoz-huang. Almost all these *shi* owe their existence to mining (mostly of coal, but also of iron ore and clay). A common feature is a considerable total municipal population (typically, over half a million) and a non-agricultural population of far less. We will consider four such places — classified in the 1980s as 'regional cities' (*quyu chengshi*) — situated in the provinces of Jiangxi and Shandong.

Pingxiang. This city on the Jiangxi-Hunan border extends over some 4,000 square kilometres, and yet within its 1970 total population of somewhat over one million, only a few tens of thousands comprised its core population, while fewer than 200,000 depended on non-agricultural activities. Pingxiang owes its extent to the dispersed coal mines (including the famous Anyuan complex) within its boundaries. The enormous area is not administered through rural county authorities subordinate to the *shi*, presumably because the territories of the pre-existing counties did not correspond to the scatter of mines.[35]

Jingdezhen. Again in Jiangxi, Jiangdezhen is the complex of ancient settlements producing China's most famous porcelain. Jingdezhen *shi*, covering around 2,500 square kilometres, in part owes its extent to the need to control labour and raw materials sufficient for its vital export-oriented production.

Zaozhuang. Until 1979, this municipality in southern Shandong controlled a huge area without any county subdivisions. In the mid-1970s a dozen towns were within its boundaries, four being around 50,000 in population. In 1979, Zaozhuang was granted control over Teng County; a dispersed pattern of coal mines is again the apparent reason for this city's arrangement.

Zibo (Zhangdian). Zibo in Shandong is chosen by one geographer as the archetype of the 'regional city'. Here the local industrial economy is based on coal, silk and porcelain in an area of 2,900 square kilometres. In all, Zibo encompasses about 600,000 non-agricultural persons, but this is only a minority (*c.* 45 per cent) of the municipal population total (*zong chengshi renkou*). The non-agricultural population is not concentrated in a single core city, but in two larger settlements (Zishan and Zhangdian — each with around 130,000) and twenty other smaller 'urban residence points' (*chengzhen jumindian*) of over 2,000 persons.[36]

Municipal Size and Annexations

A strong and positive relationship exists between municipal size and the annexation of territory. Of the cities which in their non-agricultural population are over one million (totalling twenty at the end of 1982) only two were without attached counties. According to Chinese atlas sources of the mid-1970s, Harbin *shi* incorporates only a small agricultural area and the townships of Sankeshu and Songpu. Possibly the absence of annexation here is recognition of the impossibility of achieving food self-sufficiency in the harsh sub-Siberian climate of Heilongjiang. It may also be accounted for by the large number of southerners in Harbin: the city's demand for rice rather than wheat, sweet potatoes and other northern staples may have established a pattern of importation from other parts. Similarly, only one of Heilongjiang's six other second-order *shi* — Yichun — has attached counties.

The other million-population city with no *xian* is Changchun, capital of Jilin. Changchun lost its five counties in 1982, a most puzzling occurrence in view of the current trend towards greater — not lesser — annexation. Thus at an administrative stroke, Changchun's total municipal population shrank by around four million.[37]

As might be anticipated, the 26 capital cities of provinces and autonomous regions, being in the main relatively large centres, are well endowed with attached counties. In 1982, apart from Harbin and Changchun, only Shijiazhuang (Hebei), Guiyang (Guizhou) and Nanning (Guangxi) were without any *xian*. Three of these did, however, possess some non-*xian* agricultural tracts: Nanning with three towns and eight people's communes in its suburban districts (*jiaoqu*), Guiyang, having a large area encompassing nine small towns and the Huaxi reservoir. For similar reasons as those examined above in the discussion of Cultural Revolution Nanjing, many provincial seats added counties in the 1970s. Guangzhou went from two to six, Jinan from one to three, and important regional centres which had previously got by with no *xian* were finally allowed by the State Council to annex (Shenyang *c*. 1976, Wuhan and Chengdu in 1979).

As a measure of their dominance, 12 of the 26 provincial-level seats had the most attached *xian* of any of the cities in their respective provinces, while in six provinces the capital's number of counties was equalled by one or more other cities. In eight cases, the provincial seat had fewer counties than did other cities, and sometimes by a wide margin. The most outstanding instance is in Shaanxi Province, where the capital Xi'an with its single county is dwarfed by the coal-mining 'regional city' of Baoji with its eleven attached *xian*. Table 3.3 illustrates the degree to which attachment of counties has occurred in China's provincial capitals.

Table 3.3: Annexation of Counties by Capital Cities of Provinces and Autonomous Regions, 1982

(A)	0	N	1	2	3	4	5	6	7	8	9	10	11
(B)	2	3	6	7	4	1	0	1	1	—	—	—	1

Note: Line (A): number of attached counties from 0–11 (N = territory other than a complete county authority attached to the city); Line (B): numbers of actual capitals in each of the categories of Line (A). Lhasa is the city with eleven counties.
Source: ZXQJ, 1983.

Regional Variations in Annexation

Prior to the administrative reforms introduced in 1982, there was much inter-provincial variation in the extent of municipal annexations of rural territory. This variation seemed to result not so much from differing socio-economic characteristics (population density, level of urbanisation or industry, and so on) as from arbitrary local custom. Even a single region such as the North-east displayed striking contrasts. On the one hand, as we have remarked, Heilongjiang has had only one city with attached counties, this being Yichun rather than the capital of Harbin. On the other hand, there is Liaoning Province with its pattern of comprehensive annexation. Low rates of annexation have been evident in Henan, where only one out of the six second-order *shi* had attached counties, in Jiangsu (one out of seven), in Hubei (two out of six), in Guangdong (three out of ten) and in Guangxi (one out of four).[38]

Only second-order municipalities (prefectural equivalent) have possessed the right to annex counties, and regional variations in annexation therefore depend on the distribution of such municipalities. In Hebei, for example, just two *shi* (Shijiazhuang and Tangshan) out of a total of twelve had second-order status at the end of 1982. Even they lacked attached counties, and Tangshan was until the early 1980s also without any non-*xian* rural tract.[39]

Figure 3.1: Liaoning Province, 1982: An Extreme Case of Municipal
Annexation of Territory

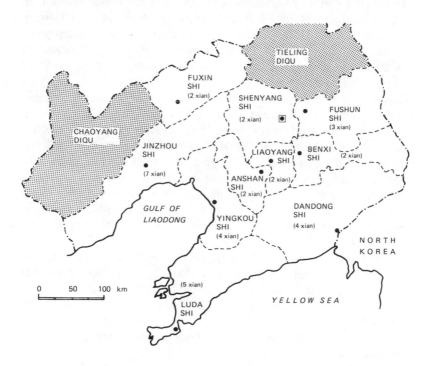

KEY

_._-._-.	provincial boundaries
- - - _ - -	prefectural and municipal boundaries
◉	provincial capital — Shenyang *shi*
●	cores of the various enlarged municipalities
(7 xian)	nos. of counties (*xian*) within the municipalities

Note: There were two standard prefectures (Tieling *diqu* and
Chaoyang *diqu*); all remaining (unshaded) territory was within the
various municipalities.

At the other end of the spectrum from Hebei is Liaoning Province with its extreme degree of annexation. In 1982, of Liaoning's forty-five counties, only thirteen fell under prefectural administration. Many of the enlargements (see Figure 3.1) were carried through in the Cultural Revolution: Luda (Dalian) grew from one to five counties, Benxi from one to two, Fushun from one to three, Shenyang from zero to two, and so on. There is evidence of a considerable scramble for the thirty-two *xian* which have been shared out between Liaoning's now ten second-order municipalities. Dandong, a border town of no outstanding economic significance in itself, controls a 225-kilometres swathe of territory divided into four counties. Their combined population in 1982 was 2.06 million, in contrast to the just over half million in the city proper. And a considerable part of this latter figure may well have been made up of agricultural persons resident in the core city's three *shiqu* (city districts). Before 1972, Dandong *shi* had been of even greater extent; in that year it lost two further counties to Luda and Benxi.[40]

The city-region is, therefore, of varied administrative and spatial form. Its existence represents a major complication in the definition and quantification of China's urban population.

The Aggregate Urban Data — An Analysis of the Official Disclosures

This section will consider the major official disclosures of aggregate urban data. As with much of our information on the People's Republic, the urban figures are fraught with problems: they are elusive, incomplete, contradictory, and rarely explicit as to their basis of definition. For many vital series on the economy, China's central statistical agencies have, in recent years, performed major exercises of retrospective reconstruction. The urbanisation statistics have, to a degree, shared in this. But as we shall see, the urban data disclosures since 1980 have failed to establish unified criteria of urbanness, and the retrospective series has, thus, to be built up through a process of deduction.

It could be argued, of course, that in a relative sense we know a great deal about China's urban proportions of the last few decades. The century of foreign intrusion, civil strife and natural calamity which preceded the Communist takeover of 1949 had made China a land of shifting populations. Under these circumstances, the calculation of total urban size had become a very imprecise science. For instance, one foreign estimate for 1917 put the total at 141 million, while another writer claimed just 100 million for 1930. At 124 million (1943), and 146 million (1946), the two official government firgures for the period immediately prior to the Communist victory show a slightly greater consistency.[41]

Since 1949 there have been two main means by which government agencies in China have kept track of population statistics. The most important has been the system of household registration (considered in chapter 2); of secondary utility have been the national censuses conducted in 1953, 1964 and 1982.

Interpreting the Urban Data of China's Three Censuses

The 1953 Census. The 1953 census found a total of almost 583 million Chinese, a figure some 20 per cent higher than expectations based on earlier Chinese and Western estimates. At 77.26 million, the urban total was, however, around half the figure which projections from the 1940s estimates might have suggested. The census counted urban residents in 5,568 places, 164 of which were municipalities (accounting for 56 per cent of the urban total). Of the remaining 5,404 urban places, the great majority (4,228) were in the size-class 2,000 to 20,000. These settlements accounted for 32 per cent of the urban aggregate. Neither of the two major Western studies of the 1953 census were able to establish the precise definitional basis of its urban enumeration.[42] A major problem in this respect is the extent to which agricultural persons were included in the urban count. As we have seen, even in 1953 the then municipal boundaries included large numbers of farmers. Some official accounts suggest that most rural persons were omitted from the final urban count. However, judging from other sources, such exclusions seem arbitrary. A footnote to a Chinese wall-map of 1956 is vague: 'Where the suburbs (of a municipality) are too big, the agricultural population in these suburbs is subtracted *when possible* . . .'[43] (Emphasis added.)

This difficulty did not end with the 164 *shi* of 1953. Compared with later counts, the 1953 census incorporated a very large number of small settlements as urban places. Most of these were rural townships overwhelmingly oriented to farming. It seems to be the case that, in those five thousand or so minor settlements of under 20,000, substantial numbers of classified agricultural persons were counted. It is probable that for many such places, eligibility for inclusion in the urban count in the first instance may have rested indirectly on their inflated sizes due to the agricultural population within their boundaries.

It has been generally understood that China's standard definition of urban population was provided in a resolution of the State Council of 1955. This ostensible definition followed the Soviet practice of mixing size and population-composition characteristics. To be considered 'urban', a settlement had to have a total population of over 2,000, of which at least half were engaged in non-agricultural pursuits. Smaller places of between 1,000 and 2,000 persons could be counted as urban, provided 75 per cent of their populations were registered as non-agricultural. In order not to exclude those important administrative centres which could not meet these size-class/occupation requirements, any people's committee at county level or above was also deemed an urban place.[44]

An important question is how far these 1955 criteria have been applied by the Chinese authorities in the period until the 1982 census. Two recent sources have a bearing here. Firstly, the extended bulletin on the 1982 census noted that all those living in municipalities (*shi*) and towns (*zhen*) were included regardless of their occupational status. The explanatory preface then goes on to detail the criteria for the establishment of *zhen* and *shi*:

> As specified by the State Council, a town is a centre of industry and commerce or handicrafts with a population over 3,000, of which more than 70 per cent are not involved in agriculture; or a place with a population of 2,500 to 3,000 of which 85 per cent are non-agricultural people, which is under direct administration of county government. In minority areas, a town could be a centre of industry and commerce or handicrafts with a population of less than 3,000 and non-agricultural population below 70 per cent which is under direct administration of county government.[45]

The presentation of such information in the bulletin implies that the possession of *zhen* status is the cut-and-dried basis for inclusion in the 1982 census urban total. In fact, analysis of the 1982 data proves that this is not the case, for a number of *zhen* are excluded totally from the urban count. We will later elaborate on this point.[46]

A second recent source considers the 1964 census and its basis. It describes Central Committee and State Council directives of 1963 which stated that for future purposes, any place of 3,000 or more inhabitants where the non-agricultural population was 70 per cent or over *might* be granted the status of town (*zhen*). Smaller settlements of 2,500 to 3,000 people could also qualify providing a larger proportion — 85 per cent — was non-agricultural.[47] These criteria are of course identical to the ones referred to in the preface of the 1982 census bulletin quoted above. In other words, the *zhen* criteria post-1963 and those of the early 1980s are unchanged. The same article also describes some 1955 criteria for *zhen* eligibility which are identical to those of the familiar 1955 rule (see above).

To summarise then, Chinese analysts of the urban data are inclined to assume that the official criteria for urbanness in general are always those which determine what may or may not become a *zhen*. This is in fact mistaken; while the 1955 rule may also actually define the then-current standard for urban population, this is not necessarily the case for the subsequent modifications of the rule. As we shall see, it is clear that in the case of the 1982 census, there is a distinction between the *zhen* rule and the general definition of what constitutes urban population.

But now to return to the 1953 census and the meaning of its urban statistics. In 1955, it was the *zhen* criteria which defined the lower limit of urbanness in general but was this the case for the 1953 census? Two questions present themselves: firstly, were all the over 5,000 urban places counted into the 1953 urban aggregate either designated municipalities or towns? The census counted 5,568 urban places, 164 of them being *shi* and 5,404 being other urban places. This latter figure in fact corresponds to the known number of designated *zhen* for 1953. Thus the answer is that the census only included as urban places those settlements which had particular status in the vertical system as described earlier in the present chapter.

The second question is whether the *zhen* size conditions of the 1955 rule were those which applied in 1953. We know that in 1949 there were 1,896 places that bore the status of *zhen*.[48] By the time of the 1953 census, this number had more than doubled — to 5,404. Yet by 1956 — and presumably because of the application of the 1955 rule which was one with higher size-class conditions than the one it replaced — the number of *zhen* had been reduced to 3,672.[49] Thus the answer to the second question is that, while the principle

Table 3.4: Urban and Total Population, 1949–57 (1957 Disclosures)

	Total	Urban	
		(no.)	(%)
1949	541.67	57.65	10.6
1950	551.96	61.69	11.1
1951	563.00	66.32	11.8
1952	574.82	71.63	12.5
1953	587.96	77.67	13.2
1954	601.72	81.55	13.6
1955	614.65	82.85	13.5
1956	627.80	89.15	14.2
(1957	642.00	92.00	14.3)

Note: Absolute figures in millions; the tables in chapter 4 are based on later disclosures which broadly correspond to the figures above, except in the following: *total population* — for 1954, 1956 and 1957 the 1983 figures are a little larger; *urban population* — 1953: 78.26; 1954: 82.49; 1956: 91.85; 1957: 99.49. (Note that all these later figures are greater, and except for 1957, by only a small margin. This can probably be explained by better compilation due to hindsight rather than by the use of different criteria of urbanness.)
Source: *Tongji gongzuo (Statistical Work)*, no. 11 (14 June 1957), as cited by Ullman, 'Cities of Mainland China: 1953–59' in G. Breese (ed.), *The City in Newly Developing Countries* (Prentice Hall, London, 1972), Table 2, p. 90; for 1957: *Jihua jingji (Planned Economy)*, no. 8 (1957), pp. 23–5.

that all designated municipalities and towns should be included in the urban count was applied in the 1953 census, the size-criteria for determining the lower order of urban settlements — the *zhen* — were different to those of the 1955 stipulations.

With this clear change in *zhen* criteria, it is obvious that there must be a discontinuity between pre- and post-1955 aggregate urban data.[50] But this discontinuity is not apparent in the available data. In 1957 China's urban population totals from 1949 to 1956 became officially available. The figure offered for 1953 was 77.67 million, much in line with the mid-year census total of 77.26 million. The urban totals for the preceding and following years (71.63 and 81.55 million respectively) are equally plausible. As Table 3.4 shows, there is no sharp discontinuity in the series, excepting perhaps that the 89.15 million of 1956 represents a considerable increase on the previous year's 82.85 million. But the explanation for this lies in factors to be explained. In any case, had the 1955 rule been applied (with its large minimum requirements and fewer *zhen* qualifying), a smaller rather than a larger urban aggregate might have been anticipated.

The problem presented by this absence of a discontinuity is not, however, a serious one. In 1956 there were over 1,700 fewer designated towns than at census time. Obviously the application of the 1955 criteria would have eliminated those places that were smaller. If, for the sake of argument, we assume that all those *zhen* excluded were considered by 1953 definition to have been of 2,500 inhabitants, then the combined loss to aggregate urban population would only have been around 4 million.

The 1964 Census. That China had conducted a nationwide census in 1964 was only confirmed officially in the early 1980s. Even then, only a very few of the major figures became available to foreign researchers. As we have seen, in December 1963 — and presumably as part of the preparatory work for the census (30 June 1964) — the Party Central Committee and the State Council issued a new set of rules concerning the designation of *zhen* which considerably raised the minimum size qualifications from the conditional 1,000 and 2,000 of 1955 to 2,500 and 3,000. The 1964 census, therefore, continued to apply the *chengzhen* notion of urbanness of the 1950s. But if the practice of counting only *shi* and *zhen* as repositories of urban population were continued, the new size criteria should have caused a further (and more marked) discontinuity in the urban series after 1964. The 1964 census urban total of 97.91 million was published for the first time in September 1981.[51]

It is difficult to evaluate the order of reduction in total urban population due to the new size-class criteria. We do not know the number of *zhen* immediately before and after the introduction of the new 1963 rule, though a considerable reduction 'from over 4,000' before its application is remarked on by one Chinese writer.[52] The aggregate urban figures adopted by the present author for the few years in question are as follows:[53]

1960: 130.73 million
1961: 127.07 million
1962: 116.59 million
1963: 116.49 million
1964: 99.17 million

Is the anticipated discontinuity reflected here? We would anticipate a reduction in the urban aggregate due to higher size-class qualifications, but this was a period when China's absolute urban total — however measured — was rapidly declining due to the adoption of the strict decanting measures of the 'back to the villages' campaign. The drop between 1963 and 1964 shown here is remarkable, and indeed might be partially accounted for by a change in criteria. Yet the number of urban dwellers prised out of the towns and cities around this time was also truly remarkable. In truth, it is impossible to draw any clear conclusions as to influence of these various factors on the particular urban statistics in question, and the entries in Table 4.6 must be judged accordingly.[54]

The 1982 Census. The first news of the 1982 census results came in a bulletin issued by the State Statistical Bureau and published in the *People's Daily* of 27 October 1982. (The full results are presented in Appendix Table A3.1, and Appendix Table A3.2 contrasts the 1982 census results province by province with 1981 year-end urban data.) At first sight, the urban figure of 206.59 million seemed extraordinarily high. And the number of urban places counted in the census — 2,664 *zhen* and 236 *shi* — seemed inexplicably low. To begin to make sense of these data it is necessary to introduce some comparative aggregate urban figures for the period 1978–81:[55]

    1978: 119.94 million
    1979: 128.86 million
    1980: 134.00 million
    1981: 138.70 million

Where did the additional 70 million urban dwellers spring from between the end of 1981 and census time in the middle of 1982? The answer to this conundrum was not offered by the census compilers. Indeed, even key urban planning ministry personnel interviewed in 1982 and 1983 were unable to give adequate explanations.[56]

The English-language weekly *Beijing Review* did make a brave effort to clarify the matter in an article entitled 'Answering Our Readers: Why the Jump in Urban Population Between 1981 and 1982'.[57] Unhappily, *Beijing Review's* explanations merely added to the confusion. Nevertheless, I shall quote them in full because they do point up the issues which have to be examined to make sense of the 1982 census data:

i. Different methods of calculation. The 1981 calculation includes only those who are non-rural population (whose food-grain is supplied by the state), but the 1982 calculation includes people whose homes are in the countryside but who have resided in cities or towns for more than one year. *This is the principal reason causing the difference.* (Emphasis added.)

ii. More cities and towns. In 1981, the country had 229 cities and towns. Seven new cities had been added when the 1982 census was taken.

iii. Births and new residents. Some of the difference in the six months between calculations can be accounted for by natural growth (births) and people moving into cities and towns.

Let us now consider these explanations one by one.

Firstly, 'different methods of calculation': indeed, this was the principal cause of the disparity, but not for the reasons given by *Beijing Review*. The actual reasons require some elaboration. Almost all of the first-order and second-order municipalities have an inner core of 'urban districts' (*shiqu*) and — as has been described earlier — an outer ring of attached counties. The *shiqu* themselves divide administratively and functionally into an inner band of 'urban districts' (*chengqu*) which are unambiguously city-like (that is, the built-up area), and the outer or suburban band (*jiaoqu*). The latter are usually mainly urban in character, but since they lie on the periphery of the city, their boundaries unavoidably include some agricultural areas and persons. The *chengqu* and *jiaoqu* are customarily divided into several different named districts, which constitute the lowest-but-one tier of urban government.[58]

These administrative divisions suggest three different ways of enumerating urban population. The first would include all the city districts (*shiqu*) plus all the population of the counties belonging to the municipality. Obviously, large numbers of rural dwellers would be counted in by this method.

A second method would entirely exclude the population of the attached counties (even though some was made up of truly urban inhabitants in satellite towns and county seats, and so on). Here, then, only the residents of the urban districts, the *shiqu*, would be counted as urban. But this method too would present complications, for the *shiqu* are made up of both core (*chengqu*) and periphery (*jiaoqu*) districts. In many cases, the *jiaoqu* boundaries extend far into the surrounding countryside, and encompass large numbers of registered agricultural population.

A third administratively-defined means would be to count only those people living in the innermost ring — the *chengqu*, that is, the city districts of the *shiqu*. This method would also be most unsatisfactory, for numbers of truly urban inhabitants would be excluded because they happened to live in the suburban districts.

A far more satisfactory means of quantifying the functionally-urban part of municipal population is provided by the household registration system. As has been described, this divides the population into 'agricultural' or 'non-agricultural', depending on the way in which staple grain is supplied. Registration is independent of the various administrative boundaries discussed above, though in some municipalities it may correspond closely to them. Thus, a functional definition of municipal urban population would take in all the persons of non-agricultural registration, regardless of whether they lived in the truly-urban core or the mixed land use urban periphery. To be even more functionally precise, the non-agricultural populations of the satellites and townships in the counties belonging to the municipality could also be grafted on to the urban total.

As we shall see, some Chinese assessments of urbanness have indeed made use of precisely such notions. But the 1982 census — for unexplained reasons — chose not to do so. Let us illustrate the orders of discrepancy which these various definitions of urbanness present. Table 3.5 list three differing 'urban' population totals for the twenty Chinese cities which in 1982 had over one million non-agricultural persons in their urban districts (*shiqu*).

Considering firstly the proportion of the *shiqu* population that is non-agricultural (column 3/2), we can see that it ranges from a low 57 per cent in the case of Chengdu to 99 per cent for Shanghai. The overall average is 81 per cent. The folly in taking the total reported municipal populations as a true measure of urban size (a common practice of both Chinese and foreign analysts of the urban data) is most evident in the entries of column 3/1. Here we can see that if the combined figures are averaged, 45 per cent of these large cities' populations actually comprised of non-agricultural persons living in the urban cores. Again, there is great variation — ranging from a mere 23 per cent in Changchun to 65 per cent in Wuhan (we cannot fairly include Harbin's high figure of 84 per cent here as that city was peculiar as a million-population city in not having attached counties).

This exercise can be extended to cover all China's municipalities.

Table 3.5: China's Twenty 'Million Cities', 1982 — Three Functional/administrative Modes of Evaluating Their Populations

	1	2	3	3/2	3/1
Beijing	9.19	5.55	4.77	86	52
Tianjin	7.78	5.13	3.92	76	50
Taiyuan	2.20	1.75	1.28	73	58
Shenyang	5.14	4.02	3.03	75	59
Dalian	4.72	1.48	1.24	84	26
Fushun	2.06	1.19	1.04	84	50
Anshan	2.52	1.21	1.03	85	41
Changchun	5.75	1.74	1.34	77	23
Harbin	2.55	2.55	2.15	84	84
Shanghai	11.81	6.27	6.22	99	53
Nanjing	3.74	2.13	1.74	82	47
Jinan	3.35	1.32	1.04	79	31
Qingdao	4.26	1.18	1.08	92	25
Wuhan	4.18	3.23	2.73	85	65
Guangzhou	5.61	3.12	2.38	76	42
Chengdu	4.02	2.47	1.41	57	35
Chongqing	6.51	2.65	1.94	73	30
Kunming	1.98	1.43	1.02	71	52
Xi'an	2.94	2.18	1.61	74	55
Lanzhou	2.40	1.43	1.08	76	45
Totals/averages	92.71	52.03	42.05	81	85

Note: Columns 1, 2 and 3: millions; columns 3/2 and 3/1 in percentages.

Column 1: total municipal (*chengshi* or *quan shi*) population (including all population in the *shiqu* and in the attached *xian*);

Column 2: total *shiqu* population — that is, the *chengqu* and the *jiaoqu* including all the agricultural population in the latter;

Column 3: total non-agricultural in the *shiqu* (that is, the *chengqu* plus the *jiaoqu*) *only*;

Column 3/2: the percentage of the *shiqu* population of each municipality that is non-agricultural;

Column 3/1: the percentage of the total municipal population that is non-agricultural population resident in the *shiqu*.

The ordering of the twenty cities is in accordance with the standard provincial listing (State Council decision, 1 January 1981).

Source: TJNJ, 1983, pp. 35–102, and p. 108. (Elsewhere it is reported that in 1982, Changchun — the capital of Jilin province — was deprived of all its attached counties; this fact is ignored for present purposes.) Anshan and Fushun column 1 entries: 1982 census data used (interview sources in Liaoning, October 1983); for Kunming column 1 entry: estimate based on BKNJ, 1981, p. 59.

Using 1981 year-end data, and based on the 229 *shi* for which the information is available (of a total of 233 at the time in question) their total combined *shiqu* population (corresponding to column 2 in Table 3.5) was 138.82 million. Their combined *shiqu* non-agricultural population, however, stood at only 93.78 million. That is to say, only 68 per cent of all municipal population was actually composed of non-farming inhabitants of their city cores: of the 138.82 million, 45 million were registered as farming folk.[59]

Now to return to the question which was raised by *Beijing Review*'s interpretation of the reasons behind the very high urban figure in the 1982 census. While different methods of calculation are a factor, they are not those presented by the journal. A clue to their true nature lies in the use in the census communiques of a term — *shizhen renkou* (literally, 'population of municipalities and towns') — not previously used in the Chinese sources. In the years before the 1982 census, the customary apellation had been *chengzhen renkou* ('population of cities and towns'). The definition on which this term was based was in principle identical to that of the 1950s. That is, it included all the persons (whether non-agricultural by registration or agricultural by registration) in those towns deemed urban places (principally the *zhen*), along with the non-agricultural persons only of the municipalities. The 1982 census dealt with the population of towns in a similar fashion, but approached the municipal populations from an entirely different angle. We have seen that administratively, the first- and second-order *shi* divide into municipal districts (*shiqu*) and attached counties. The *shiqu* in their turn are formed of the *chengqu* or core city districts, and the *jiaoqu* or peripheral city districts. The 1982 census *shizhen* definition includes the total population of the *shiqu* — that is to say, substantial numbers of agricultural persons in the *jiaoqu* are now counted as urban people. This is, in short, the reason for the 1982 census's apparent discovery of some 70 million more urban dwellers than there had been at the end of 1981.

In order to illustrate the degree of overstatement of urban population derived from the *shizhen* definition, let us look again at Table 3.5. The ratios of column 3/2 show that for China's 'million cities', the 'truly urban' figures are inflated by an average of 23 per cent. For all the 229 municipalities (1981), the exaggeration is of a far greater order — *48 per cent*.

But how about the other component of the new *shizhen* definition — the *zhen*? We are informed that of the census *shizhen* total of 206,588,582, 144,679,340 (or around 70 per cent) were accounted for by 236 *shi*, and the balance of 61,909,242 (*c.* 30 per cent) by 2,664 *zhen*. Just as for the *shi*, this combined *zhen* total includes very large numbers of agricultural inhabitants.[60] Sixty-three million persons counted in the aggregate *shizhen* figure of over 206 million (that is to say, about 30 per cent) were in fact registered agricultural population.[61]

Utilising the same ratio as for the 1981 year-end municipal data, we can estimate that:

Firstly, of the 61.91 millions in the 2,644 *zhen* of the 1982 census enumeration, 16.51 million (26.7 per cent) were agricultural;

secondly, of the 144.68 million in the 236 *shi* of the census 46.49 million were agricultural;

and thus thirdly, of the 206.59 million census *shizhen* total, 144.59 (70 per cent) were 'truly urban', 98.19 million being in the municipalities and 45.40 million in those *zhen* and other towns included. (That is to say, of the 'truly urban' total, 68 per cent were in the municipalities while the remaining 32 per cent were in the towns.

We can now, finally, move on to a new item for consideration. By way of a reminder, the second of the *Beijing Review* explanations for the much-expanded census urban total was that the 1982 count *included more cities and towns*. This assertion fails to stand up to closer examination. Once again, the tortuousness of the Chinese data demands a rather involved clarification.

It is certainly true that the census included more municipalities than the previous urban count of the end of 1981 (viz., 236 as opposed to 229). The reasons are two-fold. On the one hand, the 1981 figure excludes four *shi* which had not sent in their returns to the State Statistical Bureau. On the other, three more *shi* were designated in the first months of 1982. The increment from these seven cities amounts to a million or two — relatively insignificant in terms of the huge census discrepancy.

Contrary to the explanations of *Beijing Review*, the 1982 census actually counted in several hundred fewer *zhen* than had been enumerated in the aggregate urban data of the preceding years. In 1982, the total number of settlements regarded as urban came to precisely 2,900, and 2,664 of these were stated to be *zhen*. Yet in previous years the number of *zhen* reported was some 150 greater. The immediate suspicion was that the 1982 census had yet again broken with tradition, and for some reason excluded a number of designated *zhen*. To reiterate, the minimum requirements of *zhen* eligibility in the 1980s are identical to those of the early 1960s (a minimum of 3,000 inhabitants, providing 70 per cent or more are non-agricultural, or 2,500–3,000 with at least 85 per cent in this category). We know that for the 1953 census, requirements of a similar principle determined the urban count. Probably, they did, too, in the case of the 1964 census. The situation regarding the 1982 census, however, is less clear, for no clarification is offered in the available sources.

It would seem that the inclusion or otherwise of small settlements in the 1982 urban count was determined by quite rigid application of two conditions. The first of these concerns status in the vertical system of places: only designated *zhen* were considered eligible. The second condition concerns the size of settlements; only places that strictly conformed to the established size criteria could be considered as urban places. Implementation of these two conditions has meant the exclusion of some designated *zhen* purely on grounds of size.

As far as the first condition is concerned, since 1977 at least it had been customary to extend the definition of urbanness beyond the *zhen*. The purpose was to embrace a number of county seats (a tier of the administrative field system) which had never been granted *zhen* status. Such anomalies have various origins. In some cases, the reason was over-zealous interpretation of the ruling on *zhen* size qualifications. But for the most part, the omission of these county seats was due to administrative quirks. Most reports speak of 'over 370' such places in the past few years; the exact number appears to have remained constant at the 377 reported for 1979. The 1982 census denied all such places an urban standing.

As for the existence of the second condition (stern adherence to size criteria), the evidence lies in the pre- and post-census reports of the global figure for *zhen*. Just six months before the census, there were around 150 more *zhen*. Just six months after it, there were also about 150 more. It is entirely unlikely that such great (and equal) numbers of towns had their charters revoked in the first six months of 1982 and restored (or granted anew) in the last part of that year. The circumstantial evidence that exclusion occurred is therefore overwhelming. The only reasonable explanation for such exclusion is that the places in question did not meet the conditional size thresholds described earlier.

Table 3.6 shows the number of settlements of various kinds encompassed by the pre-census standard definition of 'urban' in China. As well as including all the *zhen*, the definition also allowed the non-*zhen* county seats to be counted. Here is unambiguous

Table 3.6: Designated Urban Places and Other Non-*zhen* Places, 1979–82

	1	2	3	4	5
1979	2,851	377	3,228	216	3,444
1980	2,882	377	3,259	223	3,482
1981	2,843	377	3,220	233	3,453
Census	2,664	0	2,664	236	2,900
1982	2,819	377	3,196	245	3,441

Note
Column 1: total designated towns (*she zhen*);
      2: total non-*zhen* county seats (*xian cheng*);
      3: total — 1 plus 2;
      4: total designated municipalities (*she shi*);
      5: total 'urban places' by pre-census reckoning.
All figures are year-end (except for 1982 census).
Source. All information on the number of municipalities derived from or confirmed in relevant ZXQJ.
    1979: private communication from personnel of now-defunct State Administration for Urban Construction (*Chengshi jianshe zongju*) in Beijing.
    1980: RMRB, 6 June 1981.[62]
    1981: RMRB, 27 April 1983 (the combined population of the *zhen* is given as 44.77 million).
    1982: Li Mengbai, CXJS, no. 12 (1983), p. 16.

proof that the 1982 census — far from being based on more settlements — in fact had a much narrower foundation than had become customary in the years immediately preceding it.

Finally, the third part of *Beijing Review*'s explanation for the high urban figures in the 1982 census is that there has been natural increase of population and some net immigration. This is undoubtedly true, but the increments arising from these two factors within a six-month period are extremely slight in comparison with the seventy-odd million 'new' urban population. Especially so at a time when the urban birth rate had been reduced to a low pitch and the great wave of post-Mao returnees to the urban areas had all but subsided.

Generalisation of the 1982 Census Urban Criteria

Evidently, the State Statistical Bureau intends henceforth to use the census *shizhen* definition as a standard. The *1981 Statistical Yearbook of China*[63] did not present a full year-by-year aggregate urban series; but the two figures offered for recent years — namely 1978 and 1981 — conform to the 1963/1982 *zhen*/urban rule

Table 3.7: The Contrasting Urban Criteria, Selected Years 1949–82

	chengzhen interpretation of urban		*shizhen* interpretation of urban		'extra' urban
	no.	%	no.	%	
1949	57.65	10.6	57.65	10.6	–
1953 census	na	na	na	na	na
1957	99.49	15.4	99.49	15.4	–
1964 census	97.91	14.1	127.10	18.3	29.19
1965	101.70	14.0	130.45	18.0	28.75
1975	111.71	12.2	160.30	17.3	48.59
1978	119.94	12.5	172.45	17.9	52.51
1981	138.70	13.9	201.71	20.2	63.01
1982 census	–	–	206.59	20.6	–

Note: Percentage data: of total population. All absolute figures are in millions.
Source: The *chengzhen* data are from TJNJ 1982, p. 89. JJNJ 1982, p. V1–3 has exactly the same figures for the six years presented in TJNJ 1982, and adds two more — 1975 and 1979. The 1964 census figure here is from TJNJ 1983, p. 93.
    The *shizhen* figures are selected from TJNJ 1983, p. 103, where the entire series 1949 to 1982 is laid out. In TJNJ 1983, p. 109, a different *shizhen* total is offered for the 1964 census: 130.46 million. And for the 1982 census we have 210.83 million. The reason behind these increases (3.36 and 4.24 million respectively) is that some tabulations include all the armed forces as urban. This is of interest in itself, as it implies that demobilised PLA personnel are basically regarded as urban, whereas their origins are basically rural. There are, of course, implications here for the past and future urban growth series.

(modified, as has been explained, by the addition of 377 non-*zhen* county seats).

    The *Statistical Yearbook of China 1983* (TJNJ 1983 — published in that year, with 1982-end data) tells a very different story.[64] To begin with, for the first time ever, a complete urban series back to 1949 is provided. But in a peculiar and entirely unacknowledged exercise in partial revision, the 1983 edition presents data based on two entirely different sets of urban criteria within the very same table. The 1949 to 1963 year-end global urban figures are consonant with the *chengzhen renkou*-type of urban definition on which the disclosures for the 1950s and for the 1964 census were founded. But figures in the 1983 *Statistical Yearbook of China* (TJNJ 1983) for the period 1964 to 1982 are unashamedly based on the highly inflationary 1982 *shizhen* concept. The urban series presented under a column headed *shizhen zong renkou* ('combined *shizhen* population') is therefore marked by a striking discontinuity between 1963 and 1964.

In the wake of the 1982 census, a revision along the same lines appears for the 1964 census urban total — which (as has earlier been explained) was registered in the 1982 edition of the Yearbook TJNJ 1982) at 97.910 million. This was, of course, in accordance with the *chengzhen* interpretation of urbanness.[65] The census communique of 27 October 1982, in detailing the *shizhen* census total, had noted that it was exactly 79,485,541 persons greater than in the 1964 census — meaning that the latter's urban total came to some 127.10 million. Here again, then, huge numbers of municipal agricultural inhabitants were being counted as urban. Table 3.7 contrasts the official urban data for the years available as presented according to the more plausible (and preferable) *chengzhen* (and modified *chengzhen*) definition on the one hand, and the inflated, implausible (yet nevertheless now-standard) *shizhen* definition. Apart from the *Yearbooks*, Table 3.7 draws on the Zhongguo jingji nianjian 1981 (JJNJ 1982 — *Economic Yearbook of China 1981*) published in 1982. The last column indicates the growth of the definition-caused urban inflation since 1964.

A Summary of Urban Criteria, Practical Definitions, and Post-1982 Census Trends

The attributes of China's urbanness have been examined at length, both in terms of the general city-region concept and the actual problems of data disclosures and changing definitions. Now is an appropriate point at which to summarise the latter. So as to render the discussion on urban definition less abstract, the chapter will conclude by taking a closer look at the morphology of a particular city — Nanjing.

Summary of the Urban Definitions and Data Disclosures

Firstly, the actual release of urban information by China. Until very recently, the only detailed and apparently authoritative information on the size of urban China related to the early 1950s. The urban figure for the 1953 census fitted into a similarly-based series issued in 1957 which gave the aggregates from 1949 to 1956. Though some hearsay reports on urban dimensions immediately before and after the 1958 Great Leap Forward have been available since the early 1970s, essentially there was no hard information released during the approximately two decades between 1957 and

1979. This long period was one in which the Chinese were satisfied to talk generally of 'resident points' (*jumindian*) rather than specifically about urban places and rural places. In a sense, this preference for vagueness suited the ideological priorities of the times: the slogan of 'eradicating the three great differentials' and learning from the Daqing spatial model were Maoist substitutes for the routine of planning and they required no firm notion of urban and rural. Yet, at the same time, China's leaders were careful to ensure that the urban-rural distinction continued to be clearly enshrined in the registration and rationing systems. While the higher echelons of political-economic planning have all along regarded the registration particulars as an indispensable tool, demographic and spatial planning — in so far as it was practised at all — was denied a definite concept of urbanness and the data consequent upon it.

The year 1979 was a turning point. It brought both the rehabilitation of urban statistics *per se*, and their open publication. In 1981, a gross urban figure for the 1964 census was at last released. And in the following year, some incomplete totals for various years from the 1950s to the 1970s appeared in different yearbooks. Then, of course, came the results of the 1982 census which have caused so much confusion. Finally, towards the end of 1983 the *Statistical Yearbook of China 1983* appeared with its eccentric tabulation of aggregate urban data right back to 1949.

Secondly, there is the complex question of urban definition. Disregarding the vague notions of the Cultural Revolution, and the spurious data published in 1980–1 (in, for instance, the *Encyclopaedic Yearbook of China*[66]), three broad definitions of 'urban' can be identified, as follows:

The chengzhen *Definition*. This includes only those places which have been designated municipalities (*shi*) and town (*zhen*) in what we have earlier termed the vertical system of urban places. It counts all such places. For the municipalities, only their non-agricultural population is enumerated as urban. For the *zhen*, the position is less clear cut: in the 1953 census, agricultural persons may have been included; in the data for 1977 to 1981, they were not. The number of *shi* has, generally, risen year by year. The number of *zhen*, however, has fluctuated wildly with changing size-class criteria.

Sometimes the *chengzhen* definition has taken account of the non-agricultural populations of settlements lying within their enlarged boundaries. On other occasions, these increments have been counted separately. The manner in which this factor is considered has made no difference, of course, to the national urban total. The *chengzhen* definition applied to the 1953 census and to the contemporary and retrospective accounts of urban size for the 1950s.

The Modified chengzhen *Definition.* This is identical to the above except in one respect: the almost 400 county seats which had failed to attain *zhen* status are included in the urban count. Their inclusion is pragmatic, as it considers functional criteria above simply bureaucratic ones. The modified *chengzhen* definition held for the 1977–81 data officially released before 1983. Thereafter, the urban totals for these years were adjusted upwards, in accordance with the *shizhen* standards.

The shizhen *Definition.* This breaks entirely with all previous practices. For the designated towns, it withholds urban recognition to some out of hand — on the grounds that they do not meet the *zhen* size qualifications. And it takes a wider view of those towns which it does include by counting in their registered agricultural populations. At the same time, the new definition strips all non-*zhen* county towns of their erstwhile urban status (held under the prior modified *chengzhen* criteria). As for the municipalities — all are included regardless of their total populations (however assessed). But the *shizhen* view is to class all the inhabitants of the municipal districts of all *shi* — that is, their combined total *shiqu* population — as urban. This results in a very great inflation of the national urban total. Since the announcement of the 1982 census results, the *shizhen* definition appears to have been adopted as standard. The 1982-end urban population is expressed thereby, and it is also the basis for a revised series back to, and including, the 1964 census.

Some Post-1982 Census Views of Urban Definition

The findings of the 1982 census have intiated a discussion amongst urban geographers and planners regarding the quantification of urban population in China.[67] Both the census criteria, and those which govern the designation of *zhen* and *shi*, have come under increasing scrutiny.

Of central concern is the counting of registered agricultural population in urban totals. The inclusion of some 16 million agricultural persons in the census *zhen* total, for example, is broadly considered to be an appropriate measure. Here the agricultural/non-agricultural populations distinction is regarded as an academic one for urban planning and construction, though no urban specialist would suggest that it should be abandoned in its role as a determinant of mode of grain supply (that is, state commodity grain or non-commodity grain supplied through the rural collective). Implied here is the need for a functional approach which departs from traditional divisions and their rigid equation of the non-agricultural part of the population with the urban sector, and the agricultural part with the rural sector. This question has a particular bearing on the work of physical planners in a period of renaissance of town planning and urban construction.

As evidence of the need for a more pragmatic approach, geographers such as Hu Xuwei[68] examine the changing economic base of small towns where residents of agricultural and non-agricultural registration live cheek by jowl. Baiguan *zhen*, for example, county seat of Shangyu *xian* (Zhejiang), is the location of production brigades of the rural commune system. In the Baiguan brigade, two-thirds of the labour force is engaged in non-agricultural activities — small industries, transport, construction services, and so on. Their revenue amounts to 85 per cent of all brigade income. From the urban geographer's viewpoint, 'obviously it is unreasonable to exclude this section of so-called "agricultural population" from the total urban population . . . [as] they jointly make use of all manner of urban facilities'.

The census's inclusion of very substantial numbers of agricultural persons within municipal urban populations is held to be a more complicated matter. The general view is that it would be 'irrational' to exclude those agricultural residents living on the immediate fringes of the municipalities from the total urban count. They may 'wear the agricultural hat', but for all practical purposes they are 'hidden urban inhabitants'. They make use of urban facilities, and planners cannot therefore exclude them of technical grounds from the municipal population. None the less, in circumstances where the urban districts (*shiqu*) are excessively extensive (stretching far into the countryside), the designation of large numbers of peasants as 'urban' gives rise to a 'great misapprehension'. This situation arises in particular where a *shi* has been formed around dispersed mining operations. Liupanshui municipality in Guizhou (elevated to *shi* status in the mid-1970s) is the classic case. Here, of the total *shi* population of 2,020,000, only 287,000 (14 per cent) are registered as non-agricultural persons. Furthermore, they are scattered around numerous urban nodes.

At provincial level, it is Zhejiang which is regarded as the worst offender in this respect. Many of the recently-chartered *shi* have commandeered large areas of non-*xian* rural territory. The third-order cities of Shaoxing, Jiaxing, Huzhou, Jinhua and Hengzhou do not even possess *shiqu*, let alone rural counties, yet in none of these places does the non-agricultural population exceed 25 per cent. A comparison of the resulting urban growth figures for Zhejiang and neighbouring Jiangsu Province shows the compound distortion which arises from this situation between 1964 and 1982, Zhejiang's nominal urban population rose by 125 per cent, but for Jiangsu, where more conventional urban administrative demarcation has prevailed, the increase was only 25 per cent.

On the other hand, the design of the 1982 census unreasonably excludes certain settlements which have all the attributes of urban places. For example, not all the county seats were registered as urban places. This anomaly is highlighted by the fact that several hundred of those *zhen* actually included were not county seats. From the functional and also the political standpoints, these places, coming as they do under county rule, are clearly subsidiary in the urban hierarchy to the county seats, regardless of *zhen* designation.

A related problem identified by China's urban specialists concerns the criteria determining status in the vertical system of cities. These are faulted on two grounds: the level at which the size standards are presently pitched, and the arbitrary manner in which they are applied. In illustration of the latter problem, it is pointed out that the almost 400 non-*zhen* county seats (excluded in the 1982 census from the urban count) are concentrated in a few regions. For instance, of the 139 county seats in Hebei Province, only 55 have *zhen* status. The 1963/1982 *zhen* regulations stipulate a minimum population of 3,000, of which 70 per cent should be non-agricultural. Yet there are places which more than meet such standards but are arbitrarily denied designation. One settlement in Hebei which is neither a county town nor a *zhen* nevertheless has a total population of almost 11,000, with a non-agricultural ratio of around 70 per cent.

Such irregularities are felt to seriously distort and devalue the overall urban figures. In Hebei's case, the outcome is that at 9 per cent, the 1982 urban proportion is a serious understatement of practical reality; it is even smaller than the 1957 figure (11.8 per cent). In practice, therefore, some provinces interpret the *zhen* size rules as they wish, many applying a minimum standard of 10,000, half at least of which must be non-agricultural, before *zhen* status is conferred. While little is understood about the implications of the *zhen* system for local government finance, the fact that certain provinces are slow to designate *zhen* may arise from a desire to avoid further responsibilities of financial support.

Similar reasons may be behind the reluctance of provincial authorities to abhore to the stipulations regarding the chartering of *shi*. The 1963/1982 rules specify that, with some exceptions (minority and border areas, places of special economic importance, and so on), all concentrations of population of over 100,000 where non-agricultural population is more than 70 per cent should be granted municipal status. The 'Provisional Directive on City Planning Norms' lays down that all *shi* over 200,000 should be promoted to the second-order category. And yet, in practice, these rules are widely disregarded. Many regions insist on at least 100,000 *non-agricultural* inhabitants as a minimum *shi* requirement.[69]

It is widely agreed that in the current period of rapid industrial and agricultural change, economic and physical planning in China demand a satisfactory means of distinguishing between the rural and urban spheres. Whatever reforms are introduced into the system of identifying and counting urban population, they should incorporate a recognition of the continuing distinction between town and country. In other words, there is little sympathy today for the vague and voluntarist approach of the Mao period which cloaked its inability to develop urban-rural criteria in utopian rhetoric. One present-day reformer reminds us of the State Council directive 'On Distinguishing between Urban and Rural Areas' (7 November 1955):

> Because the urban and rural populations' ways of life are quite different, all aspects of government work should distinguish between urban and rural areas. Urban and rural population must be tabulated separately.[70]

Hence, with regard to the question of whether (for example) China's over 50,000 commune seats should be considered urban places, the prevailing view is that these 'rural market towns' (*nongcun jizhen*) fall firmly within the rural sphere. They lack all the political, economic, technological and cultural attributes of urbanness as it is conceived of in China of the 1980s. They simply do not possess that essential quality of urbanity.

The more prescient observers agree that China's urban administrative system, and the discrimination of urban from rural population that is consequent upon it, should be reformed and standardised throughout the nation. For the *zhen* qualifications, for instance, one geographer believes that the size threshold (one of the minimum 'urban' standards) should be raised from the present 2,500 and 3,000 (depending on the non-agricultural ratio) to 5,000. Considerations both of the occupations of residents and status as a county seat should be entirely set aside. If there are 3,000 souls in the settlement of 5,000 who — whatever their household registration — have worked for a set period in stable non-agricultural employment — then that place should be considered urban and all its population included in aggregate urban population. In minority and border areas, and other special circumstances, the thresholds could be lowered to 2,000 and 3,000 persons respectively. The reformed system would establish an unambiguous means of determining whether or not a settlement were counted as urban, and it would be based entirely on the possession of *zhen* status. As for the municipalities, some recommend that their threshold should be lowered from the present (and largely ignored) 100,000 to 50,000. The general view, though, is that the present size criterion should be retained, otherwise too many towns lacking both basic urban facilities and the less tangible urban ambience would gain *shi* status. Certain cities already possessing municipal charters should redraw their suburban districts (*jiaoqu*) in order to exclude excessive numbers of registered agricultural persons living at a distance from the city proper. Having introduced these new standards, it should become a statutory requirement for each province to apply them faithfully.

The Morphology of a Municipality — Urbanness in Nanjing[71]

This chapter will draw to a close by illustration of the complexities involved in classifying urban population in the real world. Nanjing Municipality is the capital of Jiangsu Province in the rich and populous region of East China; historically, the city has frequently served as China's national capital. Indeed, for much of the first half of the present century Nanjing took on that role for the

Guomindang and the Japanese puppet government. In the decades before the Communist victory of 1949, Nanjing remained a city of almost no modern industry. Over the past thirty years, however, it has cast aside its traditional administrative role and become one of China's key industrial cities. It is now a vital producer of petrochemicals, automobiles, heavy machinery, and a wide range of light industrial goods. Indeed Nanjing's industrial prominence means that today it is one of the 17-odd major centres which bear the title of 'keypoint city' (*zhongdian chengshi*). We cannot, here, do full justice to the city's historical attributes and past urban growth; our concern is the present-day morphology and population distribution of Nanjing municipality.

As well as being one of the twenty-six provincial/autonomous region seats in the administrative field system, Nanjing is — not unexpectedly — also a *shi* of the second order. As such it bears the right to directly annex and govern rural counties. Nanjing has three of these — Jiangning, Jiangpu and Luhe. The core city divides administratively into the familiar *shiqu* or city districts. In Nanjing there are ten in all, six urban districts (*chengqu*) and four suburban districts (*jiaoqu*). The *shiqu* themselves break down into a number of *jiedao*, the lowest formal tier of the urban administrative hierarchy.

Earlier, we have considered the 1981-end and 1982-end municipal data which separate city population in first- and second-order places into three bands: the entire city, the entire population of the *shiqu*, and the non-agricultural population of the *shiqu*. By subtraction of the second figure from the first, we have a fourth band accounting for the population of the county or counties attached to the municipality. Table 3.8 shows the situation for Nanjing at the end of 1982. But a closer look reveals the inadequacy of this degree of breakdown, and in so doing brings into even sharper relief the difficulties of determining urbanness on the ground.

Figure 3.2 shows the extent and divisions of Nanjing. The municipal boundary stretches some one hundred kilometres from north to south, and 50 kilometres east to west, the whole area being divided diagonally by the Changjiang (Yangzi River). Beginning at the hub of the several concentric zones, first there are the six urban districts or *chengqu*. They are closely-packed residential, commercial and light industrial areas and unmistakably urban in appearance.

Next, there are the four suburban districts, both urban and rural in character and population. The innermost ring of three of these

Table 3.8: Four-band Funtional/administrative Division of Nanjing
Municipality's Population, 1982

	Population (millions)	Area (km²)
10 Municipal districts total	2.13	867
10 Municipal districts non-agricultural population only	1.74	—
3 Attached counties total	1.61	3,851
Total municipality	*3.74*	*4,718*

Source: TJNJ 1983, pp. 79 and 108.

forms a continuation, an overflow, of the distinctly urban core
districts. Along the major transit routes leading out of the city,
much ribbon-development has occurred in the past decade. The
people who live here are predominantly non-agricultural. On the
northern bank of the Changjiang lies the old-established railway
engineering town of Pukou. Abutting the southernmost urban
district of Qinghuai, the built-up area extends into the suburban
district of Yuhuatai without any visible discontinuity. A similar
situation is to be found in the north-east of Nanjing, where Gulou
urban district blends into the suburban district of Qixia. Extending
finger-like into this inner zone of the suburban districts are
vegetable fields belonging to the eleven rural people's communes of
the *jiaoqu*. Their main purpose is to supply fresh produce to the
urban population. A short step outwards brings one into a mainly
rural landscape and soon the fields are as likely to be sown to
winter wheat or summer rice as cabbages and aubergines.

Within the suburban districts there are, nevertheless, some
sizeable concentrations of urban-industrial population. Notable
amongst them is the long-established sprawl of the fertiliser plant at
Dachangzhen, situated on the north bank of the river east of the
city proper. Then there is the petrochemicals complex around
Qixiashan on the south bank of the Chang Jiang. Since the 1950s
an important oil refinery has operated here, supplied by river
tanker and by pipeline from the new north Jiangsu oilfields. In
recent years the activities of Qixiashan have been greatly
augmented by the construction of a giant chemical fertiliser plant
imported from France. And to the south-west of the city proper is
the new industrial centre of Banqiao.

These three places are all destined for further growth under

Figure 3.2: Nanjing Municipality, 1981: The Administrative Framework

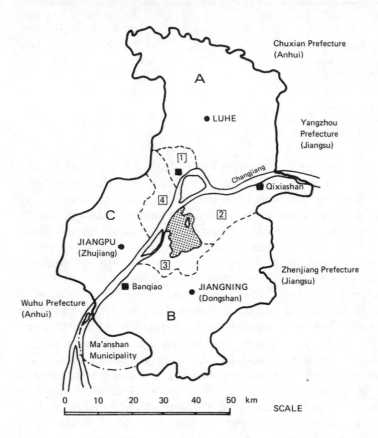

KEY

〜〜〜 BORDER OF Nanjing Municipality
– – – border of *jiaoqu* (suburban districts)
══════ Changjiang (Yangzi) River
       Urban/Administrative Division
⬡   six *chengqu* (city districts): Xia Guan, Gu Lou, Xuanwu, Jianye, Baixia and Qinghuai
1 2 3 4 four *jiaoqu*: 1. Dachang, 2. Qixia, 3. Yuhuatai, 4. Pukou
A B C three *xian*: A. Luhe, B. Jiangning, C. Jiangpu
●   *xian* seats
■   proposed or *de facto* satellite towns (Dachangzhen in Dachang suburban district)

Table 3.9: Detailed Functional/administrative Divisions of Nanjing, 1982

Division	Area			Population		
	km²			m.		
	rural	urban	total	rural	urban	total
6 Urban districts	0 +	83	= 83	0 +	1.23	= 1.23
4 Suburban districts	534 +	250	= 784	0.42 +	0.48	= 0.90
Of which						
Inner urban ring		43			0.23	
3 satellite towns		207			0.25	
Rural/villages	534			0.42		
3 Counties	3,791 +	60	= 3,851	1.51 +	0.10	= 1.61
Of which						
6 towns (*zhen*)		60			0.10	
Farm/forest land	3,475			1.51		
Villages/other	316					
Grand Total	4,325 +	393	= 4,718	1.93 +	1.81	= 3.74
	(92%)	(8%)		(52%)	(48%)	

Note: All population figures in rounded millions.
Source: i. Area: interviews with city planners 1975, 1976 and 1982 for the three main subtotals. Satellites — estimated from Dachangzhen's 110,000 (interviews, 1982) and visits to Qixia/Longtan in 1975. Six towns (three county seats and three further *zhen*) esimated at ten square km each. Remaining figures are informed estimates.
ii. Population: the main figures are all from TJNJ 1983, p. 79 and p. 108, and are all 1982 year-end. The subsidiary figures are simple *pro rata* extrapolations from various data of the 1970s and early 1980s conveyed to me in various discussions. As such, the figures for some of the minor subdivisions should be considered as notional, indicating general orders of magnitude.

current municipal plans, and if the physical planners have their way they will be granted formal recognition as satellite towns. In 1978, Dachangzhen's weight in the total urban structure of Nanjing was acknowledged by elevation to suburban district status in its own right. Formerly, Dachangzhen (literally 'big factory town') was a segment of the Pukou suburban district. Within the suburban districts there are a number of less significant settlements, the activities of their inhabitants dominated by agriculture.

Moving further out, one enters the territory of the counties. Here there is generally no outward indication of administrative attachment to a major metropolis. As one approaches the far reaches of the municipality, more and more farming folk can be found who have rarely — if ever — journeyed to the city proper. For them, belonging to Nanjing *shi* is no more than a juridical fact. (Though it must be said that the reforms inaugurated in 1979 have brought some change in this situation, the peasants being encouraged to broaden the bounds of their marketing.)

Within the three counties there are pockets of population which, under the current *shizhen* rules, are tallied as urban places. The three county seats all enjoy *zhen* status, as do at least three other sufficiently large townships located in Nanjing's three *xian*.

Table 3.9 provides the more detailed account of the spatial and population characteristics of Nanjing. Beyond pointing out that these figures show a preponderance of agricultural persons in Nanjing, I will allow the figures (read in conjunction with the map of Nanjing — Figure 3.2) to speak for themselves.

Notes

1. State Statistical Bureau, *Ten Great Years: Statistics of the Economic and Cultural Achievements of the People's Republic of China* (Foreign Languages Press, Beijing, 1960).

2. Typical were Joan Robinson, *Economic Management, China 1972* (Anglo-Chinese Educational Institute, London, 1972), or E. Wheelwright and B. McFarlane, *The Chinese Road to Socialism* (Monthly Review Press, New York and London, 1970).

3. For instance, N. Lardy, *Economic Growth and Distribution in China* (Cambridge University Press, Cambridge, 1978), or R. M. Field, 'Real Capital Formation in the People's Republic of China: 1952–1973', unpublished manuscript, July 1976.

4. See glossary of books in Chinese.

5. *Chengshi guihua (City Planning), Cheng xiang jianshe (Urban-Rural Construction), Renkou yanjiu (Population Research)*, and so on. See glossary of Chinese journals.

6. Amongst the range of statistics unavailable in useful forms during the Cultural Revolution, those relating to population matters were notable. Indeed, China's leaders were quite capable — in their interviews with foreign journalists — of losing a hundred million or more of their citizens within a few weeks.

7. Published in many places, but most prominently in RMRB, 27 October 1983.

8. At least four were in current use by central government bodies in the early 1980s — the public security authorities, the agencies responsible for the rationing system, the labour ministry, and the urban planners.

9. Interviews conducted at the Ministry of Urban-Rural Construction and Environmental Protection, June, 1982.

10. Shen Bingyu, 'Urbanization in China: Policies and Population Redistribution', unpublished MA thesis, Brown University (USA), Sociology Department', June 1981, p. 3.

11. The 1980 figure cited here is even more odd: 230.65 million as opposed to the official — and more or less plausible — figure of 134 million (see chapter 4).

12. DGB, 12 June 1982. The World Bank figure is unattributed.

13. *Demographic Indicators of Countries, Estimates and Projections as Assessed in 1980* (UN Department of International Economic and Social Affairs, New York, 1982), p. 254.

14. L. Orleans, *Every Fifth Child: The Population of China* (Eyre Methuen, London, 1972), p. 70; T. Shabad, *China's Changing Map* (Praeger, New York, 1972), p. 36; Cheng-siang Chen, 'Population Growth and Urbanization in China, 1953–1970', *Geographical Review*, vol. 63, no. 1 (January 1973), p. 66; Sen-dou Chang, 'The Changing System of Chinese Cities', *Annals of the Association of American Geographers*, vol. 66, no. 3 (September 1976), p. 399 (Chang accepts Orleans's figure without qualification).

15. World Bank, 'China: Socialist Economic Development', 9 vols (World Bank internal document, Washington, June 1981).

16. *Demographic Yearbook 1981* (UN Department of International Economic and Social Affairs, Statistical Office, New York, 1983), Table 6, pp. 203–74.

17. *Nongye wei jichu, gongye wei zhudao*, Communique of the 10th Plenary Session of the 8th Party Central Committee, 28 September 1962 (RMRB, 29 September 1962, reported in GCPP, no. 0895, p. 268).

18. Zhou Xiantang, JWTS, no. 5 (1982), p. 41.

19. See chapter 8.

20. ZXQJ 1983, and RMRB, 9 January 1983. The prefectural and county equivalents are those administrative units at equivalent level — for example, *zizhizhou* and *meng* — at prefectural level, *zizhixian* and *qi* at county level. They are so designated because they have predominantly non-Han populations and therefore (nominal, at least) autonomy. Note that the prefectural level in many provinces has — in the mid-1980s — been practically abolished in an experiment which places all their subordinate counties under the second-order municipalities. A further important change is the restoration of the township (*xiang*) level in the administrative field system, a move which will change the roles of both the commune seats which are selected as township seats, and of those which are not. Note that any particular settlement may be the location of more than one tier in the field system. Very often, the governing bodies of tiers not adjacent in the hierarchy may be spatially contiguous. For example, I once lived in a rural town which was a county capital, but not the seat of the people's commune which ruled over the immediate countryside. Yet this town was the locus of one of the production brigades of that commune. There are numerous such anomalies throughout the system.

21. The legislative basis was enshrined in the State Council's 'Decision on the Establishment of Municipalities and Towns' of 9 June 1953 (reported in M. Ullman, 'Cities of Mainland China: 1953–1959', in G. Breese (ed.), *The City in Newly Developing Countries* (Prentice Hall, London, 1972), p. 89.

22. Figures for the municipalities compiled from the provincial tables in ZXQJ 1983.

23. Li Mengbai, CXJS, no. 12 (1983), p. 16.

24. RMRB, 27 October 1982. Shanghai *shi* stood at 11.86 million.

25. ZXQJ 1983.

26. Principally the 2,843 *zhen*, but also the several hundred non-*zhen* county seats which qualified in the urban count. Figures on differing urban totals mainly from TJNJ 1982, p. 89.

27. Examples of this are manifest. Take a typical case in which the present writer was personally concerned: a university department was engaged in the preparation of a new dictionary — a tiresome enough business in China where each entry's explanation has to be reconsidered in the light of the latest political campaign. With thousands of hours invested, it transpired that an almost-identical project was underway in a neighbouring college. Efforts could not be pooled, however, as the university came under the educational departments while the college belonged to the

military. There were simply no formal channels of communication between the strands of the two separate vertical hierarchies.

28. TKP, 2 June 1983.

29. Shandong University, Jinan, and Licheng County (1979). The same county administration, despite its formal subordination to the municipal authorities, had for many years been illicitly tapping power lines belonging to the city's power plant. When finally discovered, and presented with a bill running into several million *yuan*, the defiant response of the county leadership was to embark on a sabotage campaign. Regularly, electricity cables were severed and key units suffer a blackout. In this case, though, the dispute was within the same vertical segment, and rights of redress could eventually be asserted.

30. Referred to here is the situation before 1982 — see chapter 8 on the dissolution of the prefectural tier.

31. *New China New Agency*, Beijing, 17 September 1959.

32. Local custom seems to have governed the method of acquiring land: in some areas (eg, Shandong), the *shi* have acquired rural tracts as large as counties, yet the county administrations have been abolished.

33. Provincial capital of Jiangsu and, as the ex-Guomindang capital of China, eager to present a contrite and most revolutionary face.

34. From issues of the ZXQJ 1978–1983, and ZFDJ 1977, sections 3–34.

35. Cheng-siang Chen, 'Population Growth and Urbanization in China, 1953–1970', p. 65. The population figures for Pingxiang are for 1970: total population over 1 million, core population 40,000, with an agricultural population of 730,000 and a non-agricultural population of only 170,000. Information on other cities in this section is taken from the ZFDJ 1977, as well as from various interviews and discussions in China 1975–80.

36. Information on Zibo from interviews with planners in 1982, and in Dong Liming, GSGH, no. 12 (1983), pp. 19–20. In the 1982 census, Zibo's total municipal population was given as 2.23 million.

37. Derived from ZXQJ 1982 and 1983, TJNJ, 1982, pp. 27–8, and ZFDJ 1977.

38. All information for the end of 1982 — see ZXQJ 1983.

39. In many other respects the urban order in Hebei is eccentric, the probable common reason being the weight of the great metropolitan centres of Beijing and Tianjin. Their magnetic influence on migrants, and on regional allocation of resources, seems to have repressed urban growth and power within Hebei.

40. Information from ZXQJ 1983, and visit to Liaoning, October 1983.

41. Orleans, 'The Recent Growth of China's Urban Population', p. 46.

42. Twenty years ago, two American scholars provided major studies of the urban data for the 1953 census. The work of Ullman and Orleans made use of a number of secondary sources — including Soviet writers who had been closely involved in the 1953 census. Orleans, ibid.; Ullman, 'Cities of Mainland China: 1953–1959'. The ensuing analysis draws extensively on these two articles.

43. Ullman, ibid., p. 82; see his footnote on the same page for the original source.

44. *Guowuyuan guanyu cheng xiang huafen biaozhen de guiding* (State Council Directive on the Criteria for Distinguishing between City and Countryside), *Tongji gongzuo tongxun (Statistical Work Bulletin)*, no. 12 (1955), p. 24, cited in Ullman, 'Cities of Mainland China', footnote 16, p. 89.

45. Department of Population Statistics, State Statistical Bureau, *The 1982 Population Census of China (Major Figures)*, (Economic Information and Agency, Hong Kong, 1982), Preface, explanatory note 3.

46. Other Chinese specialists seem confused here. See J. S. Aird's appraisal of Li Chengrui's interpretation in 'The Preliminary Results of China's 1982 Census', *China Quarterly*, no. 96 (December 1983), p. 615.

47. Hu Xuwei, CSGH, no. 3 (1983), pp. 25–6.

48. Ye Shuzan, 'Urbanization and Housing in China', *Asian Geographer*, vol. 1, no. 2 (1982), p. 1.

49. Ullman, 'Cities of Mainland China', Table 1, p. 86, and Table 3, p. 91.

50. Here I disagree with Ullman (ibid, p.90) who states: 'it is probable that the definition observed in tabulating the urban totals for the 1953 census was essentially the same as that used for other years.'

51. Li Chengrui, *Population Censuses in China* (State Statistical Bureau, Beijing, 1981), pp. 4–5, cited in J. Aird, 'The Preliminary Results of China's 1982 Census', p. 615. This figure was confirmed later in TJNJ 1982, p. 89.

52. Hu Xuwei, CSGH, no. 3 (1983), pp. 25–6.

53. See chapter 4, Table 4.2 and Table 4.6.

54. 1982's census reports, and subsequent announcements, have given widely differing accounts of the 1964 census urban results, as well as of the urban totals in the interviewing years.

55. For 1978: BKNJ 1980, p. 626; 1979: Zhu Zhuo, RKYJ, no. 3 (1980), p. 11; 1980: TKP, 12 June 1982; 1981: TJNJ 1982, p. 89.

56. Discussions with personnel of the Urban Planning and Design Academy of the Ministry of Urban-Rural Construction and Environmental Protection, June 1982 and November 1983.

57. BR, no. 7 (14 February 1983), p. 28. As it happens, 'our readers' was largely repeated canvassing by the present writer.

58. Above these districts is the municipal government itself, and below them are the state organs of the *jiedao* committees — the latter often poorly rendered as 'neighbourhood' committees.

59. This information results for various calculation on the data to be found in the population sections of TJNJ 1982.

60. For information on the inclusion of *zhen* agricultural persons, see RMRB, 16 November 1982.

61. Li Mengbai, CSGH, no. 12 (1983), p. 17.

62. There appear to be two typographical errors here — first, the year is given as 1980, but there are a number of different sources which confirm the above entries for 1979; a second concerns the number of *zhen*, which I believe should not be 2,882 as in the Table, but 2,482. In any case, the increase in *shi* between 1977 and 1982 (29) more or less matches the decrease in *zhen* (32) during the same period.

63. TJNJ 1982.

64. TJNJ 1983.

65. Explained under the sub-heading 'Summary of Urban Definitions and Data Disclosures' later in this chapter.

66. BKNJ; both the 1980 and 1981 editions contain some bizarre urban totals for the provinces.

67. It is of some significance that there is not really a standard equivalent for 'urbanisation' in modern Mainland Chinese usage. Overseas Chinese Mandarin usage is generally *dushihua*, which is closer in meaning to 'metropolitanisation'. In the 1970s, *chengshihua* started to be used in China, though it implies the growth of the major cities. Since 1981, many writers have fallen in with a new hybrid — *chengzhenhua* — and this is said to suit the 'Chinese road' to urbanisation better than the above expressions, for it gives recognition to the sub-municipal settlements. None of these three terms is to be found in contemporary Chinese dictionaries.

68. I shall draw here on the writings of a number of specialists, notable amongst them an article entitled 'A Close Analysis of China's Urbanisation Level' by the Beijing University geographer Hu Xuwei (in CSGH, no. 2 (1983), pp. 27–8/26.)

69. Zhou Guangyang, JZXB, no. 4 (1983), p. 34.

70. Cited from the 1955 'State Council Directive on Criteria to Distinguish

Between City and Countryside' (*Guowuyuan guanyu cheng xiang huafen biaozhun de guiding*), cited by Bu Juecha, CXJS, no. 12 (1983), pp. 21–2.

71. Nanjing is intimately known to this writer: he was resident in the city between 1975 and 1977.

4 THE PRC: A SERIES FOR URBAN POPULATION GROWTH, 1949–82

Urban Population — Its Meaning

The previous chapter discussed the complex issue of definition of urban population in post-1949 China. The urban series to be presented here draws on this discussion. In outline, the situation is as follows. For the 1950s and for 1964, the urban population totals are those already introduced in the previous chapter. The Cultural Revolution period (1966–76) has demanded some informed estimation. Thereafter, until 1981, the year-by-year urban totals are based on pre-1982 census official figures, modified to take account of the growing error due to poor household registration records in the aftermath of the Cultural Revolution. The 1982 figure is again an estimate, as official sources after mid-1982 take on the new enlarged notion of urbanness, the *shizhen* definition.

That is to say, the entire series offered in this chapter adopts the more limited idea of urban population, officially recognised (if only implicitly) over most of the period 1949 to 1982. This is, namely, the *chengzhen feinongye renkou* ('non-agricultural population of the (designated) municipalities and towns') definition. As we have seen, this is administratively delineated: basically, it counts in only those settlements that have acquired status as *shi* and *zhen* in the vertical system of urban places. These designated settlements are, in turn, defined by minimum population and household registration criteria. Within the municipalities, only non-agricultural population is enumerated as urban. Within the *zhen*, this is true for the data of the 1970s, if not too for that of the 1950s.

In the time series there are two factors which might be expected to give rise to discontinuities. The first is changes in *zhen* qualifications (1955 and 1963). The second factor is the relaxation of the urban criteria (at a point some time after 1964 and before 1977) to permit the inclusion of non-*zhen* county seats. The series ignores the former problem for lack of adequate information, but it does take account of the latter.

103

The Three-phase Division and Its Choice

The aggregate urban figures are subdivided into three phases: 1949 to 1960, 1961 to 1976 and 1977 to 1982. As we shall see, the selection of these subdivisions highlights certain disjunctions in the population data. It is, therefore, to a degree self-serving. Even in an economy intent on implementing socialist planning, however, the process of urbanisation is far from being a simple matter of the subjective choice of planners. The immature practice of national central planning in China does not permit the *a priori* selection of 'urbanisation level' as an independent variable. Rather, the latter emerges *a posteriori* from a complex of economic and political factors determined by both internal and external forces.

The periodisation of China's urbanisation adopted in the present chapter reflects such factors. For the first phase, the starting point of 1949 should arouse no objections. Even the most stubborn empiricist would have difficulty in sustaining an argument which held that the declaration of the People's Republic of China merely changed superficial categories — that underneath the old China soldiered on unaltered. The end-point of the first phase — 1960 — is more open to question. Those Chinese appraisals which make a tripartite division of the post-1949 era generally take the first as lasting from 1953 to 1963, though this conforms neither to the official economic planning phases (1963 was the first year of the then 3-year 'economic readjustment' period) nor to the major events and policy changes which marked Chinese society and government at the time.

An examination of the fluctuating growth in China's gross value of industrial output (GVIO) lends support to the choice of periodisation. The year 1960 saw the end of a decade in which the economy had been rapidly patched up, radically restructured and expanded by the highly effective First Five Year Plan, and then rudely subjected to the frenetic leapfrogging of 1958 and 1959. With an official average annual increase in GVIO of 24.2 per cent (peaking in 1958 when there was a 55 per cent increase over the previous year), the 1949 to 1960 period is one of erratic, but nevertheless extraordinary, industrial growth. The break between 1960 and 1961 is starkly evident in the gross value of industrial output data: taking 1952 as equal to 100, the level of GVIO at the end of 1960 was 535.7; by the end of the following year it was a mere 330.7.[1]

The swift downturn in GVIO reflected the general crisis in Chinese society in the immediate aftermath of the Great Leap Forward. Another vital symptom of crisis is seen in the official total population figures for the period which show a combined net reduction of 13.5 million in 1960 and 1961. The unavoidable conclusion is that well over 20 million people died prematurely — of starvation and its induced diseases.[2]

Lastly, the choice of 1960/1961 division is also reinforced by the figures for China's total state labour force. The accelerating rate of growth of *zhigong* ('staff and workers' — basically, the state-sector workforce) towards the end of the 1950s was put into rapid reverse in 1961, and it was three years before the decline was checked. At the end of 1960 there were 59.69 million *zhigong*; twelve months later only 51.71 million.

So the beginning of 1961 was marked by sudden and substantial changes in a range of social and economic indicators, symptomatic of the general crisis which stimulated a sweeping transformation in the Party's handling of the economy in the early 1960s. The consequent developments bring the 1960/1961 division into even sharper relief.

The choice of 1976 for the termination of the second phase may seem obvious. The death of Mao heralded great changes, but they were delayed until late 1978 and the 3rd Plenary Session of the 11th Party Central Committee. It might be asked why the 16 years (1961–76) of the second phase are not subdivided to allow the Cultural Revolution (1966–76) to stand out as a discrete period. Here, both the chosen year of ending and the disclination towards a further subdivision are strongly supported by the urban data themselves: between the beginning of 1961 and the end of 1976, the pace of urban growth was either powerfully negative or approximately static. At no time in these 16 years did China's aggregate urban population show an annual growth rate which exceeded the rate for population as a whole. *This is in the sharpest contrast to the first and third of the chosen phases.* Throughout their combined 18 years, in only one (1955) was the urban rate of growth exceeded by that of total population.[3] The dominant feature of negative or only very slow growth of urban population of the second phase is, broadly, an expression of both political and economic constraints of the time. They were manifested in the stern application of those various measures aimed at extracting large numbers of people from China's towns and cities.

The second phase is also highlighted by various economic indicators. For 1961 to 1976, the average annual rate of increase of GVIO was 7.2 per cent — far below that of the first phase (24.2 per cent). As well as the sharp drop from 1960 to 1961, the early Cultural Revolution years saw decreases in industrial output. After 1968, GVIO growth remained positive, though the ensuing years until 1976 are characterised by wild fluctuations. For example, 1974's 0.3 per cent in GVIO growth was followed by a 15 per cent figure for 1975, down again to 1.3 per cent in 1976.

Table 4.1: Three-phase Periodisation — Some Defining Characteristics

	Gross value industrial output			State labour force (*zhigong*)		
	1 beginning	2 end	3 p.a. av. %	1 beginning	2 end	3 p.a. %
1952–60	100	536	24.2	16.03	59.69	19.5
1961–76	536	1,232	7.2	59.69	86.73	2.6
1977–82	1,232	2,116	9.5	86.73	112.81	4.5
1952–82	100	2,116	12.2	16.03	112.81	7.5

Note: GVIO columns — at 1952 = 100: 1 ratio at beginning of phase; 2 ratio at end of phase; 3 average annual percentage increase for phase (series based on adjusted prices). NB: 1949 = 41, 1962 (year-end) = 331.
    Zhigong columns — 1 number (m.) at beginning of phase; 2 number (m.) at end of phase; 3 average annual percentage increase for phase.
Source: TJNJ 1983, pp. 16–19, and p. 120.

While the new economic and social policies of the post-Mao period were not consolidated until the late 1970s, the sea-change of 1976 seems a suitable starting point for the third phase. As we have remarked, 1977 marks the point at which urban population growth suddenly began to outstrip that of total population, and the economy settled down to a more stable, if modest, rate of growth. The GVIO figures for the years 1977 to 1982 show an average annual growth of 9.5 per cent, with far less annual fluctuation during the preceding phase. Not unexpectedly, the period from 1977 also features a sharp but consistent rise in the numbers of *zhigong*. Table 4.1 shows the situation regarding increase of GVIO and *zhigong* over the three phases, the first being adapted to begin at the end of 1952 after the economy had been stabilised.

Phase 1: 1949–60

Table 4.2 gives a year-by year account of China's total and urban population growth for this first phase, as well as figures for implied net migration. The information will now be elaborated.

Table 4.2: Phase 1 (1949–60): Growth of China's Total and Urban Populations and Implied Net Migration to Urban Areas

Year 1	Total Popn. 2	% incr. 3	Urban Popn. 4	% of total 5	% incr. 6	Urban RNI 7	Expec. Urban 8	Net Mig. 9
1949	541.67	—	57.65	10.6	—	—	—	—
1950	551.96	1.9	61.69	11.2	7.0	1.9	58.75	2.94
1951	563.00	2.0	66.32	11.8	7.5	2.3	63.12	3.21
1952	574.82	2.1	71.63	12.5	8.0	2.8	68.17	3.46
1953	587.96	2.3	78.26	13.3	9.2	3.1	73.85	4.41
1954	602.66	2.5	82.49	13.7	5.4	3.4	80.95	1.54
1955	614.65	2.0	82.85	13.5	0.4	3.1	85.08	−2.23
1956	628.28	2.2	91.85	14.6	10.9	3.0	85.37	6.48
1957	646.53	2.9	99.49	15.4	8.3	3.6	95.16	4.33
1958	659.94	2.1	107.21	16.2	7.8	2.4	101.91	5.30
1959	672.07	1.8	123.71	18.4	15.4	1.9	109.19	14.52
1960	662.07	−1.5	130.73	19.7	5.7	1.4	125.47	5.26

General note: a. Absolute figures are all in millions; b. all data are rounded; c. aggregations of the above data used later in the text are based on roundings of a different order to give greater accuracy; d. as the details of sources indicate, generally data are confirmed by a number of similar or almost similar Chinese compilations. Except where the series offered is clearly based on different criteria, the practice has been to accept the most recently disclosed data.

Sources/Notes:
Column:
  1: All data are year-end.
  2: China's total mainland population.
  These data exclude Overseas Chinese and residents of Taiwan, Hong Kong and Macao. They do include the armed forces, however (many series exclude the PLA).
  TJNJ 1983, p.103 (also TJNJ 1982, JJNJ 1982, BKNJ 1980); previous to these the most cited source for the 1950s was *Tongji gongzuo (Statistical Work)* no. 11 (1957). There are minor discrepancies between the latter and the series dating from the 1980s. For example, 1954 is given as 601.70.
  Note the 1.5 per cent fall in total population during 1960. See also Sun Yefang cited in Reuter report, *Guardian*, 24 April 1981.
  3: Simple annual percentage rate of increase of 1.
  4: China's total mainland urban population (see 2 above). The definition of urban population used here is explained earlier in the present chapter. All urban data here are from TJNJ 1983, p. 103; corroborations/variations:
1954: *Tongji gongzuo* (see note 2 above) gives 81.55 million.
1957: also, BKNJ 1980.
1958: also, RKYJ, no. 1 (1981), p. 20.

1959: Tian Xueuyan, in ZRKL, p. 71, gives a very different figure (indirectly through a percentage reference) of 103.64 million. This would seem quite inadmissible in view of what we know about the scale of population movements during the Great Leap Forward.

    5: Urban population as a percentage of total population (1).

    6: Simple annual average rate of increase of urban population.

    7: Urban rates of natural increase of population.

These figures are available in greater detail in the original sources, which are all TJNJ 1983, p. 105, except for 1950–53. Rates for these years are from Tian Xueyuan, 'A Survey of Population Growth since 1949', in Liu Zheng (ed.) *China's Population: Problems and Prospects* (New World Press, Beijing, 1981), Table 10, p. 46.

    8: Expected urban population at year-end. These figures are calculated from the previous year-end's urban population total (column 4) and the urban rate of natural increase for the current year (column 7).

    9: Implied net migration to the urban areas. The definition of 'urban area' is for present purposes taken as synonymous with 'urban population' under the relevant usage (see discussion on the changing basis of definition, chapter 3). Entries in column 9 derive from subtraction of column 8 from column 4. Note 1955's negative entry.

Total Population

The establishment of the People's Republic brought to an end China's millennial low rate of population growth. Between 1840 and 1949, there had been an average annual increase of only around 2.6 per thousand, bringing the total figure up from perhaps 400 million to the 540-odd million of the late 1940s. As might be imagined, the slow rate of increase derived from a high birth-rate and an almost equally high mortality rate.[4]

The vast improvements in nutrition, public health, and education seen since 1949 have caused a steady fall in China's mortality rate. Apart from a brief interlude around the time of the Great Leap Forward, this decline has continued through to the 1980s, bringing the rate from around 20 per thousand at the time of the Liberation to the present 6 or 7 of the 1980s. Over half of the improvement came in the first decade after 1949.[5]

The falling death rate of the early 1950s was matched by a rising birth rate, peaking in 1954 at 38 per thousand, and remaining over 30 throughout the first decade of the People's Republic.[6] In short, in the eleven years of the first phase, China's total population rose by 20 per cent; in absolute terms, the additional population in this short space of time was not too far short of the entire increment of the preceding century. In only two years was the rate of natural increase less than 2 per cent. One was 1960, for which the recently released data attest to the devastation wrought in the wake of the Great Leap: in that year China's population was reduced by 1.5 per cent.

Urban Population

The growth in China's urban size in this first phase was even more extraordinary — an annual average rate of increase over four times that of total population. By 1960, aggregate urban population had more than doubled; indeed, of all the increase in national population, over 60 per cent was accounted for by the urban increase. With the exception of 1955, the growth rate was always above 5 per cent, and in 1959 it exceeded 15 per cent.

Natural Increase. In the 1950s, superior conditions in the urban areas meant that the mortality rates in them were somewhat below those of the villages. At the same time, urban birth rates were higher, for the structure of the city populations was generally younger than in the countryside, this being compounded by the youthfulness of the majority of rural-to-urban migrants (see Table 4.3).

Table 4.3: Urban and Rural Rates of Natural Increase of Population, Selected Years

	Urban	Rural
1952	27.9	19.1
1955	31.4	19.1
1957	36.0	21.7
1959	18.5	9.2

Note: Rates of natural increase per thousand.
Source: Tian Xueyuan in Liu Zheng and Song Jian (eds), *China's Population: Problems and Prospects* (New World Press, Beijing, 1981), p. 46.

The Role of Migration. The impact of migration on urban population growth increased greatly towards the end of the first decade of the People's Republic. Before 1953, net migration accounted for over 70 per cent of total urban growth. This was a time of few formal controls on population movements. The great land reform movement of this period pulled large number of urban dwellers back to the villages where they could stake their claims. On the other hand, substantial numbers of people who had taken refuge in the countryside during the years of turmoil before 1949 were to return to urban residency. And some of the better-off rural classes cleverly removed themselves to the towns and cities, where property in the form of shops, warehouses and small factories excited less ire from the new regime than did rural landlordism.

The year 1955 is the only one showing any net migration *from* the urban areas. This occurred because of the stern application of new rules on migration combined with the first great efforts to rid the cities of unwanted urbanities, many of them recent migrants. The rapid and substantial reassertion of movement in the opposite direction in 1956 is in great part due to rural 'push': the setting up of the advanced rural producers' cooperatives in 1956 was probably intended to absorb some of the unwanted millions who had drifted to the cities and towns in the preceding years. But the disruption which it brought in the countryside displaced large numbers of farmers, and the new apparatus of migration controls was inadequate to the task of keeping many of them out of the urban areas. In the event, this suited the changes in economic policy of 1956 — changes which readjusted the emphasis of the state's investment in favour of the large cities of the eastern seaboard.

The emergence of the sending-down campaigns in the mid-1950s has been chronicled in chapter 2. Despite the fact that hundreds of thousands (if not millions) were despatched from the urban areas in 1957 as a consequence of the anti-rightist movement of that year, there was nevertheless a considerable aggregate urban increase arising chiefly from migration.

The first of the Great Leap Forward years (1958) is customarily blamed for having sucked 20 million peasants into the towns and cities.[7] The recent data, however, put 1958s urban population growth at around 8 million, with a further 16.5 million being added in 1959. This is due in part to a time-lag in registration procedures, but mostly to the fact that the main impact of the new policies was felt only in early 1959.

Obviously, the broad explanation for the fantastic rise in urban population during the first decade of the People's Republic is the expansion of non-agricultural economic activities. In the period 1952 to 1960, the index of GVIO rose from 100 to 535.7, while (ignoring for a moment the disaster years of 1959 and 1960) the growth in agricultural output value was only about 5 per cent annually.[8] For the Great Leap Forward itself, the close relationship between rates of sharp upward and downward swings in the industrial and agricultural employment figures are displayed in Table 4.4. There is no exact proportionate increase between industrial workforce growth and urban population expansion because of the fact that much of the former remained of nominally rural registration. Note the enormous rise of 1958 in the heavy industrial workforce. This is mirrored in a one-year increase in heavy industry's gross output value of 78.8 per cent.

Table 4.4: Employment and Urban Population Growth, 1957–9

	Industry		Agriculture		H. industry		Urban Population	
	(m.)	(%)	(m.)	(%)	(m.)	(%)	(m.)	(%)
	1	2	3	4	5	6	7	8
1957	14.01	6.8	193.10	93.2	5.57	39.8	99.49	15.4
1958	44.16	22.2	154.92	77.8	35.50	80.4	107.21	16.2
1959	28.81	15.0	162.73	85.0	n.a.	n.a.	123.71	18.4

Note: Columns 1 and 2: total industrial workforce; 3 and 4: total agricultural workforce; 5 and 6: heavy industry and % of 1; 7 and 8: urban population, and % of total population. All absolute figures in millions.
  Source: Columns 1 to 4 — TJNJ 1983, pp. 120–2; 5 and 6 — Lin Gang, RKYJ, no. 1 (1981), p. 20; 7 and 8 — as for Table 4.2.

In comparison with 1959, 1960s urban growth of around 7 million (5.7 per cent) was modest. The implied net immigration into the cities — totalling over five million, was the tail-end of the massive impulse of the Great Leap, compounded by the sudden appearance of a crisis on the agricultural front. The net loss to agriculture of over 15 per cent of its workforce between the beginning of 1958 and the end of 1959 had resulted in a drastic reduction in China's grain harvest. In the three years 1958 to 1960 it fell by 26 per cent.[9]

Apart from the labour shortage, other factors were to blame for the crisis. In many areas, the crops of 1958 and 1959 — as they stood in the fields at least — may have been better than usual. This fact was stridently proclaimed in the official eulogies of the time. But often they simply went unharvested for lack of hands. Or a rash and commandist local leadership obsessed by the need to propel China directly into 'communism' ensured that time-honoured farming practices were ignored — with disastrous results. Peasants were allowed for a brief period the hitherto undreamt of indulgence of eating their fill in free communal kitchens. And added to these man-made difficulties were the afflictions of drought and flood.[10]

At the time of the Great Leap Forward, the existing urban population was only producing an annual increase of the workforce of perhaps 1.25 million.[11] This was far below the requirements imposed by extremely high targets in the iron smelters and engineering enterprises spawned by the Great Leap Forward. Having exhausted the supply of hitherto-unemployed women, and the fund of voluntary labour, urban units actually sent their recruiting agents to the villages. The carefully constructed machinery of migration restraints of the pre-Leap era had been cast to the winds.

Phase 1: Summary

Table 4.5 contrasts China's total and urban population changes over the period in question. While the former expanded quite

Table 4.5: Phase 1 (1949–60) — Summary of Total and Urban Population Growth

Phase					increase
	beginning (m.)	end (m.)	phase (m.)	phase (%)	p.a. (%)
Total	541.67	662.07	120.40	22.2	1.85
Urban	57.65	130.73	73.08	126.76	7.78

Note: All absolute figures in millions (m.); p.a. (%) = annual average increase based on increases for individual years.
Source: See Table 4.2.

rapidly, its growth over the eleven years is dwarfed by that of urban population. China's pace and scale of urbanisation during the first decade of the People's Republic is without parallel.

Analysis of the complex urbanisation process in terms of 'pull' and 'push' factors is generally unsatisfactory, for often the dialectical interweave between the two is obscured. In the case of China's extraordinary urban growth in the 1950s, however, these notions are compelling. The First Five Year Plan and the Great Leap Forward embodied quite different approaches to the development question, yet they shared a common purpose: accelerated industrial growth. Their effect in terms of urbanisation was also alike: to exert powerful forces of pull on the rural population. Of all the urban increase of 73 million between 1949 and 1960, it is calculated that almost 70 per cent was caused by net migration.[12]

It is sometimes claimed that a central purpose of the Great Leap Forward was, through the establishment of the rural people's communes, to erode the economic causes of the urban-rural differential at source. The Great Leap has also been characterised as the antithesis of over-centralised and urban-centric 'Soviet-style' planning. In these respects, the movement suggests an 'anti-urban' flavour. But the reality was a huge reinforcement of the urban-industrial sector at the expense of agriculture. The pull of the cities became irresistible, and as a direct consequence, over 20 million villagers were sucked in.

The tremendous urban growth of the late 1950s was not matched by investment in the urban fabric. The consequence was a sharp deterioration in urban living conditions, and (by 1960) a gross imbalance between demand for and supply of urban jobs. Neither is the concept of 'over-urbanisation' a very satisfactory one, for it implies universalities and absolutes. But it would seem entirely applicable to China's urban condition of the late 1950s and early 1960s.

The events of 1958 and 1959 (seen in post-Mao China as 'left errors') turned upside down the mechanisms of economic planning which had been so carefully constructed during the First Five Year Plan. By and large, the damage was neutralised by the economic liberalisation of the early 1960s. But the excesses in urban growth were less easily expunged. The sixteen years of the second phase (1961–76) were to see the fierce application of measures designed to remedy the over-urbanisation of the 1950s and to maintain China's aggregate urban population at supportable levels.

Phase 2: 1961–76

Total Population

The food shortages caused by the Great Leap Forward continued into 1961, when China's total population showed a further reduction. In 1962, however, there was a swift restoration of agricultural production and a new surge in the birth rate. By 1963, it had leapt to what was to prove a historical high of 43.37 per thousand. At the same time, the mortality rate had shrunk away to 10.4 — or around the same as before the 'three bad years' (1959–61). The high rate

Table 4.6: Phase 2 (1961–76): Growth of China's Total and Urban Populations and Implied Net Migration to Urban Areas

Year 1	Total population 2	% increase 3	Urban population 4	% of total 5	% increase 6	Urban RNI 7	Expec. urban 8	Net mig. 9
1961	658.59	−0.50	127.07	19.30	−2.80	1.0	132.07	−5.00
1962	672.95	2.18	116.59	17.33	−8.25	2.7	130.52	−13.93
1963	691.72	2.79	116.46	16.84	−0.11	3.7	120.95	−4.49
1964	704.99	1.92	99.17	14.07	−14.84	2.6	119.44	−20.27
1965	725.38	2.89	101.70	14.02	2.55	2.2	101.32	0.38
1966	745.42	2.76	102.66	13.77	0.95	1.6	103.32	−0.66
1967	763.68	2.45	103.49	13.55	0.81	1.6	104.30	−0.81
1968	785.34	2.84	104.51	13.31	0.98	1.8	105.35	−0.84
1969	806.71	2.72	105.48	13.08	0.93	1.5	106.08	−0.60
1970	829.92	2.88	106.54	12.84	1.00	1.6	107.17	−0.63
1971	852.29	2.70	107.51	12.61	0.92	1.6	108.29	−0.78
1972	871.77	2.29	108.27	12.42	0.70	1.4	109.02	−0.75
1973	892.11	2.33	109.63	12.29	1.26	1.3	109.62	0.01
1974	908.59	1.85	110.45	12.16	0.75	1.0	110.73	−0.28
1975	924.20	1.72	111.71	12.09	1.28	1.0	111.51	0.20
1976	937.17	1.40	112.43	12.00	0.64	0.9	112.76	−0.33

General note: See Table 4.2.
Sources/Notes:
Column:
    1: All data are year-end.
    2: China's total mainland population. Definition as for Table 4.2 above.
    TJNJ 1983, p.103; TJNJ 1982 is in agreement, though earlier disclosures differ somewhat. The probable reason is uncertainty in the past as to whether to include the armed forces.
    3: Simple annual percentage rate of increase of column 1.
    4: China's total mainland urban population. The definition of what constitutes urban population in this series is explained earlier in the present chapter.
1961: TJNJ 1983, p. 103.
1962: TJNJ 1983, p. 103 (Wu Youren, ZRKL, Figure 1, p. 100, has 111.00 million).
1963: TJNJ 1983, p. 103; R. Y. Kwok, Urban-Rural Planning and Housing Development in the People's Republic of China, PhD thesis, University of Columbia, 1973 (Xerox University Microfilms, Ann Arbor, 1974), p. 46, cites a figure of 110 million.
1964: This is the point at which the TJNJ 1983 series on urban population becomes confused. That is, within the same table (p. 103) there are urban data which are based upon two quite differing definitions of urbanness. The year 1964 is the dividing point and thereafter the urban data are defined by the 1982 census criteria (the shizhen definition) explained in chapter 3. The 1964 year-end urban total here is an estimate based on an incremental growth from the 1964 census figure (mid-year) at the urban rate of natural increase. It is assumed that during 1964 urban population rose after a nadir of 97.10 million at census time (note the fluctuation from 1963 to 1965).
1965: JJNJ 1982, p. V1–3 (also TJNJ 1982); as an example of the divergence of the TJNJ 1983, p. 103 series after 1963–end, the latter gives the inflated figure of 130.45 million for 1965–end.

1966–74 inclusive: these are estimates based on proportions of the magnitude of year by year *shizhen* growth as given in TJNJ 1968, p. 103. The method of calculation is to iterate through these proportions to fit the two ends which are known from official disclosures and accepted by this writer as valid. This procedure is acceptable because the factor which accounts for the inflation of the *shizhen* data is the inclusion of agricultural population (*nongye renkou*) residing within districts (*shiqu*) belonging to municipalities, and within the designated towns. During the period in question (1966–74), there were almost no new municipalities granted charters, and few new city districts added to the existing municipalities.

1975: JJNJ 1982, p. V1–3.

1976: estimate based on an extrapolation similar to those described for 1966–74; it corresponds to the figure of 112 million mentioned to the author in an interview July 1982 at the Nanjing Institute of Geography, Chinese Academy of Sciences.

    5: Urban population as a percentage of total population (column 1).

    6: Simple annual average rate of increase of urban population.

    7: Urban rates of natural increase of population.

1961–3, 1972: TJNJ 1983, p. 105.

1964, 1965, 1971: TJNJ 1982.

1966: (Editorial), RKYJ, no. 1 (1981), p. 7.

1975: Tian Xueyun in Liu Zheng, *China's Population: Problems and Prospects*, Table 10, p. 46.

1976: estimates related to rates in TJNJ 1983, p. 105.

    8: Expected urban population at year-end. These figures are calculated from the previous year-end's urban population total (column 4) and the urban rate of natural increase for the current year (column 7).

    9: Implied net migration to the urban areas. The definition of 'urban area' is for present purposes taken as synonymous with 'urban population' under the relevant usage (see discussion in the previous chapter on the changing basis of definition). Entries in column 9 derive from subtraction of column 8 from column 4. Note that the only positive entries are for 1965 and 1975.

of natural increase of population began to alarm the authorities, and for the first time since 1949, directives promoting birth control were issued. In 1963, a 'planned births' agency was established under the State Council and at provincial and local levels.[13]

    The hesitant family planning campaigns which they promoted met with moderate success in their first three years, but along with other 'non-political' campaigns, they were brought to an abrupt end in 1966. None the less, urban birth rates remained depressed during the Cultural Revolution, largely because of the atmosphere of instability and the dislocation of family life caused by the sending-down movements. In the rural areas, however, the suspension of birth control campaigns kept the birth rate at a relatively high level during the late 1960s.

    The year 1971 saw a renewed determination on the part of the central authorities to limit China's population growth. 'Late, sparse and few' (late marriages, long gaps between births and few of them at that) became the rule. In 1972 (and for the first time since the early 1960s), the birth rate started to fall away. By 1976, it was a little under 20 per thousand, in contrast to the 33.43 per thousand of 1970. The birth boom of the early 1960s and the chaos of the Cultural Revolution meant that despite the success of the family planning programmes post-1971, the annual average rate of population increase in our second phase was 2.2 per cent — rather higher than the 1.85 per cent of phase 1.

Urban Population

The brunt of the post-Great Leap Forward crisis was borne by China's rural areas. Even in the worst year (1960) the urban population continued to show a positive rate of natural increase (around 14 per thousand compared with the rural rate of − 9.23). A turning point was marked in 1963, for thereafter rural birth rates increasingly outstripped those of urban China. Only in 1974 did this gap begin to narrow slightly.

In 1960 China's registered urban population exceeded 130 million, and sixteen years later, after an almost 300 million increase in total population, it was just 112.43 million. Urban rates of natural increase were indeed rather lower than in the 1950s, but they were nevertheless positive throughout. The quite extra-ordinary reduction in China's total urban size was caused by the mass deportations of the early 1960s and of the post-1968 years. During the entire period 1961–76, there was a decline in the urban population's share in total population — taking it down from 19.7 per cent at the end of 1960 to a mere 12 per cent sixteen years on.

The severe problems of over-urbanisation brought about by the Great Leap Forward invoked drastic action. When Zhou Enlai presented the National People's Congress with a ten-point programme aimed at resolving China's economic crisis, the fourth point was 'to reduce urban-population and the numbers of workers and officials to an appropriate extent by persuading those coming from rural areas to return to rural production.'[14]

As has been described in chapter 2, the great *huixiang* campaign (initiated in 1962) principally targeted those millions of new workers and their dependants who had transferred from agriculture in 1958 and 1959. Many had already lost their jobs by 1961 as enterprises shed their labour through retrenchment or complete collapse. The scale of the cutbacks can be appreciated from the following figures: at the height of the Great Leap, there were 263,000 industrial enterprises nationwide, but by 1965, only 158,000 remained.[15]

There is some confusion in the data as to the timing of the greatest wave of sending-down. Reports suggest that the 20-million-strong *invasion* of the cities had happened within 1958, when in fact it was spread over the three years (1958 to 1960). Similarly, the evacuation of an equal number is often ascribed to the 1958–61 period, whereas the information in Table 4.6 registers the most spectacular annual drop in urban population as occurring in 1964. In that year alone, there was a net loss due to migration of 20 million persons.[16] Nevertheless, of the entire urban population reduction of 30 million in the four years 1961 to 1964, about half was achieved by the end of 1962. And the implied net migration loss in 1961 and 1962 was indeed almost 20 million, around 14 million of which belongs to 1962.

The low net migration loss in 1963 from the urban areas is an interregnum. The *huixiang* doubtless continued right until 1966, though at a more gentle rate. Increasing buoyancy in agriculture combined with continuing retrenchment in industry provided a dual impetus. The former is not so evident in the GVAO data now available, but the liberal rural economy did encourage under-reporting of harvests. As for industry, whereas in 1958 it had become dominated by the heavy sector, which then accounted for over 80 per cent of the workforce, by 1965 the balance had been restored to one of rough parity with light industry in numbers employed.[17] This adjustment was responsible for a slight increase in the industrial workforce, from the post-Leap low of 16.32 million in 1963 to 1965's 18.28 million.[18]

Yet the increased labour demands of industry could not keep pace with the growth in the urban working-age population. Already in 1962 (alongside the *huixiang*) the government had anticipated these pressures deriving from the urban age-structure by reintroducing the various youth resettlement schemes which had lapsed for several years. The effect nationally can only be guessed at from the snippets of information available. In 1963–4, for example, Shanghai and some nearby cities in Zhejiang reportedly sent out 130,000 young people 'to support border construction'.[19]

China's second nationwide census was conducted in mid-1964. It is probable that the pre-census checks on personal registration indentified some millions of illegal urban residents who had previously managed to escape detection. In the circumstances of the time, the majority would have been summarily ejected from the cities. Additionally, the Socialist Education movement of 1963–4 removed millions from the cities, most temporarily, but — as the 1964 entries in Table 4.6 suggest — some for good.[20]

The great majority of the 17 million young people sent out to the villages and small towns between 1966 and 1976 automatically relinquished their urban registration. Not so, however, for the tens of millions of older people (Party cadres, members of the intelligentsia) shifted from the cities and towns. Their stints in the 'May 7th cadre schools', on college-run farms (or, in less fortunate cases, in the various correction camps) were not usually to be permanent; urban household registration, and even one's urban salary, could be retained during an absence of some years from the city.

After 1972, the scale of net emigration from the urban areas (seen in Table 4.6) becomes less pronounced. One reason is the steady return-trickle of sent-down youth. Some came illicitly, others were recruited by labour-starved urban units under the guise of being true peasants, or came in to take up courses in higher education which were restarted in 1972 and 1973. Without doubt, hundreds of thousands came back each year for such reasons (and large numbers too without any officially-acceptable excuse). In an attempt to offset the increased pressure on urban resources created by the returnees, the response of many city authorities was, in fact, to spread the net wider to embrace categories of urban youth who previously had been exempt from sending-down. This factor contributed to the negative rates of migration to the urban areas being almost consistently maintained until 1976.[21]

Though, as we have earlier seen, the movement of population from city to countryside continued on a massive scale throughout the Cultural Revolution, it is not reflected in the net migration data (Table 4.6, final column). Indeed, the annual loss from the urban areas does not exceed 800,000 persons. The reason is that movement was almost equal in both directions. Some sources for the 1980s claim that growing unemployment in the late 1960s was the single most important reason behind Mao's 1968 call to the youth to leave the cities for the countryside. On the other hand, we now know of the substantial recruitments of peasant labour by urban units which were occurring simultaneously with the mass sending-downs.[22] At the time of the Cultural Revolution, this fact was consistently denied by officials.[23] In so far as there were identifiable categories of persons officially transferred to the urban areas during the Cultural Revolution, urban planners interviewed by this writer have conceded that they were restricted mainly to one: the

Table 4.7: The Rapid Increase in the Industrial Workforce, 1970– 2

	Light industry	Heavy industry		Total
1970	1.31	3.13		4.44
1971	0.85	3.38		4.23
1972	1.10	1.53		2.63
Total	3.26	8.04	=	11.30

Note: All figures are net annual increases, millions of workers.
Source: Lin Gang, RKYJ, no. 1 (1981), pp. 20–1.

relatives and friends of the new layer of officials thrown up in the course of the intense power struggle.[24]

The true picture is very different. During the ten years from 1967 to 1976, urban enterprises needing manpower were not permitted to meet all their requirements by local recruitment. The 'naturally-produced' workforce amounted to around 16 million in the Cultural Revolution period, but too many youngsters were being shipped out to the countryside and border areas. The solution imposed on urban units by central state labour regulations was to look to the nearby rural areas for their new workers. Thus, while 17 million young people were lost to the cities and towns in the Cultural Revolution, 13–14 million peasants are now said to have been drawn simultaneously into the urban workforce. Certainly a small proportion of this number were sent-down youth passing themselves off — with official connivance — as peasants. But the great majority were true peasants. The unavoidable conclusion is that the removal of entire cohorts of urban youth, and their replacement by less demanding peasant youngsters, was a calculated political move.[25]

Favourable climatic conditions meant that 1969 and 1970 were good years for China's agriculture, increases in its output value being 23.8 per cent and 25.7 per cent respectively.[26] Post-1949 developments in China indicate a link between the size of the agricultural surplus and industrial/urban growth. Recent Chinese studies of urbanisation claim that the good performance of agriculture in the late 1960s was directly responsible for the increases in the urban labour force (and of industrial output) which were seen in the early 1970s. The significant expansion in the industrial workforce is detailed in Table 4.7. Of course, not all the rise of 11.3 million in the industrial labour force had direct implications for the aggregate urban figures. A part of the increase took place in non-urban places (especially light industry based on agricultural raw material), and some was met by a heightening of the urban labour participation rate. Nevertheless, the figures suggest substantial transfers from the rural areas to the cities and towns.

With a gross outflow of 17 million youth between 1966 and 1976, and an inflow around 14 million peasants, it is not surprising that Table 4.6 shows an implied loss from the urban areas during the period amounting to 5.47 million persons. The implication here is, of course, that few of the peasant recruits were able to bring their family dependants with them to the cities, a fact confirmed by the observations of the present author.[27]

Phase 2: Summary

Table 4.8 outlines the changes in total and urban population at the beginning and end of the second phase. The swing-of-the-pendulum analogy is not infrequently used by Chinese when ruminating on their recent history. In the context of any discussion of the changes

Table 4.8: Phase 2 (1961–76) — Summary of Total and Urban Population Growth

	Phase		Increase		
	beginning (m.)	end (m.)	phase (m.)	phase (%)	p.a. (%)
Total	662.07	937.17	275 10	41.6	2.2
Urban	130.73	112.43	– 18 30	– 14.0	– 0.8

Note: All absolute figures in millions (m.); p.a. (%) = annual average increase based on increases for individual years.
Source: See Table 4.6.

in urban population, it is most apt. The enormous urban growth rates of the first decade of the People's Republic — in terms of both their scale and pace, unprecedented in modern industrial revolutions — were followed by a contraction in China's aggregate urban population of almost equal dimensions. The excessive forces of urban 'pull' of the first phase provoked the powerful 'reverse push' of the 1960s and early 1970s. It is no coincidence that the (consecutive) volumes of net migration (in both directions) were very similar: between 1949 and 1960, the calculated increase in aggregate urban population due to net migration amounted to

49.22 million. In the second phase the decrease due to net migration adds up to 48.78 million. As will be seen next, after 1976, the violent migratory fluctuations between city and countryside were to be continued in a third phase.

Phase 3: 1977–82

The urban data for the final phase, 1977 to 1982, are offered in Table 4.9. As with the previous phases, the detailed explanation of the origins of the aggregate figures is to be found in the notes to the table. The outstanding features of the phase are firstly, much slower total population growth rates than in the Cultural Revolution, and secondly, increases in urban population which have been almost as dramatic as in the 1950s.

Table 4.9: Phase 3 (1977–82): Growth of China's Total and Urban Populations, and Implied Net Migration to Urban Areas

Year	Total population	% increase	Urban population	% of total	% increase	Urban RNI	Expec. urban	Net mig.
1	2	3	4	5	6	7	8	9
1977	949.74	1.34	116.17	12.23	3.33	0.9	113.46	2.71
1978	962.59	1.35	122.78	12.76	5.69	0.9	117.22	5.56
1979	975.42	1.33	133.57	13.69	8.79	0.9	123.86	9.71
1980	987.05	1.19	140.28	14.21	5.02	1.0	134.84	5.44
1981	1000.72	1.38	146.55	14.64	4.28	1.1	141.87	4.68
1982	1015.41	1.47	152.91	15.06	4.34	1.3	148.46	4.45

General note: See Table 4.2 above.
Sources/Notes:
Column:
  1: All data are year-end.
  2: China's total mainland population.
  As for the Tables for Phases 1 and 2, totals are for China's 29 provinces/regions/ municipalities only. The army are not excluded as they have been in many series in recent years. All figures are from TJNJ 1983, p. 103.
  3: Simple annual percentage rate of increase of column 1.
  4: China's total urban population. The definition of what constitutes urban population in this series is explained earlier in the present chapter and in chapter 3.
  For the years 1978–82 there are firm official figures for China's aggregate urban population within the present — and favoured — definition of urban. These figures are, however, inadequate, for they fail to take account of the many unregistered permanent urban dwellers, nearly all of whom are recent immigrants or re-immigrants.
  The available data are adequate to an estimation of the numbers resident in China's towns and cities (that is, in those urban places included within the official

category of urban population adopted here) who were identified in the pre–1982 census registration excercise of late 1981 and early 1982. The 1982 census urban data are based on criteria which differ from the previously disclosed aggregate urban totals in two vital respects, viz., firstly, their inclusion of very large numbers of agricultural population (*nongye renkou*) in the municipalities as well as in the towns (the *shizhen* definition), and secondly, their exclusion of all population (whether agricultural or non-agricultural in registration) in certain settlements included in pre-census aggregate urban counts.

In order to take account of these discrepancies and find the appropriate increments to add to each year's urban total it has been necessary to follow an involved procedure which is now outlined:

First, the 2,900 settlements counted in the 1982 Census (2,664 *zhen* and 236 *shi*) had a combined population, termed *shizhen* of 206.59 millions. Within this figure, 63 million are actually agricultural population (*nongye renyou*), meaning that the urban population in its preferred definition (*feinongye chengzhen renkou* — see discussion in chapter 3) amounted at 1982 census time to 143.5 million. The source of this information is Li Mengbai, CSGH no. 12 (1983), p. 17.

To this figure we must add — in order to achieve the urban definition which is taken as standard in the present series — the urban parts (that is non-agricultural parts) of those settlements included in the pre-census aggregate urban counts but excluded in the census. These settlements are of two categories: on the one hand there are the 377 county seats (*xiancheng*) not designated as towns (that is not *she zhen*) and, therefore, automatically excluded in the census urban count. (Why these relatively important urban places have not been granted town status is one of the mysteries of the Chinese urban administrative system.)

Additionally, the 1982 census also excluded 155 settlements which did have the necessary town status but were found lacking in another respect: they were under the size limit allowed by the census designers.

The aggregate populations of these categories of excluded urban places are based on estimates of average size of both of them: 15,747 for each of the 377 non-*zhen* county seats (based on information on small town size given in RMRB, 6 June 1981, and apparently referring to 1979), and 1,500 for each of the 155 *zhen* excluded from the census count on grounds of their diminutive size. Addition of the urban population in each of these categories gives a total mid-1982 urban population figure of 149.67 million.

Second, the calculation of the unregistered urban population increment: at the end of 1981 the official total urban figure (by *chengzhen* definition) was 138.70 million. By census time six months later it is estimated that this would have grown to 139.74 million (rate of natural increase of 1.3 per cent). Now by 1981, the immigration wave which began in the late 1970s was rapidly falling away. It is assumed here that the rate continued to drop in 1982, and on the basis of the trend identified in previous years it is estimated here that in the half year between the end of 1981 and census time about 1.30 million net migrants were added. This figure is now added to the 139.74 million total, the origin of which I have just explained.

In short, from the basis of these extrapolations it is estimated that the census found 8.63 million in China's urban areas who had previously not had urban registration. This total must now be interpolated for the years 1977–81, to give the urban totals given in column 4 of the table. This interpolation is done on the assumption that illegal residence (that is, lack of urban registration) began to be a prominent factor after the death of Mao. Of course, this is to a degree an arbitrary assumption, as it is well known that many *shang shan xia xiang* youth had filtered back into the urban areas before 1976.

On the other hand, the really massive influxes began only in 1978, with the return of millions who had been ejected from the cities as long before as 1957. The estimate for each year's unregistered increment is a ratio which reduces geometrically from 1982 back to 1977.

As for the urban total for 1982, it is estimated on the basis of three variables: a rate of natural increase of urban population of 1.3 per cent, a figure for net immigration based on trends of recent years (2.59 million), and an element for further unregistered population, estimated too from recent trends (1.57 million).

The above calculations for urban population 1977–82, tedious though they are, have been necessitated by the 1982 census finding which (implicitly) put aggregate urban population some 10 million ahead of the 1981 year-end figure of 138.7 million. I am in little doubt that this huge discrepancy arises from the factors I have outlined here. Further elucidation can be found in the text of the present chapter.

As a matter of comparison, corroboration and record, the official unweighted figures (in millions) are as follows:

1978: 119.94 (TJNJ 1982, p. 89).

1979: 128.86 (as for 1978, and confirmed to me by staff of the now defunct City Construction Central Bureau (*Chengshi jianshe zongju*) in Beijing, June 1982).

1980: 134.00 (Hu Xuwei, CSGH, no. 3 (1983), p. 27).

1981: 138.70 (TJNJ 1982, p. 89, and numerous journal sources).

5: Urban population as a percentage of total population (column 1).

6: Simple annual average rate of increase of urban population.

7: Urban rates of natural increase of population.

These figures are available in greater detail from the sources specified:

1977–9: Hu Huanyong, RKYJ, no. 4 (1982), p. 27.

1980: TJNJ 1983, p. 105 omits this year (a typographical error) and it is estimated from a report on Beijing's births in 1981 in *Beijing Review*, no. 1 (4 January 1982), p. 14, as well as from various other cities' reports.

1981 and 1982: TJNJ 1983, p. 105. Although the rates in TJNJ 1983 are classified under the heading 'Municipal' (*shi*) it would appear that in recent years there are few differences with rates for urban population as a whole.

8: Expected urban population at year-end. These figures are calculated from the previous year-end's urban population total (column 4) and the urban rate of natural increase of population for the current year (column 7).

9: Implied net migration to the urban areas. Entries in column 9 derive from subtraction of column 8 from column 4.

Total Population

With the exception of the 'three bad years' which followed the Great Leap, the six years after 1977 were characterised by annual rates of population growth lower than at any time since 1949. The average rate was 1.34 per cent, compared with 2.20 per cent for the preceding phase and 1.85 per cent between 1949 to 1960. The reason is, of course, stringent application of China's well-known 'one-child' policy. Yet despite this, 1979 marks a historical low in the birth rate. The rise thereafter is due to the age-structure of China's population, and it is expected to continue at least until the end of the 1980s. The origins lie in the birth bulges of the mid-1950s and early 1960s.

Urban Population

The post-Mao period has seen a spectacular surge in China's urban size. While in the six years of the third phase total population rose by less than one tenth, aggregate urban population at the end of 1982 was around one-third greater than at the beginning of 1977. Since natural increase has played only a minor role here, and is more than usually consequent upon migration factors, we will come to the latter first.

A Note on Data Problems. A major complicating factor in the post-Mao urban data is that of unregistered urban residents. It can be deduced from the 1982 census data that the 1982 census enumeration included over 8 million previously unregistered inhabitants (an explanation for this figure will be found in Table 4.9). This is despite claims in the post-census accounts that the pre-census household registration data were proved to be highly accurate.[28] The urban data in Table 4.9 assume that the census incorporated all previously unregistered persons.[29]

Almost all the pre-census unregistered inhabitants derived from the 1970s, and most arrived in the towns and cities illegally after 1976. They were drawn from all those groups evicted during the previous two decades, and especially the sent-down youth. The unregistered element also included peasants taking their chance in the city, and — as has been described in chapter 2 — families of officially-transferred ex-peasants. The pre-census enumeration would also have discovered numbers of 'secret babies' — born outside the strict quotas of the one-child programme and not registered by their parents for fear of punishment. Some would be second generation 'black people' — children of illegal immigrants into the urban areas. The kind of thing which went on in the period before the census is suggested by the following report:

> Some people in Lanzhou, for the purposes of the census, adopted illegal children who they claimed were foundlings but in fact belonged to friends and relatives and were born outside the plan. Some were even sent in from the countryside to be 'foundlings'.[30]

As we have seen, there were several developments which brought a sharp upturn in illegal peasant entry into the urban areas in the pre-census period. They were, namely, the increasing impotence of the grain rationing system as a mechanism of migration control (brought about by the greater urban affluence and the blossoming of the free peasant market for food), new policies encouraging peasants to leave the land and seek employment opportunities elsewhere, not to mention the general relaxation in the overall political climate. It seems likely that a high proportion of the illegal newcomers identified by the preparatory registrations of the 1982 census were allowed to effect a change in their registration before the census. Many had already integrated into the urban labour force, and their expulsion would have caused much inconvenience to those urban units which had illicitly taken them on.[31]

The unprecedented urban housing construction programme initiated by the State Capital Construction Commission in 1978[32] quickly re-established the system of temporary and contract workers abandoned as a 'revisionist' practice during the early stages of the Cultural Revolution. A good part of the labour force was brought in from the countryside. In Beijing and Shanghai in 1980, for example, the temporary population (*zanzhu renkou*), comprising temporary workers (*linshi gong*), contract workers (*hetong gong*) and 'visitors', came to 10.3 per cent and 4.2 per cent respectively of total registered urban population.[33] From such an enormous reservoir of would-be city-dwellers, the seepage into *de facto* urban status before the census must have been significant. It is suggested that the census provided the occasion for a considerable number of such people to become *de jure* urban citizens.

All these factors, then, account for the more than 8 million addition to the official total urban population of 1981 which can be identified through close analysis of the available data as the total number of those whose household registration was converted by the census procedures.

Legal Migration to the Urban Areas. The great bulk of the urban increase during the third phase is accounted for by the officially-sanctioned return to the urban areas of millions of persons removed during the previous periods. The evidence provided in Table 4.9 is of a combined figure for net immigration to the towns and cities between 1977 and 1982 of almost 33 million. Because of the continuation of some emigration from the urban areas during the period, it is estimated that the gross figure for legal entries during the period was some 10 per cent greater.

As has been described in chapter 2, a number of distinct groupings have made up the influx into the cities since 1977. Firstly, many cities have reported the return of practically all their sent-down youth of the Cultural Revolution years.[34] It was announced with an air of finality in January 1982 that all those educated youth 'who should be called back to the cities have already returned'. Officials of the new planning ministry in Beijing confirmed in 1982 that the relevant authorities were not countenancing any renewed wave of re-entry, and the matter was now closed. For the nation as a whole, it is estimated that perhaps 12 million of the 17 million youth who left the towns and cities during the Cultural Revolution have been permitted to return by 1982.[35]

The second most numerous group to return to the cities legally has been that of the sent-down cadres and professional personnel, some of whom had lost their urban status as long ago as the late 1950s.

Thirdly, legitimate recruitment of peasants direct from the villages has been only on a limited scale, though many young people from rural areas have been brought in to the urban areas by the expansion of higher education. Indeed, urban planners in Chengdu, provincial capital of Sichuan Province, claimed that expansion of higher education was the single greatest contributor to urban growth in that city in 1978 and 1979.[36]

Other peasants have come in under the *dingti* or retirement/ substitution arrangement. In 1979, the Party issued directives aimed at getting workers in the cities to take early retirement, allowing their children (including those not already in the urban areas) to take over their jobs. In many cases, the substitution was made, but the parent was unwilling to retire to his or her native village as had been suggested. The effect was a net increase in the urban population.[37]

A further source of indirect but legal peasant entry into the urban areas has been through armed forces demobilisations. It has, of course, been customary for most members of the PLA — recruited overwhelmingly from the villages — to be demobilised in the urban areas. Since 1978, the task of allocating those demobilised has fallen to the new Ministry of Civil Affairs. The new attractions of farming life, and changes in demobilisation policy, have meant that only around one third of the annual total of about one million ex-forces personnel now assume urban status. Taking into account the overall reduction in the ranks of the PLA of the early

1980s, it is estimated that the 1977 to 1982 period saw a total addition to China's urban population from this source of about four million.[38]

Movement from the Urban Areas. The 1977 to 1982 phase did not see a complete end to migration from the urban to the rural areas. In the Hua Guofeng interregnum (late 1976 to late 1978), there was every sign that the youth sending-down would continue apace. In December 1978, a national conference on youth placements outlined four options for urban school-leavers: continuing with study, settling in rural areas, 'aiding construction' in border regions, or taking up city jobs.[39]

In late September 1979, the resolve to substantially continue these decanting programmes was seen in an announcement that by the end of that year 800,000 youngsters were to have been sent out. But the unprecedented clamour of young protesters trying to get back to the cities probably made this high target unattainable.[40] Beijing reported that in 1979, only 10,000 young people had left the city proper, and nearly all had gone only as far as the capital's rural outskirts. As a rough guide to the situation nationwide, an extrapolation of this rate suggests that only 270,000 would have been excised from the urban scene in 1979.

By 1980, pronouncements and claims about youth rustication were no longer evident in the news media, and it may be assumed that the outflow had become insignificant. The main exception in 1981 and 1982 was provided by the increasing numbers of young people caught up in the anti-crime wave, and sent off to remote labour camps, many of them located in Qinghai province.[41]

Natural Increase. After 1979, the birth rate for the nation as a whole began to edge upwards, the reason being the age-structure of China's population. As for the urban birth rate, it increased at a rather greater rate, the factor of population age-structure being greatly exaggerated by the wave of youth returnees. Of the 17 million rusticated youth of the Cultural Revolution period, by 1978 just 900,000 had married. Getting back to the city had always been difficult for a single person, and almost impossible for a couple if they wished to remain together.[42] Thus the millions of young (or in some cases, not so young) people returning in the late 1970s were nearly all unmarried, yet of marriageable age. The resulting situation in Beijing is probably typical of urban China in this period:

in 1979, there were almost twice as many females entering marriageable age as in the previous year. In Chinese custom, marriage is for immediate procreation. In 1977 there were 86,000 live births in Beijing, in 1978, 109,000 and in 1979, 118,000.[43]

Phase 3: Summary

Table 4.10 contrasts the small addition to China's total population with the massive leap in the urban size. In the six years, almost half the increase in the former has been accounted for by the latter. As for the figure for implied net immigration, this is equal to a massive 90 per cent of all the urban growth over the period.

Table 4.10: Phase 3 (1977–82) — Summary of Total and Urban Population Growth

| | Phase | | Increase | | |
	beginning (m.)	end (m.)	phase (m.)	phase (%)	p.a. (%)
Total	937.17	1,015.41	78.24	8.35	1.34
Urban	116.17	152.91	36.74	31.63	5.24

Note: All absolute figures in millions (m.); p.a. (%) = annual average increase based on increases for individual years.
Source: See Table 4.9.

The problem of estimating China's urban dimensions according to the criteria established has been compounded by the various categories of unregistered urban dweller. A large proportion are assumed to have been legitimised in their urban status by the process of the 1982 census.

By the mid-1970s, most of China's major urban centres were displaying all the optimistic signs of slow and stable population growth. Some detailed research on Shanghai, for example, did not find the pyramidal age-structure associated with underdevelopment (high birth rates and mortality rates falling away). Instead, the age-structure had taken on the rectangular profile (a roughly equivalent percentage of population at each age-group) more typical of an industrially advanced nation.[44] This was, of course, in part due to enhanced life expectancy. But the chief factor was the expulsion of over a million young people in the preceding seven years. With the wheel now come full circle, and returnees making up for lost time by marrying and having children, the demographic transformation of the urban areas claimed for the early 1970s has proved to be no more than a mirage.

Conclusions

China's volatile aggregate urban population figures for the entire 33 years from 1949 to 1982 are summarised in the percentage data of Table 4.11. The overall picture of change indicated by the summed data shows an almost threefold rise in the urban total, while China's population as a whole has not doubled. How do the

Table 4.11: Phases 1 to 3 — Summary of Total and Urban Population Growth

	Total population growth			Urban population growth		
	p.a.	(%)	phase	phase	(%)	p.a.
1949–60	1.85		22.20	126.76		7.78
1961–76	2.20		41.55	− 14.00		− 0.83
1977–82	1.34		8.35	31.63		5.24
1949–82	**1.93**		**87.46**	**165.24**		**3.14**

Note: All figures in percentages: per annum (p.a.) figures are calculated on a year-by-year basis.

rates of growth indicated here compare with other parts of the world? For all the less-developed nations (excluding China) in the 1950 to 1980 period, there was slightly greater total population growth (103 per cent compared with China's 87 per cent), and considerably greater urban population increase (238 per cent as against 165 per cent). The index of urban population growth to total population growth derived from these rates of increase is 2.3:1 for the less-developed nations as a whole and 1.9 for China.[45]

Such comparisons do not, though, tell us a great deal about the internal processes of the development of each nation. What value judgment is ultimately placed on the pace of urbanisation depends on a host of factors peculiar to the individual country. Obviously, in China's case the overall growth figures also conceal the violent fluctuations which are evident between differing historical phases. It is these that the foregoing analysis has emphasised by a division into three periods.

Take, for instance the 1950s: in the developing world as a whole, the crude rate of annual urban growth was 4.76 per cent — whereas China's was a massive 11.52 per cent. While in the 1960s and most of the 1970s China saw negative or only small growth, the rest of the less-developed countries as a whole experienced steady urban growth averaging at around 5 per cent each year.

Many Chinese today regard the pre-Great Leap Forward years as something of a golden era. Urban specialists are tempted by this attitude, for the carefully-constructed controls of the mid-1950s gave way to the free-for-all of 1958, setting in motion a train of actions and responses which echoed on into the early 1980s. The spectacular evacuation of the cities in the early 1960s is unmistakably betokened by the events of the late 1950s. The rapid migration to the urban areas in the third phase is a direct consequence of the sending-down in the late 1960s and early 1970s. A further and most crucial interdependence lies in the fact that the principal actors in the migratory waves between countryside and city and from city to countryside have, in large part, been the self-same individuals.

China's urban analysts are eager to point out that, in contrast to other countries, the unique features of their system have meant that only a small part of total urban growth has been caused by migration. Because no definitive, internally consistent urban growth series has even been produced by China's own specialists, the role which they attribute to net migration varies from 20 per cent to 42 per cent (see Appendix A4.1). My own figure of 34.6 per cent is towards the top end of the scale.

This is a figure far lower than the average for developing nations in the post-war period. Yet here the comparisons must end, for no other nation state (not even South Africa, let alone Indonesia) has had the ability to reverse the migratory flow to the cities. In the 1950s, China saw a net immigration into the urban areas of 49.22 million. This was followed by an almost equal net *outflow* in the 1960s and early 1970s of 48.75 million. The final six-year phase has been characterised by yet a further net inflow — of 32.55 million. At a rough estimate, the gross inflow in the 33 years has amounted to 110 million, that is, more than the 95.26 million absolute rise in urban population between 1949 and 1982 (57.65 to 152.91 million). Had there been minimal emigration from the towns and cities to the rural areas, as has been the case in most developing nations, then China's urban population total today would be in excess of 250 million. The rate of urban growth would have been far in excess of the average for developing nations.

So it is clear that although the *overall* figures hold no hint of this, migration has been the overwhelmingly crucial factor in determining the rate of growth of China's urban population. The unique features of the Chinese case is that migration has been very much a two-way business. The particular instruments of strict control over personal mobility responsible for this phenomenon have been described in detail in chapter 2.

To the great credit of the Chinese government, the unbreakable 'iron rice bowl' long ago became synonymous with an urban existence. Almost unassailable material security — albeit at a fairly low level of consumption — is the prize of an urban life. At the same time, the rewards of rural existence have remained fragile and uncertain. The ossification of sharp differences in urban and rural worlds is the key reason for the steep gradient of migration between the two, a gradient which has given rise to stern state controls over residence and mobility.

It is only in this context that we can understand why *gross* (as opposed to *net*) rural-to-urban migration has been so massive in the People's Republic of China. In short, it is the power of state intervention in Chinese society — both in determining differential living standards and in curbing the population's migratory response to them — which so clearly marks China off from other developing nations.

Notes

1. TJNJ 1983, pp. 17–19.
2. Ibid., p. 103.
3. See Table 4.2.
4. Hou Wenruo, 'A Survey of Population Growth' in Liu Zheng *et al.* (eds), *China's Population: Problems and Prospects* (New World Press, Beijing, 1981), p. 56.
5. Ibid., Table 11, p. 57, and Table 13, p. 64.
6. Ibid., Table 14, p. 68.
7. Discussions with personnel of the Beijing College of Economics, June 1982.
8. TJNJ 1983, pp. 17–18.
9. See Table 4.3; also Lin Gang, RKYJ, no. 1 (1981), p. 19.
10. The shroud of secrecy which for twenty years was drawn over the 'three bad years' is only now being lifted. The temporary effect of the rural crisis was to drive millions more off the land and into a wandering starvation. Private accounts speak of particular large cities such as Xi'an, Nanjing and Qingdao being awash with hordes of semi-starving peasants.
11. Feng Lanrui *et al.*, ZGSK, no. 6 (1981), p. 191.
12. See Table 4.2.

13. Hou Wenruo, 'A Survey of Population Growth', pp. 58–63, provides a useful account of population policies during this period.

14. Private communication from central planners, 1979.

15. Some of the reduction accounted for by mergers. See TJNJ 1983, p. 213.

16. An article in *Dagong Bao* (Beijing), 2 February 1961, claimed that between 1958 and 1960, 20 million people had been removed from the cities and towns. I suspect that this is a case of confusing aims with realities — a characteristic trait of Chinese officialdom.

17. Feng Lanrui *et al.*, ZGSK, no. 6 (1981), p. 191.

18. TJNJ 1983, p. 122.

19. Feng Lanrui *et al.*, ZGSK, no. 6 (1981), p. 191.

20. See chapter 2.

21. By 1974, there was sufficient disquiet about every aspect of the youth sending-down programme to oblige a partial relaxation. A specially convened 'conference on educated youth' determined the following: i. single children and the chronically sick need not 'go down'; ii. those in the countryside for a two-year period or more could return provided that they were recruited by colleges or urban workplaces; iii. those with adequate proof of sickness could 'retire'; iv. youth with ageing and infirm parents could return. From the evidence at the grass roots, it seems that many places chose to ignore these guidelines in the following two years. From Feng Lanrui *et al.*, ZGSK, no. 6 (1981), p. 192.

22. Ibid., pp. 191–2.

23. In my own discussions with city planners in different parts of China between 1973 and 1980, it was always claimed that there was almost no seepage to the urban areas in the 1966 to 1976 period. Obviously urban officials were unwilling to concede any lapse in social discipline which admission of such movement would indicate.

24. It is widely understood that cadres may and will exercise their prerogative in this respect.

25. Suggested in Zhao Lukuan, RKYJ, no. 4 (1981), p. 20, and Feng Lanrui *et al.*, ZGSK, no. 6, 1981, pp. 191–2.

26. TJNJ 1983, p. 18.

27. Between 1975 and 1977, I visited many dozen urban units.

28. J. S. Aird, 'The Preliminary Results of China's 1982 Census', *China Quarterly*, no. 96 (December 1983), p. 630, cites a State Council circular of December 1982 which said there were still 'very large' numbers of people still not on the population registers.

29. The Hong Kong newspaper *Ming bao* (22 September 1982) estimated that there were 20,000 to 60,000 'black' (unregistered) people in every *shi*. Taking the mean, this would give over 9 million for the then roughly 240 *shi* nationwide. This figure is close to that deduced from the census results by this writer.

30. *Gansu ribao (Gansu Daily)*, 14 January 1983.

31. Private communications in China.

32. Described in chapter 6.

33. Including ageing peasants lodging with urban relatives, people on business and training missions, domestic tourists, and so on.

34. Feng Lanrui *et al*, ZGSK, no. 6 (1981), p. 194. Also TKP, 11 December 1980, notes that 620,000 young people were sent out from Beijing between 1966 and 1976. The paper asserts that all those sent out before 1978 had been allowed back into the city by the end of 1980, provided they had put in a proper two-year stint in the countryside.

35. Discussion at the Ministry of Urban-Rural Construction and Environmental Protection, June 1982.

36. Be that as it may, the post-1976 climate certainly brought a new recognition

of the importance of academic learning. In 1978 alone, 200 universities and research institutions were opened or re-opened, their students and staff totalling 650,000. Of the intake of such places, perhaps one-quarter involve rural-to-urban transfers which become permanent (interviews with urban planners in Chengdu, February 1979).

37. This writer took part in a 'political study' session in his unit on the Directive, February 1979.

38. XHDR, 9 April 1983, on the role of the Ministry of Civil Affairs. BR, no. 31 (1 August 1983), p. 25, on the number of demobilisations.

39. XHDR, 15 December 1978, p. 8.

40. Particularly of the Shanghai and Beijing youth in Xishuangbanna, Yunnan, and in cities such as Shihezi in Xinjiang.

41. The campaign reached a higher pitch in 1983, when tens of thousands of youth were caught in the net.

42. XHDR, 15 December, 1978, p. 8.

43. Qian Lingjuan, RKYJ, no. 1 (1980), p. 41.

44. P. Elvory and W. R. Lavely, 'Rustication, Demographic Change and Development in Shanghai', *Asian Survey*, vol. XVII, no. 5 (May 1976), p. 44.

45. Derived from UN, *Demographic Indicators of Countries, Estimates and Projections as Assessed in 1980*, pp. 58, 60, 62, and 254.

5 CHINA'S URBAN POPULATION AND ITS CHANGING DISTRIBUTION

Spatial Aspects of Economic and Population Change

The previous chapter was concerned with the pace and scale of aggregate urban growth in China. Chapter 5 will consider the form of that growth, that is its degree of concentration both in spatial and aspatial terms. The interconnected nature of these two aspects of urbanisation are apparent. In describing the priorities of the First Five Year Plan (1953 to 1957), a leading economic planner noted:

> Our present task in urban construction is not to develop the large cities on the coast, but to develop medium and small cities in the interior and to restrict appropriately the expansion of the large cities. The present blind or unplanned development of the coastal cities is a phenomenon that has to be corrected.[1]

As in the case of aggregate urban growth, the degree of concentration/dispersal of China's urban population has been broadly decided by patterns of industrialisation. And the resulting distribution of urban population amongst cities of different size-classes (referred to here as aspatial distribution) is, to a degree, dependent on changes in its distribution over space. Before turning to the aspatial characteristics, therefore, we will examine regional changes in China's urban population distribution, and the forces behind these changes.

The Physical Framework and Economic Heritage

Regional economic conditions in the territory of modern China have always varied enormously. The overwhelming cause is natural conditions. Over one third of the national territory is made up of great mountain chains. Around one quarter is high and inhospitable plateaux. About one fifth is composed of great basins, most of them arid and infertile. Ten per cent is taken up by hill-land, mostly punctuating the mere 12 per cent of China's territory which is classified as plains.

134

China's relief can be likened to three great steps descending from west to east. The first is the Qinghai-Tibet plateau, comprising perhaps one quarter of the national territory. Here is the 'roof of the world', with an elevation of 5,000 to 6,000 metres and 40 peaks over 7,000 metres. The second step takes in the plateaux and basins of Inner Mongolia, the north-west loess lands, the Yunnan-Guizhou Plateau in the south-west, and the Tarim, Junggar and Sichuan Basins. Much of this step is between 1,000 and 2,000 metres above sea level. The bottom tier is China's eastern seaboard: the lowlands of the North-East China Plain, the North China Plain, and the middle-lower Changjiang (Yangzi) Plain.[2]

It is a chastening experience to board a train in Urumqi, capital of Xinjiang in the far north-west, journey south-eastwards through stone desert, through sand desert, through classic badlands, and in three days scarcely see any sign of mankind and his endeavours. In this particular great wilderness of China — and it is just one of several — aridity is the decisive factor. This is in enormous contrast to eastern China, where it is nigh-impossible to be beyond hailing distance of one's nearest neighbours and to beyond a stone's throw of water.

China's geographers are fond of demonstrating the great regional divide by ruling a straight line between Heilongjiang Province's Aihui *xian* in the far north-east to Yunnan Province's Tengchong *xian* in the south-west. To the left of this line lie the six provincial units of Xinjiang, Tibet, Qinghai, Gansu, Ningxia and Inner Mongolia. Here in 60 per cent of China's territory are all the highest mountain chains and plateaux, all the deepest basins and the greatest deserts, and traditionally, less than five per cent of China's peoples — most of them minority races. To the right of the line is heartland, Han China with the great fertile river valleys and plains, relatively favourable climatic conditions, and the vast bulk of China's population.[3]

When considering China's possibilities for regional development since 1949, this great east-west division must never be far from our minds. For all man's progress towards controlling the natural world, the physical constraints of the division will remain fundamentally immutable.

Not unexpectedly, the historical pattern of agricultural production has been one of great regional variation. Shortly after the Communist victory of 1949, a survey of per capita grain production showed that, whereas nine provinces lay within plus or minus 10 per cent of the national mean, six were over 30 per cent above or below it.[4] Spatial differences in industrial production were even more pronounced. The seven strictly coastal provinces had around 40 per cent of China's population, yet generated two-thirds of total industrial output value and around three-quarters of *modern* industrial output. In 1949, ten out of the 26 provincial units had no measurable manufacturing capability. Modern industry was not only concentrated in the eastern seaboard: it was centred in a small number of very large cities.[5] These great contrasts in productive capacity were compounded by enormous differentials in productivity. We find that in the early 1950s, Liaoning, Beijing, Tianjin and Shanghai had rates of per capita output of industrial production which were up to 18 times the national average.[6]

A survey conducted by the Nationalist (Guomindang) government in 1948 showed the domination over industrial production exercised by just a handful of cities — most of them coastal. Predominant amongst them was Shanghai (Table 5.1).

Table 5.1: Spatial Concentration of Industry in China, 1948

	Percentage of modern-sector industries:		
	motive power	employment	factory units
Shanghai	57.7	60.9	60.4
Cities with 5 largest shares	90.7	85.5	85.6
Cities with 8 largest shares	96.6	92.4	93.0

Source: S. Paine, 'Spatial Aspects of Chinese Development: Issues, Outcomes and Policies, 1949–1979', *Journal of Development Studies*, vol. 17 (January 1981), p. 150.

Some Features of Macro-Regional Policy

The glaring regional inequalities evoked strong responses from the new government of the 1950s. Firstly, they were a feature of the semi-colonial and feudal past which the Communists were intent on negating. Secondly, in that China's as-yet largely unexploited mineral and energy resources were thought to be in the interior, they were dysfunctional in terms of national development. And thirdly, the concentration of so much of China's industrial capacity in the eastern seaboard left China militarily vulnerable.

It is, perhaps, tempting to imagine that the above ordering reflects the priorities of China's planners. But pursuit of the goal of regional balance for its own sake cannot have been a central motivating factor in China's highly constrained and difficult development process. In the enumeration of the locational priorities of the First Five Year Plan, and in the many official commentaries which surrounded it, there was no mention of the innate socialistic superiority of spatial balance in itself. The concerns were far more pragmatic: to strengthen China's economy and free it from dependence on foreign countries by siting industry near to raw materials (and their new markets), and establishing a degree of regional specialisation.[7]

A crucial objective lay in defence strategy. The Communists had achieved their victory of 1949 through imaginative tactical retreats into China's far interior — epitomised by the Long March. Throughout the Mao years in the People's Republic, the guerilla warfare mentality remained dominant; attack by the Americans in the early years, or by the Soviet Union in the 1960s and 1970s was to be met by a second great retreat to the hills of the interior. In the meantime, not all the eggs were to be placed in the vulnerable, coastal basket. It would be overstating the case to suggest an intimate correlation between military perceptions on the part of China's leaders and the planned direction of resources. There are, though, a few obvious connections: during the First Five Year Plan (1st FYP), the coastal regions largely missed out in the allocation of construction projects. The recession of the immediate US threat, and the discovery during the first stages of the Plan of the very high costs of building up industry in interior sites, led to a reappraisal of regional strategy. The move towards a greater allocation of resources to the coastal areas was signalled in Mao Zedong's speech of 1956, *On the Ten Major Relationships*.[8]

At the time of the First Five Year Plan, the authorities in 'frontline' cities such as Canton had scarcely been able to conceal their frustration at being denied their share of industrial investments during the first years of central planning. There was general rejoicing at the new regional priorities heralded by Mao's speech.[9] Even Shanghai had been sorely neglected. During the course of the Plan, the greatest powerhouse of China's industry had, on average, received just 2.5 per cent of all national industrial investment; in 1958 the figure almost doubled.[10]

The massive uprooting of eastern enterprises and personnel and their despatch to the 'second line' of the interior under the extremely influential *san xian* or 'three lines' policy of the 1960s and 1970s is a major expression of military strategy in spatial-economic policy. Our knowledge of the real impact of *san xian* remains limited; even in the climate of greater official candidness of the 1980s, only anecdotal evidence relating to individuals and their enterprises is available. However, the primacy of military thinking in determining spatial economic strategy is little by little being acknowledged. One writer in the journal *Chengshi guihua (City Planning)* is prepared to go this far:

> After the Liberation, the actual reason for China's emphasis on even distribution (*junhenghua*) has been national defence thinking. Thus the form of urbanisation was determined *a priori* . . .[11]

Direction of Resources. In 1955, Li Fuchun, chairman of the State Planning Commission, revealed the broad locational priorities of the 1st FYP. Of its almost 700 major 'backbone' items, 68 per cent were earmarked for non-coastal provinces. These included most of the particularly important industrial projects being built with direct Soviet assistance.[12] All in all, the Plan despatched 58 per cent of total industrial investment to the non-coastal provinces. Despite a re-evaluation of regional strategy after 1956, in the 2nd FYP (1958 to 1962) and 3rd FYP (1966 to 1970), this proportion was equalled or exceeded. Only in the 4th FYP was there a slight reduction in the non-coastal provinces' overall share.[13]

The positive discrimination in favour of non-coastal provinces, reinforced by various other redistributive measures, has been complemented by a planned movement of human capital from east to west. As long before as 1912, the newly-proclaimed Republic had drawn up plans to colonise the wastelands of peripheral China. Only after 1949, though, could a real start be made. The National Programme for Agricultural Development (1956–7) laid out ambitious plans to settle and reclaim over 100 million *mu* of land in the coming twelve years. From 1955 on, surplus rural dwellers (principally those peasants who had drifted to the cities) were sent off to the North-east, Inner Mongolia, Gansu and Xinjiang.[14]

With the very high capital cost of land reclamation, and the powerful reluctance of migrants (many of whom have, of course, managed to return to their native places after a few years), the overall economic efficacy of planned transfer of human resources is hard to gauge. None the less, in various parts of Xinjiang today, cities such as Shihezi seem to be almost exclusively populated by emigrés from Shanghai. In Heilongjiang too, one can find many

Figure 5.1: The Coastal, Inland and Border Regionalisation

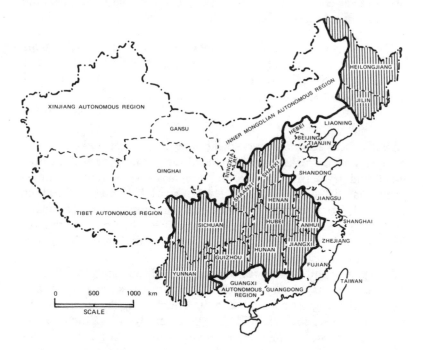

Note: Provincial-level units in each of the three macro-regions:
1. Coastal (11 provincial-level units, 13.4 per cent of China's area): Beijing, Tianjin, Hebei, Liaoning, Shanghai, Jiangsu, Zhejiang, Fujian, Shandong, Guangdong, Guangxi AR.
2. Inland (12 provincial-level units, 31.5 per cent of China's area): Shanxi, Jilin, Heilongjiang, Anhui, Jiangxi, Henan, Hubei, Hunan, Sichuan, Guizhou, Yunnan, Shanxi.
3. Border (6 provincial-level units, 55.1 per cent of China's area): Nei Monggol AR, Xizang (Tibet) AR, Gansu, Qinghai, Ningxia AR, Xinjiang AR.
Source: see, for example, Zhou Yixing, CSGH, no. 2 (1983), pp. 17–21/38.

communities in exile from various cities of East China. The records on population transfers of this kind are probably skeletal, but the overall scale is suggested by reports such as the following, from the Ningxia Hui Autonomous Region:

> Over the past 32 years, the number of people from other areas who have moved directly to Ningxia, plus their offspring since coming to Ningxia, have comprised 42 per cent of the autonomous region's total population increase.[15]

The Impact — A Broad Regional Evaluation

China's sheer scale and territorial diversity do not make regional analysis an easy task. Intra-provincial variations in natural endowment and level of economic activity may be as great as inter-provincial differences. A lesser level of spatial resolution — taking in a number of provinces — is obviously of limited value. Nevertheless, such a wrong-end-of-the-telescope view has been opted for here — much because it is indicated by the broad sweep of official macro-economic planning policies.

The geographical basis for the present regional analyses of distributional aspects of the Chinese model is more sophisticated than that of the vague 'coastal' and 'interior' division found in the general Chinese sources. Macro-regional analysis in China has, in recent years, increasingly made use of a three-fold partition. This divides China into coastal (*yanhai*) interior (*neidi*) and border or peripheral (*bianjiang* or *bianyuan*) regions. The tripartite division is delineated by geographical conditions, by history, culture and ethnicity (Figure 5.1).[16]

Changes in the Distribution of Industrial Output. A full provincial breakdown of industrial output value in 1952 and 1982 is provided in Appendix Table A5.2. Table 5.2 summarises the relative and absolute changes by the three macro-regions. The figures for absolute rise in GVIO show that the inland region has performed better than the coastal region, and the border region has greatly outpaced the inland region. Of course, the scale of these increases is partly a function of the differentials in base points. Nevertheless, the relative decline of the coastal region's share in GVIO is quite steep (a 12.7 per cent reduction proportionally). Most of it has been taken up by the inland region, though the border provinces have more than doubled their share of GVIO in the thirty years.

Table 5.2: Regional Changes in the Generation of Industrial Output Value, 1952–82

	Proportion of GVIO (and amount in million *yuan*)		Relative (and absolute) % changes
	1952	1982	1952–82
Coastal	68.5% (23,312)	59.8% (333,356)	−12.7% (1,330%)
Inland	29.6% (10,075)	36.2% (201,862)	22.3% (1,904%)
Border	1.9% (644)	4.0% (22,527)	110.5% (3,398%)

Note: The figures in parentheses in columns 1 and 2 are GVIO in million *yuan*.
Source: 1952: N. R. Lardy, *Economic Growth and Distribution in China* (Cambridge University Press, 1978), Tables A.1. and A.2., pp. 197–8; 1982: TJNJ 1983, p. 234.

Changes in the Distribution of Total Population. Table 5.3 shows that in the early 1950s, the border region, with 55 per cent of China's territory, held less than 5 per cent of total population. Here, provincial population densities ranged from one person per square kilometre across the 1.2 million square kilometres of Tibet to 25 persons per square kilometre in Ningxia and Gansu. In the three decades of the People's Republic, the border region has experience growth at a rate rather higher than the national average, and has more than doubled its total population. In the case of Xinjiang, the increase has been almost three-fold, from 4.87 million in 1953 to 13.16 million in 1982.

Table 5.3: Regional Changes in the Distribution of China's Population, 1953–82

	Proportion of population (% and millions)		Relative (and absolute) changes (%)
	1953	1982	1953–82
Coastal	42.9 (250.18)	41.1 (416.02)	−4.2 (66)
Inland	52.2 (303.94)	52.7 (533.06)	1.1 (75)
Border	4.9 (28.49)	6.1 (62.03)	25.4 (118)

Source: see Appendix Table A5.3.

The inland region, with almost 32 per cent of the nation's land area, in 1953 contained just over half of its population. In contrast to the border region with its 5 persons per square kilometre, the inland provinces' average density stood at 100 persons per square kilometre. Here, the 1982 population was 75 per cent greater than in 1953, with Jiangxi and Jilin doubling, and Heilongjiang tripling their populations. Of the three regions, it is the coastal provinces which have experienced the lowest overall rate of increase (66 per cent), only Fujian and Guangxi approaching a doubling of their populations. The relatively impressive growth of the border region's population is, of course, placed in a different perspective by the changes in regional distribution. As can be seen in the third column of Table 5.3, the overall change in population balance is minimal.

Changes in the Distribution of Urban Population

Aggregate Urban Population. Changes in the regional distribution of China's aggregate urban population are of greater magnitude than those of population as a whole (Table 5.4). It is significant that they are of similar order to alterations in the regional balance of GVIO. As in the cases of these two factors, the absolute growth in the border region is small, but the relative increase (over 300 per cent) is greater than that of the inland region, and greater by far than that of the coastal region. Of the rises in total population discussed above, the proportions due to increase in *urban* population are 12, 16 and 26 per cent for the coastal, inland and border regions respectively.

Table 5.4: Regional Changes in the Distribution of China's Aggregate Population, 1953—81

	Proportion of urban population (% and millions)		Relative (and absolute) changes (%)
	1953	1981	1953—81
Coastal	58.2 (45.08)	45.6 (63.26)	−22 (41)
Inland	38.3 (29.59)	46.5 (64.46)	21 (118)
Border	3.5 (2.70)	7.9 (10.98)	126 (307)

Source: see Appendix Table A5.4.

The absolute level of increase in the border region has been sufficient to alter significantly the *relative* distribution pattern between the three regions. In 1953, the coastal provinces had between them around 58 per cent of China's urban population. By 1981, their share had declined considerably — to about 46 per cent. The greatest gainer by far has been the inland region (up from 38.3 to 46.5 per cent).

Designated Municipalities (shi). Table 5.5 demonstrates that in the early days after Liberation, China's chief urban settlements, the *shi*, were more evenly distributed than was urban population as a whole. This was due to the larger dimensions of the coastal cities. The figures for 1982 indicate a remarkable relative reduction in the coastal region's share, to the exclusive benefit of the inland region. Of the total net increase of 79 *shi* in the period in question, 53 are located there.

Table 5.5: Regional Changes in the Distribution of China's Designated Municipalities 1953–82

	Proportion of *shi* (%) (and numbers)		Relative (and absolute) changes (%)
	1953	1982	1953–82
Coastal	43.4	36.3	− 16.4
	(72)	(89)	(24)
Inland	45.2	52.2	15.5
	(75)	(128)	(71)
Border	11.4	11.4	0.0
	(19)	(28)	(47)

Note: The figures in parentheses in columns 1 and 2 are numbers of municipalities; in the third column, they are percentage increases in the number of *shi* within the region.
Source: see Appendix Table A5.6.

Cities of Over Half a Million. Amongst the designated municipalities, it is the cities with urban cores of over half a million which are customarily noted in the Chinese sources as the vital industrial engines of the revolution. In 1982, the 48 cities in this category contained over 40 per cent of all China's urban population and over 60 per cent of the nation's municipal population.[17] Here, again, the weight of the coastal region has diminished markedly in favour of the inland and border regions. Appendix Table A5.7

Table 5.6: Border Region — Growth of Selected Cities Currently of over 500,000 Persons

	1953	1957	1982
Lanzhou (Gansou)	397,000	699,000	1,080,000
Hohhot (Nei Monggol)	148,000	314,000	515,000
Baotou (Nei Monggol)	150,000	500,000	853,000
Xining (Qinghai)	94,000	300,000	546,000
Urumqi (Xinjiang)	141,000	275,000	899,000

Source: For 1953, the census, and for 1957 Chen Cheng-siang, 'Population Growth and Urbanization in China, 1953–70', *Annals of the Association of American Geographers*, vol. 63, no. 1, Table III, p. 67.
1982: TJNJ 1983, p. 165, except for Xining. This city did not, by 1982, have a non-agricultural population of over half a million; the figure offered is for 1980 (see BKNJ 1981, p. 56). The figures for 1982 are year-end.

shows that of all the urban population in cities over half a million, in 1983, 70.5 per cent was in the coastal region. By 1982, the proportion had been reduced to 58.6 per cent. The border region, which in 1953 had no such cities, by 1982 had gained four.

A particular feature of urban growth in the border provinces has been the spectacular expansion of just a small number of urban centres. Prominent are the capital cities of provinces and autonomous regions, such as Lanzhou, Hohhot, Urumqi and Xining. These places were early on earmarked as heavy industrial growth nodes. As Table 5.6 shows, in the five years of the first great plan (1953 to 1957) many of them doubled in population. Other centres which have seen spectacular growth are located on the sites of vital mineral resources. An example is Baotou in Inner Mongolia, where the construction of a huge iron and steel complex with Soviet aid caused the urban population to be tripled during the course of the First Five Year Plan.[18] In Panzhihua, situated on the border between Yunnan and Sichuan, discovery of large quantities of iron ore in the early 1960s have given rise to a similar pattern or urban expansion. Today, the new steel city has over 300,000 inhabitants.[19]

Differential Regional Urban Growth over Time. The foregoing examination of spatial changes has only considered the beginning and end of a thirty-year process. Within the three decades, different regions have experienced markedly different paces of urban growth, this determined by the changing emphases of national planning. We are aware, of course, of the rapid urbanisation of the 1950s, the suppressed rates of growth in the 1960s and the early 1970s, and the speeding up again in the post-Mao era. At present, the data are inadequate to a full evaluation of differential *regional* growth over time. Perhaps the closest we can come is to recapitulate an important analysis which appeared in 1983 in the journal *Jingji dili (Economic Geography)*. This rests not on our three-fold division of China's territory, but rather on the six great regions used intermittently since 1949 in Party organisation and planning (Figure 5.2; unfortunately, the information here does not go beyond 1978[20]).

While the detailed regional statistics are to be found in Appendix Table A5.8, Figure 5.3 illustrates the growth of settlements of over 50,000 inhabitants during four phases. In the decade 1953–62, most of the urban places new to this category appeared in the far North-east — in Heilongjiang. The second fastest area for growth was, nevertheless, the East China region which incorporates four coastal and two inland provinces.

The primacy of military strategy in deciding national investment patterns has been referred to earlier. Here, the evidence is strong: between 1963 and 1972, the period as a whole is explicitly described as being dominated by the *san xian* military-strategic policy, which greatly accelerated growth in the South-west region — not counting Tibet. The South-west saw an average annual increase of 6.9 per cent in places coming within the 50,000-plus category, compared with a national average of just 2.9 per cent. Also noticeable is the string of new such places extending up the Gansu corridor and into Xinjiang. As will be noted from Appendix Table A5.8, during this phase the East China region came at the bottom of the table of increase.

It is clear in Figure 5.3 (iii), however, that in the *san xian* period, Heilongjiang (but not the North-east region as a whole) maintained its importance as an urban growth node. This is due to two major factors: the rapid expansion of the Daqing oilfield in the 1960s, and the immigration of large numbers of displaced Shanghaiese and others during the great sendings-down of the Cultural Revolution. Though many were sent initially to state farms, there was always a substantial seepage to local county seats and other townships. The same phenomenon is evident in Yunnan — in expansion of the towns of Jinghong in Xishuangbanna, and of the airstrip settlement and staging post for the south-western frontier of Simao. Here the residual immigrants from the east have now even managed to legitimise their presence in the local towns, and are

Figure 5.2: China's Current Delineation of Six Greater Economic Regions

Note:
North-east — Liaoning, Jilin, Heilongjiang;
North China — Beijing, Tianjin, Hebei, Shanxi, Inner Mongolia;
North-west — Shaanxi, Gansu, Qinghai, Ningxia, Xinjiang;
East China — Shanghai, Jiangsu, Zhejiang, Anhui, Fujian, Jiangxi, Shandong;
Centre-south — Henan, Hubei, Hunan, Guangdong, Guangxi;
South-west — Sichuan, Guizhou, Yunnan, Xizang.

Figure 5.3: China's Settlements Over 50,000: Four Phases of Growth

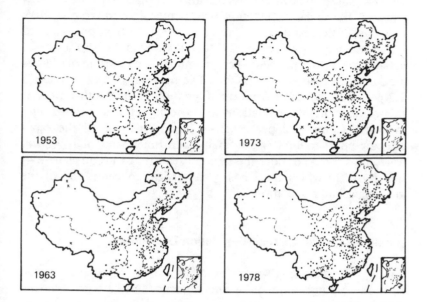

Note: The dots represent settlements over 50,000 pre-dating the phase in question. The crosses represent new such places during the phase. Differential regional growth of urban population density as measured by the number of places over 50,000 per 10,000 square kilometres is summarised in the following ordering of regions where the region with the fastest growth is first given (see Appendix 5.8. for the numbers of settlements and rates of growth by phase):
1953–62:   NE, E, NW, SW, C-S, N;
1963–72:   SW, NE, NW, N, C-S, E;
1973–78:   N, NW, NE, E, C-S, SW.
Source: Xu Xueqiang *et al.*, JJDL, no. 3 (1983), Figures 4–7, p. 210.

on the whole no longer required to labour on the farms.[21]

The third phase considered by the *Jingji dili* analysis (1963 to 1978) is judged to be one of 'rectification' (*zengdun*) of the *san xian* strategy. Particular satisfaction is evidently derived from the fact that the South-west no longer received priority attention — indeed it had become during this period the region with the lowest rate of urban growth (0.7 per cent average annual rise in urban density as measured by places over 50,000). The national rate of increase is 2.3 per cent, and apart from the stagnation in the South-west, it is fairly evenly distributed nationwide. The highest rate is now found in North China (3.2 per cent) — largely because of the rapid opening-up of coal mining in Shanxi and Inner Mongolia. We will now move on to consider the aspatial features of urban change — the degree to which there has been vertical concentration of the growing urban population.

Aspatial Aspects of Urban Population Distribution

Amongst Mao Zedong's many homilies was one especially directed to those responsible for urban management: 'It's no good having over-large cities; we should build more small cities and towns' (*Chengshi tai da le bu hao, yao duo gao xiao chengzhen*).[22] At no stage between 1949 and 1982 has the official line been anything but to restrict the population growth of the big cities in favour of the smaller settlements. From the late 1960s on, the 'small cities' strategy has usually been defined in terms of certain size-classes of *shi*. First, there are the 'large' (*da*) cities of over 500,000, nowadays usually subdivided into 'large' and 'extra-large' (*teda*). The latter have over 1,000,000 inhabitants. Beneath them are the places with from 200,000 to 500,000 (in the earlier literature, from 300,000 to 500,000), which are termed 'medium-sized' (*zhong deng*). Next down are the 'small' (*xiao*) cities of under 200,000 (earlier, 300,000). To simplify matters, these Chinese definitions will be used in the present analysis.[23]

Settlements of Over 50,000 Inhabitants

Appendix Table A5.9 provides a comparison of all places over 50,000 in population, 1953 and 1979. It will be noted that, firstly, between 1953 and 1979, the number of places over 50,000 almost doubled. As to the number in each city size-class, a slight reduction in the weight of the large and extra-large places is evident. This has been to the gain of medium-sized cities (200,000–500,000), and also to that of the smallest category of urban places. With reference to the distribution of population, a reduction in the share of the extra-large places is again evident, though there is a slight gain for the large cities, and a more pronounced gain for the medium-sized places. In terms of population, the smallest categories of urban place have lost out. In short, between 1953 and 1979, China's aggregate urban population practically doubled, but when all sizeable urban places are considered together, there is no marked evidence of an increase in concentration.

The Municipalities

Looking at the situation for the municipalities alone, a rather different picture emerges, especially if we refer not to 1979 data but to 1982 year-end figures. That is to say, the growth characteristics of these most important centres have not been typical of urban places as a whole. This is signified by the weight of the *shi* in the entire urban spectrum: in 1953, they contained 56 per cent of all China's urban population, up to 68 per cent by 1982.

As Table 5.7 demonstrates, regarding the changes in the distribution of municipalities, there has been a fair increase in the proportion taken by the places over 1 million (they have risen from nine to twenty cities; those over 2 million have gone up from three to seven). Once again, the *shi* in the medium-sized group (200,000 to 500,000) have made the greatest headway (up from 18.4 to 29.9 per cent of all municipalities), and there has been a corresponding reduction in the share of the smaller categories.

These changes are somewhat less evident in the data regarding population. For instance, in 1953 China's million cities held 40.5 per cent of all municipal population; in 1982, the figure was slightly higher at 42.8 per cent. Nevertheless, even here the share of the medium-sized class has risen by 6 per cent. Regarding the proportion of all urban population accounted for by million-city population, here there has been a significant concentration (in 1953, 22.6 and in 1982, 29 per cent). As we shall see, it is trends of this kind that especially exercise China's urbanists.

The broad conclusion to be drawn here is that for all urban places over 50,000 there has been an erosion in the dominance of the largest cities. The 200,000 to 500,000 'medium-sized' category has been the relative gainer. The slight reduction in concentration

Table 5.7: Municipal Population Distribution by Standard Size-class, 1953 and 1982

Size-class	No. of shi	Share of shi (%)	Population (millions)	Share of all urban population (%)	Share of all shi population (%)
i. 1953					
Over 1,000,000	9	5.5	17.47	22.6	40.4
500,000–999,999	16	9.8	9.38	12.1	21.7
200,000–499,999	28	17.1	7.06	9.1	16.3
100,000–199,999	49	29.9	5.99	7.8	13.8
Under 100,000	62	37.8	3.63	4.7	8.4
Totals	164	100.0	43.25	56.3	100.0
ii. 1982					
Over 1,000,000	20	8.2	42.05	29.0	42.8
500,000–999,999	28	11.4	19.93	13.7	20.3
200,000–499,999	70	28.6	21.88	15.1	22.3
100,000–199,999	70	28.6	10.55	7.3	10.7
Under 100,000	57	23.3	3.78	2.6	3.8
Totals	245	100.0	98.20	67.7	100.0

1953: Source: See Appendix Table A5.9.
1982: Source: The chief source is TJNJ 1983, pp. 103, 107 and 108. TJNJ gives 1982 year-end details for only 239 *shi*; the distribution of the extra six, which are all under half a million, has therefore been estimated. TJNJ utilises 300,000 as the ceiling for 'small' municipalities, but in keeping with current urban planning practice, here 200,000 has been used. The adjustment has been effected through information in Li Mengbai, CXJS, no. 12 (1983), p. 16. An urban population total of 145.2 million for 1982 is applied. This is an extrapolation from the previous year's growth rate and because of the need to maintain consistency with the size-class data available it differs from the urban total offered earlier.

of the urban system as a whole is not, however, closely reflected in the evidence concerning China's municipalities, which form the backbone of that system. The increased weight of the medium-sized cities testifies to the success of the policy of promotion of the smaller *shi*, many of which have consequently moved up to the higher size-class.

Redistribution of Urban Population — The Verdict

Spatial Redistribution

We have seen in the first section of the present chapter that in terms of the coastal/inland/border division, regional planning policies have been effective in producing the fastest rates of growth away from the coastal region. The inland belt, and more particularly, the remoter interior provinces, have experienced extremely rapid rates of increase in their industrial economies, and in their total and urban populations. But in most respects the relative overall shares of the border and inland regions have not changed greatly.

Despite the continuing dominance of the eastern provinces in matters of production and population, the consensus amongst China's development specialists is that redistributive goals have been successfully met. In particular there is satisfaction taken in the doubling of the share of aggregate urban population accounted for by the border region and in the remarkable expansion of provincial capitals in the peripheral areas.

Concerned attention has, therefore, turned to the question of growing spatial differentials within provinces and regions, and particularly within the coastal provinces. Table 5.8 shows the

Table 5.8: Five Major Industrial-urban Sub-regions

Region	1	2	3	4	5
Shenyang/Anshan	25,000	16	0.64	2	4.2
Beijing/Tianjin/Tangshan	40,000	27	0.68	3	4.4
Nanjing/Hangzhou	60,000	88	1.47	2	9.0
Guangzhou as centre	20,000	27	1.35	3	8.8
Chengdu as centre	30,000	44	1.47	6	9.5

Note: Columns: 1, area in square kilometres; 2, number of urban places of 10,000 persons and over; 3, urban density in terms of 10,000+ settlements per 1,000 square kilometres; 4, urban density as compared with respective province's (times); 5, urban density as compared with the national average (times).
Source: Xu Xueqiang *et al.*, JJDL, no. 3 (1983), p. 208.

most prominent sub-provincial urban-industrial agglomerations, four of which are coastal. Until the early 1980s at least, the instinctive response of the spatial planning fraternity has been that such concentration is essentially unwholesome and unnatural.

Aspatial Redistribution

The qualified satisfaction of China's planners regarding regional redistribution of urban population does not extend to the record concerning its vertical concentration. Article after article has bemoaned the 'incessant growth' (*buduan zengjia*) of the larger cities at the expense of the smaller ones. Typical is the following appraisal:

> For many years, there has existed a tendency for those living in the countryside to enter the cities, and for those residing in small and medium-sized cities to move to the large cities. Small towns have developed into medium-sized ones, and medium-sized ones into large ones. This has resulted in the big cities getting bigger and more numerous.[24]

And for the sub-municipal townships the picture is painted in even bleaker tones: 'For four turbulent decades there has been a steady exodus of small-town residents to the countryside, with the result that even most shops in small-time places have vanished'.[25]

This over-riding perception of the much-enhanced primacy of cities arises partly from the inadequacy of the data available to China's urban scholars. Many of the accounts fail to distinguish between a municipality's truly urban and quasi-urban dimensions. Obviously this creates a compound distortion, as the larger cities generally have a greater proportion of their total municipal populations in the agricultural communities within their boundaries. According to Zhu Zhuo (a prominent demographer at the Chinese People's University), State Statistical Bureau data show that the combined population of all China's designated municipalities hardly changed between 1959 and 1978. Yet the 29 cities which (by 1978) were over 1 million in their *shiqu* population[26] experienced a combined growth of 12.6 million.[27]

The line of argument which holds that there has been considerable concentration is supported by such figures as those in Table 5.9. Appendix Table A5.10 provides a full comparison of the municipal population statistics for 1982 based on the two methods of calculation — firstly, with the agricultural population of the city districts (that is, the method of the 1982 census); and secondly, the more acceptable assessment which includes only non-agricultural residents. The first method of calculation gives 38 'million cities', with 52 per cent of municipal population and 36 per cent of aggregate urban (*shizhen*) population. The second, and more acceptable basis provides just 20 'million cities', with 43 per cent of all municipal population and 29 per cent of all urban (*chengzhen*) population as judged by an internally-consistent standard.

Those concerned at what they perceive as excessive tendencies

Table 5.9: Municipal Distribution by Size-class Based on Complete *shiqu* Populations

	1953		1978	
	no.	%	no.	%
Over 2 m.	4	2.4	10	5.2
1.0 m.–1.999 m.	5	3.0	19	9.9
0.5 m.–0.999 m.	16	9.6	36	18.9
0.3 m.–0.499 m.	10	6.0	41	21.5
Under 0.3 m.	131	78.9	85	44.5

Note: Percentages are of all municipalities (here, the 1953 and 1978 totals are given as 166 and 191 respectively). Complete *shiqu* populations means both the non-agricultural and agricultural persons in the *shiqu*.
Source: Zhu Zhuo, RKYJ, no. 3 (1980), p. 13.

towards concentration of the urban population are apt to make quite spurious international comparisons. It is discovered, for instance, that both in the developing and in the industrially advanced worlds, the proportion of all urban population in places of under 200,000 is 45 per cent, whereas in China it is only 41.5 per cent.[28] One researcher makes a most extraordinary comparison with the United States. It is stated that here, the shares of all urban population accounted for by cities over one million and by those under 100,000 are half and double respectively the corresponding figures for China.

Further cause for alarm is found in the information for the very largest cities. For instance, the provincial and autonomous region seats today are very much primate cities. Of the 26 capitals, 21 are the largest urban centres within their respective province or region. Their average primacy ratio is 3.9:1. But there is considerable variation: in Hubei, Wuhan is 7 times larger than Huangshi, in Gansu, Lanzhou is 9 times the size of Tianshui and the capital of Qinghai, Xining, is 12 times greater than its nearest rival.[29]

These concerns extend beyond the population data: for instance, in 1979 the then 216 municipalities provided 74 per cent of China's gross value of industrial output, accounted for 63 per cent of the state payroll, 81 per cent of remitted enterprise taxes, and so on.[30] While a complete array of municipal economic data is unavailable, there is detailed information for those cities which in the early 1980s were granted 'key-point' (*zhongdian*) status (see Appendix Table A6.1). At the end of 1982, the 17 keypoint cities constituted only 7 per cent of all municipalities, yet had 24 per cent of China's industrial employees, and produced 38 per cent of all industrial output value. They also had 53 per cent of the nation's higher educational institutes and 18 per cent of all hospital beds.[31]

On the other hand, it should be noted that Shanghai's outstanding pre-eminence has been diminished. In 1953, the city accounted for around 8 per cent of national urban population and perhaps 20 per cent of all GVIO. Thirty years of economic development have just about halved these proportions. It should be noted that such a fact would be unquestioningly applauded in almost all the Chinese accounts, whereas the evidence of municipal concentration is generally presented as a cause for gloom and regret.

On balance, however, the pessimism regarding the vertical concentration of urban population *per se* does not seem justified by the actual figures produced earlier in this chapter. Apart from confusion regarding the urban data, one must perhaps take account of a certain propaganda element. It is a general feature of centrally-planned economies that the economic planners occupy a dominant position and those concerned with spatial implementation have to fight their corner as best they are able. Exaggeration of primacy is necessary if any resources are to be devoted to the fond objectives of urban planners. Be that as it may, it is instructive to examine some of the reasons given in the Chinese sources for the adjudged 'over-urbanisation', for they highlight the problems which confront present efforts in pursuit of a dynamic small settlements policy.

Chinese Explanations for Over-concentration of Urban Population

The Primacy of Industrial Production. From the early 1950s until the late 1970s, the official view of the purpose of urban development was uncomplicated: it was to serve the needs of industrial expansion, to turn passive 'consumer cities' into robust 'producer cities'. And in national economic planning, the growth of industrial output was considered far more important than its location at sub-regional and sub-municipal levels. The construction of cities was seen very much in terms of the construction of individual plants: 'Every authority responsible for industry independently chooses its own factory sites without consideration of location and city scale', remarked one critic in 1979. Things had got to such a pass, that 'the masses have coined a saying: "No big-wig cares a jot for planning!"'[32]

All this was, of course, despite the official line of the early 1970s that municipal urban planning had been fully restored following the first chaotic years of the Cultural Revolution.[33] The reality was that comprehensive land-use planning and development control was still regarded as a superfluous activity. An authoritative voice from the Communist Party Central College casts light on the situation:

> Even up until 1978, our long-term plan stipulated 120 projects, but it was not accompanied by any city development plans at all. *This is, in my opinion, the reason for our inability to control the growth of large cities.*[34] (Emphasis added.)

Only in 1979 did municipal planning bureaux begin to be reconstituted in their pre-Cultural Revolution form, and it would seem that even in the mid-1980s, on matters relating to major industrial plant location they are usually still the last parties to be consulted.

In the absence of a comprehensive spatial planning element at central and local levels, decisions on the siting of important industrial projects were largely left to the various ministries, and their corresponding agencies at provincial and municipal levels which oversee different sectors of industry. The strong inclination of ministry planners, whose concern is minimum cost of installation and maximum output, proximity to transport and markets, and so on, is clearly to locate new enterprises in the larger cities. From the simple viewpoint of the individual project this normally can be proved to be the optimum solution. The disadvantages which might be found by a less narrow and more *socially*-oriented cost-benefit approach are not their concern. With verticality the dominant feature in urban management, the spatial planning fraternity are obliged to mobilise arguments which rest on narrow and immediate diseconomies of scale to the individual plant:

> Some think that the conditions of the big cities are good as they have their existing infrastucture — water supply, electricity, roads, drainage — and it is therefore cheaper to build there. This was the case just after Liberation, and such views accorded with practical reality then. At that time, most of the big cities were still consumer cities and the existing public utilities could be taken up, and their potentialities tapped. But now, today, in all the big cities, the infrastructure is grossly inadequate. Plenty of

cities, for instance, have a road network dating from the 1930s and a population of the 1970s.[35]

The arguments which pit efficiency of a single plant against urban amenity has continued into the mid-1980s, and short of radical readjustment of the entire system of organisation. China's pressing needs on the production front will doubtless keep it alive in the future.

Cumulative Spirals: The Absence of Production Specialisation. Perversely, the Cultural Revolution concept of 'self-reliance' (*ziligengsheng*) is, today, said to be partially responsible for the supposed poor performance in developing smaller urban centres. At the level of the individual industrial unit, self-reliance meant not merely manufacture of much of the required production equipment, but in many cases, also the building of machine tools, large and small, needed to make that equipment.

At the urban level too, self-reliance was often taken to extremes, and today it is criticised as an unhealthy and wasteful quest for 'completeness whatever the scale of operation' (*xiao er quan, da er quan*) and 'unconditional integration' (*qiu quan qiu zong*). A classic example of these tendencies must surely be the township of Hongjiang, Hunan province. Here, the local leaders — doubtless with some support from higher authority — attempted in the first instance to construct an integrated iron and steel works. Forced to abandon this project for lack of materials, they then opted for that other symbol of industrial modernity, the automobile plant. 'It took them one year to assemble only two cars. The first got as far as 200 metres, when one of its front wheels fell off. The other car also failed to work.'[36] The experience of the present writer suggests that this tale is by no means apocryphal. Cases of this kind hardened central industrial planners against the dispersal of projects to the smaller urban places, and in the battle for ever-greater output, the hand of the big cities was strengthened accordingly.[37] In many ways, China's Cultural Revolution economic management system encouraged cumulative spirals of success. In the urban sphere, the outcome was a strengthening of tendencies towards primacy.[38]

Discrimination in the Allocation of Non-productive Expenditures. Throughout the 1960s and 1970s, the municipalities received far less in terms of non-productive capital allocations than was required to keep pace with growing demands in housing, public transport facilities, and all manner of services. The neglect of the sub-municipal settlements was even greater, and in popular perception, they mostly came to occupy a low rung on the mental ladder of liveability.[39]

The situation is well illustrated by conditions in the 12 satellite cities of Shanghai. During the 1st FYP the municipality as a whole assigned 11.4 per cent of all its capital investment to non-productive urban construction. Over the years this proportion slipped to around 6 per cent. Entrenched interests favouring the city proper meant that the satellites received far less than their fair share of a shrinking cake. The consequence was that many of the proposed neighbourhood facilities were left incomplete (*bu peitao*). The resulting situation was bleak:

> In the Anting industrial district there are plants belonging to the municipality of Shanghai, with over 13,000 employees and dependants. But there is no cinema, sports hall or anything else. The residents say that they live in a desert.[40]

It is surprising that the city proper of Shanghai, bulging at the seams with its 45,000 persons to the square kilometre, nevertheless exerts strong powers of attraction. Of the 300,000 people employed in the twelve satellites in 1979, only 45,000 had actually settled down in them. The result was a daily tide of a quarter of a million commuters between the core districts and the satellites, some of which are 25 kilometres distant. Similar problems are reported in the case of Guangzhou and its overspill town of Huangpu.[41]

In the smaller urban places, especially the 3,000-odd *zhen*, the problem of inadequate investments in the urban fabric has been greatly compounded:

> At present, many small cities and towns are locations of central government, provincial, prefectural, county and even commune units and enterprises. The structure [of decision making and management] is complex, and the inherent contradictions very inhibiting to their development.[42]

That is, in the typical sub-municipal centre, there is no single authority charged with the task of unified land-use allocation and public works. This fact is today regarded as having been a key obstacle to small-town economic development and planned population growth.

Discrimination in Personal Consumption. A further factor considered to have retarded the development of small towns is the arbitrariness of the urban rationing system. To quote at some length from a Chinese critique of the anomalies of the system:

> There are some policy stipulations which are not suited to the promotion of small and medium-sized cities. The existing division of the nation into various wage areas dates from the early 1950s, but there have been great changes since then. Nowadays, frequently the cost of living in small and medium-sized cities is greater than in the big ones. People who move to the former have to accept lower wages. For instance, in Nanning, if a 40-*yuan*-a-month-class worker moves to the county [and prefectural] seat of Hechi, then he must take a wage-cut of 6 *yuan*. But the cost of living is not necessarily less there. There are also lots of other anomalies in the rationing system. Comparing a similar grade of worker in Wuhan and one of its nearby county towns, in the latter he receives 3 or 4 *jin* of grain per month less, and one less *liang* of vegetable oil. Additionally, there are discrepancies between larger and smaller settlements in the amount spent on welfare facilities. According to the rules of the Ministry of Finance, only those living in cities over half a million are eligible for the monthly bicycle subsidy. *All these things encourage people to move to the big cities.*[43] (Emphasis added.)

Bureaucratic quirks of this kind underlie the lack of success of Shanghai's satellites, county seats and *zhen* in attracting residents from the city's congested core districts. Shanghai municipality in effect operates a three-tier household registration (*hukou*) system, of 'city district' (*shiqu*), 'town' (*chengzhen*) and 'rural' (*nongcun*). A transfer from the core city to a subsidiary urban place within the 10 counties of Shanghai entails a downgrading in household registration. Apart from the inferior living environment, there are distinct material disincentives to making such a move. For instance, in 1979, the bottom rung of the national eight-grade wage system as adjusted for Shanghai city districts was 36 *yuan* monthly. With the same length of apprenticeship, young workers in a typical county-

or-*zhen*-run enterprise within Shanghai could expect only 33 *yuan*. Their average bonus was only 56 *yuan* as against 70 *yuan*. The rules of the rationing system allowed them and their families less edible oil, sugar, fish, and so on.[44]

In the austere days of the Cultural Revolution, when the free markets of the peasants were banned and there was no alternative means of procuring daily essentials, such considerations were extremely important to the average city-dweller. They are a major factor behind the stubborn reluctance of the inhabitants of China's bigger cities to move to the smaller places. And for the existing populations of small towns and cities, and the mass of would-be peasant migrants, they presented tangible incentives to move to the metropolitan centres if ever this could be arranged.

Ideological Discrimination. Finally, and perhaps most surprisingly in view of the almost 'small is beautiful' image of Maoist economics which foreign observers of the Cultural Revolution were tempted to conjure up, *ideological prejudice* is said to have been a key factor in retarding the growth of small towns. The impact was greatest on the sub-municipal centres, especially the traditional rural marketing townships. But the attitude also extended to those small *shi* known for their strong cultural heritage. The leftist philistinism of the early 1970s held that places like Suzhou would only gain socialist absolution when their pagodas were replaced by belching factory chimneys. But even so, they were not the kind of town that a central planner in Beijing would choose for a new factory site.[45]

The establishment of small-scale agriculture-oriented industry in rural townships was certainly a key element of economic strategy during the Cultural Revolution period. The contribution of small industries to overall industrial output is shown in Appendix Table A5.11. However, a cornerstone of Maoist voluntarism was that, without constant revolutionary vigilance, a surreptitious and peaceful 'restoration of capitalism' might occur at any time. The small towns were considered to be a fertile breeding ground for the restorationist impulse. They were 'vacuums in the class struggle' (*jieji douzheng de sijiao*) and China's 'most rampant centres of capitalist activity'. So while many vital industrial undertakings were introduced into the county towns and the *zhen*, at the same time the traditional economic underpinnings of these places — commerce, petty peasant trading and services, handicrafts, and so on — were greatly constrained. In the words of one observer:

> There were lots of small towns (before the Cultural Revolution) which were relatively prosperous, with handicrafts, services, good transportation, construction industries, etc. People found life there very congenial. But as a result of the chaotic Cultural Revolution . . . they became dreary and desolate places [*leng leng qing qing*] where it is inconvenient to live and work.[46]

While we must tread carefully in interpreting such unremittingly negative verdicts, it is true that during the years of the Cultural Revolution, the scale of an urban place and its measure of officially-advertised ideological rectitude seemed to be in positive correlation. No one could ignore the fact that at the apex of the pyramid of supposed proletarian purity stood China's largest city — Shanghai. On the other hand, as for all the other reasons now given for under-attainment in urban distribution, there is necessarily an element of overstatement. The urban planning authorities — rehabilitated and intent on realisation of their small town development objectives — have to fight their case as best they can.

The Distributional Record — Concluding Remarks

By the early 1980s, the current of opinion amongst those of China's development specialists who most closely reflected the views of the leading reformers in the Party was beginning to turn openly against the notions of 'evenisation' (*junhenghua*) and 'balancisation' (*pinghenghua*) which had informed previous plans. The reason it could do so was that the military perceptions had changed, a dispersed pattern of industrial development no longer being seen as essential to national defence. The post-Mao political-military bureaucracy has been inclined to reject the notion of 'people's war'. The implications for regional planning have been swiftly drawn: in the age of accurate missile warfare, it matters little whether a factory is built in Beijing or in the remote interior. Today, there is every incentive for factory managers, and the industrial bureaux and ministries above them, to seek the optimum means of expanding output. There is no longer any necessity to forego the great economies of scale and linkage which concentration of industrial development in the advanced regions, and within them, in the major cities, can confer.

With the hidden agenda of regional policy today being deprived of its underpinnings, China's urbanists are eager that vague notions of 'evenisation' should be expunged. They are castigated as undialectical and utopian; because of stark realities of topography and climate, it should be understood that 'China's population distribution in its main outline . . . cannot be transformed'.[47]

The need for new criteria whereby broad spatial planning decisions can be evaluated is recognised by one writer. As far as population and production are concerned, the demographer Zhu Zhuo suggests that there should be two considerations:

First, whether or not the degree of development of the forces of production in a given territory or region is sufficient to meet the needs (material, cultural, etc.) of the existing population. Second, whether or not the level of development of the productive forces is consonant with the size of the labour force, and the quality [*sic*] of that labour force.[48]

There is irrationality if the population surpasses the employment capacity of a given level of productive forces. There is imbalance (*shitiao*) if population increases fall behind the development of the productive forces, resulting in under-utilisation of the available human and material resources.

Such radical re-assessment of basic locational precepts accompanies a search for new mechanisms of industrial planning. In the mid-1980s, the 'keypoint city' concept of the 1950s has been revived, and there is active promotion of new forms of regional network based on urban growth poles — the 'central city' (*zhongxin chengshi*) concept. These developments will be given detailed consideration in chapter 8.

Notes

1. Li Fuchun was speaking at the Second Session of the First National People's Congress, 5 July 1955. Cited in C. Lin, 'Urbanization and Economic Development in Communist China', Independent Research Paper, MIT, 1971–2, p. 23.

2. *Geography* (China Handbook Series, Foreign Languages Press, Beijing), pp. 12–14.

3. See Appendix A5.1 for the Aihui-Tengchong line.

4. S. Paine, 'Spatial Aspects of Chinese Development: Issues, Outcomes and Policies, 1949–1979', *Journal of Development Studies*, vol. 17 (January 1981), p. 148.

5. Lin, 'Urbanization and Economic Development in Communist China', pp. 1–7.

6. N. R. Lardy, *Economic Growth and Distribution in China* (Cambridge University Press, Cambridge, 1978), p. 11.

7. See Liu Tsai-hsin, 'Changing the Economic Map', *China Reconstructs*, May 1956.

8. *Selected Works*, of Mao Tse-tung, Volume 5 (Foreign Languages Press, Beijing, 1977), pp. 284–307.

9. E. Vogel, *Canton under Communism* (Harvard University Press, Cambridge, Mass., 1969), p. 234.

10. To 4.4 per cent. See L. T. White III, 'The Chinese Model of Urbanization: Population and Capital Aspects', unpublished paper prepared for the Annual Meeting of the American Political Science Association, Chicago, September 1976.

11. Zhou Yixing, CSGH, no. 2 (1983), p. 21.

12. There were 156 chief Soviet projects, of a total of 694 major projects in the Plan. Varying criteria were used to decide whether or not a project was 'above norm' (that is, large-scale). For example, for a steel mill, tractor plant, shipyard — those costing over 10 million *yuan*; for a cotton mill, 3 million *yuan* or over. See Liu Tsai-hsin, 'Changing the Economic map', *China Reconstructs*, May 1956.

13. RMRB, 15 December 1981.

14. *National Programme for Agricultural Development, 1956–1967* (Foreign Languages Press, Peking, 1960), p. 16; cited by H. Y. Tien, 'The Demographic Significance of Organized Population Transfers in Communist China', *Demography*, vol. 1 (1964), p. 221.

15. *Ningxia ribao* (*Ningxia Daily*), 13 January 1983.

16. The obvious anomaly in the three-regional division of China is Yunnan's exclusion from the border region — presumably on grounds of its historic role in mainstream Han culture and its relative weight in the population map. Heilongjiang also looks a little odd in its region.

17. That is to say, of *non-agricultural* population of those settlements counted as urban (*shiqu feinongye renkou*).

18. Cheng-siang Chen, 'Population Growth and Urbanization in China, 1953–1970', *Geographical Review*, vol. 63, no. 1, Table 3, p. 67; also in ZFDJ, p. 56, Baotou is shown as having a population of between 300,000 and 1,000,000.

19. XHDR, 11 April 1979, p. 11.

20. From Xu Xueqiang et al., JJDL, no. 3 (1983), p. 210.

21. Evident during a visit to the area in early 1979.

22. Cited in RMRB, 18 June 1981, but only attributed to the 1960s.

23. Normally, the implication is that these various size-classes are defined according to the numbers of non-agricultural persons resident in their *shiqu*. But there is some ambiguity on this point.

24. DZRB, 6 September 1979.

25. Ibid.

26. That is, the non-agricultural and agricultural populations in their city districts, but not including the rural inhabitants of annexed counties.

27. Zhu Zhuo, RKYJ, no. 3 (1980), p. 13.

28. Wei Jingsheng, ZRKL, p. 11.

29. Xu Xueqiang, CSGH, no. 4 (1982), p. 41; the basis of definition of urban size used here appears to be *chengzhen* population — see chapter 3.

30. DGB, 8 May 1982.

31. Extracted from TJNJ 1983, pp. 23–86.

32. Chen Weibang, JJYJ, no. 11 (1979), p. 57; in Chinese, *Guihua guihua buru changguan yi ju hua*.

33. City planners were routinely wheeled out to meet foreign visitors from 1983

on. In October of that year, I was a member of a UK city planning group which visited several cities and met 'planners'.

34. Qin Renshan, RKYJ, no. 3 (1981), p. 16.
35. DZRB, 6 September 1979.
36. BR, no. 26, 30 June 1981, p. 26.
37. Even then, irrational outcomes were not always avoided. The most notorious case is the decision of the late 1970s to build a new integrated iron and steel complex at Baoshan, Shanghai. Here there were no local raw materials, and even the site selected turned out to be marshland. After very large expenditures, the project was shelved in 1979, only to be resuscitated in 1982.
38. 'Self-reliance' has an egalitarian ring, as did many of the slogan-policies of the Cultural Revolution. In practice, they turned out to be the opposite (viz., the *gong nong bing* 'worker-peasant-soldier' system of getting to university: in the author's personal teaching experience, children of cadres dominated the system).
39. Most urban Chinese carry about with them such a mental ladder, and Shanghai is at the top. Lower down the urban hierarchy, it is very often the location of 'good' schools which provides the basis for such considerations. Most Chinese parents are keenly aware of the importance of a good education for their offspring; I have found that they will make great sacrifices in its pursuit.
40. DZRB, 15 September 1979.
41. Ibid., and DZRB 6 September 1979.
42. RMRB, 3 February 1981. For a similar appraisal, see RMRB, 18 June 1981.
43. DZRB, 6 September 1979. The 'bicycle subsidy' referred to here is paid by units to their employees who live over a certain prescribed distance away. It is usually not more than 3 *yuan* monthly. An alternative is the *jiaotong fei* or 'transport subsidy' paid for by the purchase of season tickets on public transport.
44. DZRB, 15 September 1979.
45. I heard this attitude frequently while living in the provincial capital of Nanjing, 1975–7.
46. Wei Jingsheng, ZRKL, pp. 111–12.
47. Zhou Yixing, CSGH, no. 2 (1983), p. 21.
48. Zhu Zhuo, RKYJ, no. 3 (1980), pp. 16–17.

6 URBAN CONDITIONS IN THE AFTERMATH OF THE MAO ERA — THE CASE OF HOUSING

As we have seen in chapter 5, China's urban planners are generally dissatisfied with the record on urbanisation since 1949: they regard the growth of large cities as having been disproportionately rapid, while the smaller settlements are seen to have stagnated. Clearly, the judgment of 'over-urbanisation' is closely related to the perceived ability of such places to cope with their growth. The largest cities were those which inherited the worst conditions in 1949. Though great efforts were made in the early years to solve their most outstanding problems of slum housing, environmental degradation, unemployment, non-existent public transportation and the like, the demands of the industrialisation process have been particularly felt by the 'large' cities (those over 500,000) of today. They have accounted for a great part of China's economic growth: the 38 cities of over half a million in 1978 accounted for more than half the nation's 'big and medium-sized' enterprises and 65 per cent of all industrial output value.[1]

While they may not have greatly increased their relative share of all urban population, the larger cities are likely to be those places where there are real barriers to further expansion (particularly in the supply of building land, and of industrial and domestic supply). The congestion of the big cities is manifest. Towards the end of the 1970s, urban Shanghai had an average population density of 42,000 per square kilometre, around five times that of Paris, London or Moscow, and almost three times greater than Tokyo's. This was despite the fact that none of Shanghai's housing was high-rise.[2] In general, the greater the city, the worse its overcrowding: statistics for the late 1970s show that the then 15 'extra-large' cities had gross densities which were three times greater than those of the 28 'large' cities. Within the extra-large cities were some quarters where the average density was exceeded several times over. While Beijing's overall urban core density stands at around 1,200 per square kilometre, in its Xuanwu District the rate is well over 30,000.[3]

The model neighbourhoods shown to outsiders in the 1970s were impressive in their environmental and social qualities. But the typical backstreet was another story: it was dirt-strewn, lacking in basic utilities, and lined with overcrowded dwellings in various stages of decay. This was likely to be equally the case for the post-Liberation apartment blocks as for the older, mostly privately-owned stock.[4]

In the years of the Cultural Revolution, open criticism of these conditions was rare, for it would have invited instant condemnation as bourgeois 'welfarism' (*fulizhuyi*). Only occasionally did the widespread dissatisfaction with urban living conditions surface: in the midst of a campaign supposed to vilify followers of the 'revisionist line', an anonymous wall-poster might appear which addressed the more prosaic problems of everyday life. In the eyes of most urban citizens, uppermost amongst these was the shortage of housing space. Housing supply will now be examined more closely, not merely for its own sake, but because it points up the key traits of the economic system under differing regimes of planning. Furthermore despite the important steps taken since 1978 to solve urban housing inadequacies, they will continue to represent the central obstacle to an urbanisation strategy based on the existing municipal network.

Declining Housing Conditions

The basic standard of urban housing in post-1949 China is per capita 'living space' (*juzhu mianji*), a measure which excludes all corridors, stairways, as well as kitchens and latrines (both of these only became standard provision for each household towards the late 1970s). Hereafter, we will refer simply to 'floorspace'.[5]

According to Kang Chao, in 1949 the average per capita floorspace in urban China stood at 6.25 square metres. With a more than doubling of the urban population in the 1950s, by 1962 this figure had shrunk to around 3 square metres.[6] The massive reduction of the aggregate urban population in the early 1960s, and the small increase in the absolute amount of floorspace, brought per capita floorspace back to around 5 square metres by the end of the Cultural Revolution.[7] This average concealed considerable variation. In a smaller city such as Yantai (eastern Shandong, total population around 230,000), there was still 8 square metres per person in 1978, despite a post-1949 population increase of 160 per cent and a total housing floorspace increase of just 62 per cent.[8] But in the municipalities taken together the situation was much less

favourable. In the 192 *shi* of 1978, average per capita floorspace
was just 3.6 square metres, down from the 4.5 for the same places
in 1952.[9] In the fifteen 'million cities' of 1979, the average stood at
3.9 square metres, but six of them were under the mean for all *shi*,
with the heavy industry centre of Chongqing at 3.2 square metres
and Harbin (capital of Heilongjiang) at just 3.0.[10] (See Appendix
A6.1 for all the 20 'keypoint' cities' housing standards in 1982.) It
can be deduced from this information that the worst housing conditions were to be found in the cities of under one million and over
half a million. Here, the loss due to out-migration had not been as
great in relative terms as in the larger centres.

As to the condition of the housing stock, and the shortfall in
floorspace, each locality has its own means of estimation. In
Wuhan, one of China's largest conurbations, only 14 per cent of
the city housing bureau's stock was found to be up to standard,
while much of the remainder was 'in a dangerous condition'.[11]
Even in the showplace of Beijing, where the available floorspace in
1978 was somewhat above the average (4.56 square metres as
compared with 3.6), almost one quarter of households were said in
one report to be suffering from 'severe' housing difficulties.[12]

Beyond the floorspace statistics, there is little comprehensive and
comparable information on urban housing standards. In Beijing,
for example, a survey of the early 1980s found 26,000 newly-
married couples without their own homes, 108,000 families
(around 10 per cent of the total) where male and female children
over the locally-specified age were sharing the same sleeping
accommodation, 10,000 households in which the per capita space
was less than 2 square metres for each person, and so on.[13] From a
nationwide survey in 1978, 35 per cent of municipal households
were deemed to have a 'severe housing problem' and 5–6 per cent
were 'homeless'.[14]

Causes of the Housing Crisis

In the PRC, the state has assumed the major responsibility for the
provision and administration of urban housing, and it fulfills these
functions both through the municipal housing bureau and through
the enterprises or work-units. In 1982, for the municipalities as a
whole, 28.7 per cent of all housing floorspace was operated by the
former, 53.6 per cent by the latter, and 17.7 per cent remained in
private hands — most under owner occupation.[15] For all the urban
population, the figure for the private sector was somewhat higher

— around one quarter — this because the private sector is more heavily represented in the smaller, non-*shi* settlements.[16]

The private sector being severely restricted in its sphere of operations during the 1960s and 1970s (for reasons of socialist political rectitude), the major responsibility for the poor performance on the urban housing front must, therefore, rest directly with state policy. We are by now familiar with the philistine view which the Communists brought to urban management: the purpose of urban construction was first and foremost to promote industrial production. With such a perspective, in the tussle for scarce resources urban housing was a weak contender. This was reflected in the administration of urban housing construction. Reforms of 1957 intended to put housing supply on a firmer footing were never implemented; after the Great Leap Forward, housing was even removed from the state planning system as a separate item. In common with many other branches of the executive, in the early Cultural Revolution city planning and urban housing agencies and municipal levels were dismembered, their personnel dispersed. The housing investment and floorspace completion figures to be introduced shortly indicate that the periods of greatest relative neglect of urban housing coincided with the ascendancy of Mao Zedong in the Party leadership. At these times, the rate of non-productive capital expenditures — of which urban housing takes the major part — went down dramatically.

Traditional peasant views have also played a role in the degeneration of the physical fabric of China's cities. The ex-peasants who in many cases became the new urban-industrial managers, were unable or unwilling to accept that city existence, by its very nature, demands certain publicly-provided expenditures and installations. Public transportation, sewerage systems, centralised maintenance of buildings — all these were superfluous in the village but less dispensible in the new, urban setting of the revolution.

Deep-seated attitudes regarding the *maintenance* of buildings have also played a crucial part in limiting the supply of housing. In Chinese tradition, a dwelling, or a public edifice such as a temple or pavilion, might well be permitted to deteriorate almost to the point of collapse before receiving remedial attention. Consequently, in China today there are very few buildings of genuine antiquity, though there are many completely rebuilt facsimiles of ancient buildings which in popular regard are 'original'. Transferred to the setting of the modern cities, such attitudes have had a disastrous impact. After decades of war and disruption, China's cities in 1949 were in a parlous physical state. Buildings which had long lacked basic maintenance were now subjected to the pressures of increased occupancy, and little attention was given to their upkeep and repair. After heavy rainstorms — not to mention earth tremors (for instance, in Beijing and Tianjin in 1976) — large numbers of buildings could be expected to come to an untimely end.[17]

Most vulnerable have been private dwellings, which are usually the poorer and smaller structures which the state did not wish to requisition in the 1950s. During the 1960s and 1970s, it was well-nigh impossible to procure building materials to effect essential repairs. No market for private purchase of such materials existed, and everything had to be 'back door' — scrounged or filched from state units. And during the Cultural Revolution, it was extremely unwise for a private household, or a tenant of a public housing authority, to set about essential repairs and maintenance. Such efforts would be branded as self-promoting and bourgeois, and most people would far sooner put up with appalling inconveniences in their homes than risk political condemnation.

Taken on its own, the new floorspace added in the urban areas would seem adequate to the rise in population. Appendix Table A6.2 demonstrates this point by comparing cumulative urban floorspace construction and cumulative net increase in urban population from 1949 to 1980. By 1962, 3.7 square metres had been built for each additional urban citizen, and this increment rose steadily to 8.2 square metres in 1980.

However, from the information now available, it appears that the gross reduction in housing stock in the years between 1949 and 1978 amounted to over 200 million square metres — equivalent to one third of all the space newly constructed during the same period and sufficient to accommodate almost one quarter of the present urban population at the average space ratios of today. It seems unlikely that more than 15 per cent of the loss has been caused by deliberate demolition for the purposes of planned urban renewal.[18] If we subtract the gross depreciation figure from the cumulative floorspace construction figure for 1980, it turns out that there has been only 5.7 square metres of new living space supplied for each additional urban dweller over the 31 year period.

Policies Since 1976

The post-Mao regime has brought very different attitudes to every aspect of the construction of a socialist society in China. Under Mao — as for Stalin before him — there was a tendency to see the purpose of production as being enhanced future production. The essential disposition of economic strategy during the periods of Mao's hegemony were as follows: a high accumulation rate, a powerful emphasis on heavy industry (especially the iron and steel sector), neglect of agriculture in general but an obsessive concern with grain output, and a deep antipathy towards non-productive capital expenditures associated with the urban sector.

In 1979 occurred the hesitant emergence of a discussion which had long been taboo. It centred upon the fundamental purpose of production in a socialist society. Initially (and as a means of political insurance) the debate was couched in Mao's own terminology by using his metaphor of a body with its skeleton (*gutou*) and its flesh (*rou*).[19] Gradually, it was argued, the obsession with output of the basic industries (and with only one element of the agricultural sector — grain) had so reduced the flesh, and so reinforced the skeleton, that the body in its entirety was on the point of expiry.

The long-prevailing official perspective on the cities is summarised by the *Guangming ribao*:

> For many years, urban development has been regarded as nothing more and nothing less than the industrialisation of a city. The formula of transforming consumer cities into producer cities was put forward by our Party long before the cities were entered. It was directed towards the situation in the old society, in which their productive capacity was low . . . But over a long period to grant this formula primary status is totally unscientific.[20]

An indignant report on the neglect of Beijing put matters more directly: 'man is a consumer and not merely a producer' and in the city these consumption needs are many and varied — 'electricity, heating, grain, clothing, transport, culture, recreation, health, and, above all, housing.'[21]

The post-Mao regime is no less driven by the desire to rapidly develop a strong and modern industrial base than was its predecessor. This is seen in the ambitious plans unveiled at the beginning of 1983 to quadruple China's industrial and agricultural output by the year 2000. But it differs remarkably in its chosen means. In so far as the Communist Party has a constituency to which it must be responsive, it is very much an urban rather than a rural one. The CPC leaders who emerged in the late 1970s were well aware that after two decades of deteriorating urban conditions (housing and the urban fabric as well as wage standards), suppressed demand for improvement could only be ignored at the regime's peril. They also understood that chaotic urban conditions were not conducive to ambitious economic plans of the 'four modernisations'. In terms of re-allocation of the state's resources, the urban housing sector has emerged as the single greatest beneficiary.

The Statistical Evidence

The Investment Record

Integral to the operation of the 6th FYP (1981−5) was the period of 'economic readjustment' (*jingi tiaozheng*) introduced in late 1978, and extending into the early 1980s.[22] The policies of readjustment were to prove a genuine departure from those of the preceding decade, when high accumulation rates, the dominance of light over heavy industry, and low rates of investment in non-productive capital projects were the order of the day. It is the record in the latter which will be examined here, alongside the proportion given over to housing. The second column of Table 6.1 (which shows the average proportions of all capital investment given over to non-productive projects) demonstrates the clear relationship between periods of Maoist ascendancy (the 2nd, 3rd and 4th FYPs) and the decline in non-productive investment. Of course, as the data in the first column indicate, changes in the relative rates do not necessarily imply absolute changes in the same direction. Nevertheless, the absolute amounts of non-productive investment did not recover to their 1st FYP level until early 1970s.

What is really remarkable is the dramatic resurgence in non-productive investment in the 5th FYP, and the sustained surge in the 6th FYP. The proportion of all basic capital investment which it accounted for rose from 18.8 per cent in 1976 to an unprecedented 45.5 per cent in 1982. Apart from 1981, when the state budget was much reduced due to changes in the revenue gathering system, the

Table 6.1: Proportion of all State Basic Capital Construction Investment in the Non-productive Sector and State Housing

Period	Non-productive investment		Housing investment	
	1 m. yuan	2 %	1 m. yuan	2 %
Restoration 1950−2	887	34.0	277	10.6
1st FYP 1953−7	3,879	33.0	1,076	9.1
2nd FYP 1958−62	3,529	14.6	991	4.1
Readjustment 1963−5	2,895	20.6	970	6.9
3rd FYP 1966−70	3,160	16.2	786	4.0
4th FYP 1971−5	6,176	17.5	2,015	5.7
5th FYP	12,245	26.1	5,546	11.8
1976	*7,063*	*18.8*	*2,284*	*6.1*
1977	*7,890*	*20.6*	*2,630*	*6.9*
1978	*10,475*	*20.9*	*3,921*	*7.8*
Readjustment 1979	*15,834*	*30.3*	*7,728*	*14.8*
1980	*19,961*	*35.7*	*11,166*	*20.0*
6th FYP 1981	*19,048*	*43.0*	*11,119*	*25.1*
1982	*25,263*	*45.5*	*14,105*	*25.4*

Note: Non-productive investment (*fei shengchanxing touzi*) is that part of the state's 'basic capital construction' funds devoted mainly to urban utilities, cultural, educational, and social service installations, urban utilities and housing, public buildings, commercial enterprises, and transport and communications construction.

Non-productive investment: column 1 — annual average amount in millions of *yuan* during the respective planning period, prices adjusted; column 2 — average percentage of all basic capital construction investment devoted to non-productive projects during the respective planning period.

Housing investment: column 1 — annual average amount in millions of *yuan* given over to public housing investments by all urban agencies involved (both housing bureaux and enterprises) during each period, prices adjusted; column 2 — average percentage of all basic capital construction investment taken by housing during the respective planning period; note that the unit cost of housing floorspace construction has more than doubled during the period (eg, 1957: 47 *yuan* per square metre; 1980: 113 *yuan* per square metre).

Source: Derived from TJNJ 1983, pp. 323, 339, 359.

relative rise in non-productive investment has been closely reflected in the absolute figures.

The pattern of housing investment has closely mirrored these changes throughout, the worst relative performances occurring in the course of the 2nd FYP (1958–62) and in the 3rd FYP (1966–70), when the lowest absolute expenditures in housing were experienced. There is a parallel extremely sharp climb in the funds devoted to urban housing construction in the late 1970s, so that by 1982 this sector accounted for one quarter of all funds which the state mobilised for capital construction. Comparing the annual sum allocated to housing during the 1st FYP with 1982, we can see that there has been a thirteen-fold increase (at constant prices). This comparison cannot be taken at face value, because the cost per square metre of new housing more than doubled between the mid-1950s and the early 1980s. Still, the figures attest to an considerable determination to tackle the accumulated problems of China's cities after two decades of studied neglect, and a real trans- formation of time-honoured political and economic priorities of the post-1949 Chinese state. We shall now examine the record in terms of actual floorspace provided.

The Record in Housing Construction

The production of urban housing floorspace during the 1st FYP was impressive: it accounted for 35.5 per cent of all construction (Table 6.2). This proportion dropped away in the 2nd FYP, a far greater share being accounted for by industrial buildings, offices and warehousing, though the actual housing completions in the 1958 to 1962 phase were maintained at a slightly higher level than during the previous five years. The really dramatic fall began in the period of economic readjustment (1963 to 1965) which separated the 2nd from the 3rd FYP. Though housing accounted for a rather higher proportion of all new floorspace during this period, annual average completions shrank to just 14.2 million square metres. The productionist ethos of the early Cultural Revolution (1966–70) meant a further decline in housing's share: now it was just 26.8 per cent of all constructed floorspace, and the actual amount built each year stood at 10.8 million square metres, or around half the figure for the 1st FYP years. The surge in the urban population in the early 1970s, and an improved performance of the industrial economy in general, meant a big increase in this figure during the 4th FYP (1971–5). Nevertheless, during the Cultural Revolution as a whole, only 18-odd million square metres were completed annually.

Table 6.2: Housing Floorspace and Other State Building, 1949–80

	Total 1	Floorspace 2	3	Housing 1	Floorspace 2	3
Restoration 1950–2	n.a.	n.a.	n.a.	n.a.	4.5	13.4
1st FYP 1953–7	53.3	24.9	75.1	35.5	18.9	108.0
2nd FYP 1958–62	76.3	44.6	55.4	28.9	22.0	218.1
Readjustment 1963–5	36.2	34.2	65.8	39.4	14.2	260.8
3rd FYP 1966–70	40.3	37.0	63.0	26.8	10.8	314.8
4th FYP 1971–5	76.6	39.5	60.5	32.8	25.2	440.5
5th FYP	100.1	30.0	70.0	46.9	47.0	675.4
1976	*69.1*	*37.9*	*62.1*	*35.0*	*24.2*	*—*
1977	*76.2*	*36.9*	*43.1*	*37.1*	*28.3*	*—*
1978	*90.1*	*33.9*	*66.1*	*41.6*	*37.5*	*—*
Readjustment 1979	*120.0*	*26.6*	*73.4*	*52.1*	*62.6*	*—*
1980	*145.0*	*23.0*	*77.0*	*56.8*	*82.3*	*675.4*
6th FYP 1981	*129.4*	*17.4*	*82.6*	*61.1*	*79.0*	*754.4*
1982	*143.6*	*16.5*	*83.5*	*62.8*	*90.2*	*844.6*

Note: Total floorspace: column 1 — in millions of square metres; column 2 — production-oriented floorspace (factories, warehouses, and offices) as a percentage of column 1; column 3 — non-production-oriented floorspace (educational, medical institutions, housing, and other buildings) as a percentage of column 1.
Housing floorspace: column 1 — housing floorspace as a percentage of total floorspace constructed; column 2 — average annual housing floorspace constructed, in millions of square metres; column 3 — cumulative total (at end of period concerned) in millions of square metres. It should be borne in mind that in the early 1950s the Soviet standard of 9 square metres of living space per person was applied to new construction. By the end of the 1950s this target had been halved; in the early 1980s, the norm stood at around 12 square metres per person for *newly-built* housing.
Source: TJNJ 1983, pp. 339, 357; for the cumulative completion figures, extrapolated from 1980s total in He Gongjian, JHLT, no. 6 (1980), p. 14; there has been considerable disagreement between various sources regarding the completion figures of recent years. The data in the TJNJ seem to be the most authoritative and reliable, and in every case they are supported by some of the other disclosures.

This record has to be set against the post-Mao performance in housing completions. In September 1978, the State Capital Construction Commission organised China's first-ever national housing conference. The purpose of the conference was to set targets for the immediate future, and work out the means of financing housing construction. The declared objective was to build more housing in the coming seven years than in the entire preceding 28 years of the People's Republic.

The effectiveness of the new housing programme is evident in the contrast between the 1978 completion figure and that of 1979 (37.5 and 62.6 million square metres respectively). Briefly, the mechanisms which allowed such a vast order of increase in construction within a period of one year are firstly, a return to strongly coordinated planning at the municipal level (the readoption of the 'six uniteds' — *liu tongyi* — organisation of finance, construction and allocation) and secondly, increased local means of financing housing. The latter are closely linked to the new policies of industrial management, whereby an individual enterprise has markedly greater autonomy over production and internal accounting, and retention of self-generated funds which can be used for various purposes including the welfare of its workforce. Whereas in the old system, the greater part of the public housing appropriation was supplied through the state budgetary system (that is, from above), by 1981 the local enterprises for the first time provided over half of the expenditure. In some provinces their share was as high as 70 per cent.[23]

From an average of 25.2 million square metres during the early 1970s, the 1976 to 1980 (5th FYP) period has seen a quite extraordinary rise in annual completions: by 1980 the figure had trebled, to 82.3 million square metres. And the trend continued upwards, to reach a historic high of over 90 million square metres in 1982.[24]

So unlike most of the extravagant targets set for industry and agriculture in the period just prior to the introduction of the 'economic readjustment', the plans for housing were not to be quietly abandoned. Though in 1983 the government announced a scaling down of the remainder of the 6th FYP's housing programme, the attainment by the end of 1985 will be not far short of the cumulative total for 1950 to 1977. This was 493 million square metres, and by the end of the fourth year of the proposed seven-year planning period, 314 million square metres had been completed. The contemporary space allocation standard for new housing stood at some 12 square metres per person; this total has therefore been sufficient for the needs of 26 million people.[25] Additionally, an equal number had their dwellings improved in the same period.

The Impact of Recent Housing Programmes

Urban Growth Since 1976

Between 1949 and the end of 1982, China's aggregate urban population rose by over 95 million. Over 40 per cent of this net increase took place in just six years — between 1977 and 1982. As Appendix Table A6.3 shows in detail, this spiral of urbanisation is reflected in the designation of new *shi*. In 1977 the total came to 190, and by 1982 it had risen to 245; the proliferation of *shi* gathered pace in 1983, when a further forty county seats were raised to municipal status.[26]

During Hua Guofeng's brief chairmanship of the Party, the Cultural Revolution policies of decanting urban population and maintaining strict controls on migration were still very much to the fore. When China's 1979–85 housing programme was announced in September 1978, the subsequent sharp rise in the urban population was not anticipated. Clearly, modest increases in the urban total would have produced a very substantial improvement in the overall housing situation. But with a net immigration of almost 25 million people into the urban areas in just four years (1979–82) and an upturn in the birth rate after 1979, this was not to be.[27]

Nevertheless, the vast housing programmes have enabled the cities and towns to keep slightly ahead of the ever-growing urban population. The situation is illustrated in Table 6.3.

But the slight improvement in housing provision in all China's urban places has not been evenly spread. While housing statistics for each size-class of settlement are unavailable, housing conditions in China's largest cities have, if anything, deteriorated during the period of the late 1970s and early 1980s. In 1979, the average floor-space available to the inhabitants of China's then 15 cities of over 1 million was 3.9 square metres, whereas the figure for the urban population as a whole stood at 5.4 square metres.[28]

According to data for the 17 keypoint cities of 1982 year-end (including all the 'million cities' of 1979 plus two more), the average available floorspace for the *shiqu* population as a whole

Table 6.3: Urban Population and Available Floorspace, 1977—82

	Total urban population (millions)	Total housing floorspace (millions m^2)	Per capita availability (m^2)
1977	116.17	607.6	5.2
1978	122.78	651.2	5.3
1979	133.55	720.4	5.4
1980	140.28	810.0	5.8
1981	146.55	880.1	6.0
1982	152.91	960.6	6.3

Note: Total urban population — all urban places (*shi* and *zhen* and non-*zhen* county seats — see chapter 3 for precise definition); total urban housing floorspace — living space only, the figures adjusted for depreciation at a nominal 1 per cent annually, and extrapolated from the 1980 year-end figure of 810 million square metres; note that the 1981 per capita floorspace figure is slightly at odds with the figure of 5.3 square metres given in CR (June 1983), p. 23.
Sources: Urban Population: see chapter 4, Table 4.9; 1980 floorspace total — RMRB, 8 May 1981, and other annual figures taken from TJNJ 1983, p. 339, adjusted on the basis of a simple 1 per cent rate of depreciation.

was just 3.6 square metres. This contrasted sharply with the all-urban average of 6.3 square metres. And Tianjin, Chongqing, Shenyang, Chengdu, Harbin and Lanzhou all had under 3 square metres (see Appendix Table A6.1). These figures overstate the amount of floorspace available to the non-agricultural, or truly urban, inhabitants of the city districts, for the peasants invariably have less-crowded dwellings. The stagnant, or even worsening conditions in these large centres did not arise from a neglect of the new housing programme. Indeed, most of them undertook particularly large-scale projects in the 1979 to 1982 period. These can, for instance, be seen in Beijing's Tuanjiehu scheme, in Jinan's huge Qilishan project, and the Dachangzhen new town development in Nanjing. Rather, they reflect the fact that China's great metropolises ejected a larger proportion of their citizens in the previous era, and have thus had to re-accommodate a greater influx in the post-Mao years.

The intractability of the urban housing question has driven China's political leaders to novel solutions. By the early 1980s, the private housing sector was no longer officially regarded as an unseemly birthmark left over from the old society. Indeed, the new policy was to applaud private ownership as a correct manifestation of socialist property relations. Not only should the existing private sector be nurtured, but the state housing stock should be subjected to 'commodification' (*shangpinhua*). In 1984, the China Housing Construction and Development Corporation decided to try to accelerate the selling off of public housing by establishing pilot schemes in four cities.[29] It would seem unlikely that the Chinese public will leap at such opportunities, though the Overseas Chinese community will continue to invest in the special projects — the 'overseas Chinese new villages' — built for them on the outskirts of major cities of southern China. The main reason is the lack of purchasing power of the average urban household, and the suspicion that private housing may be requisitioned by the state at some future point.

In the post-1982 circumstances of smaller housing budgets, and chronic under-financing of housing administration and maintenance at the municipal level, privatisation was regarded as a means of raising immediate funds for further housing rehabilitation and capital programmes. But the continuing housing problems of the larger cities are not merely financial. For these places in particular, land availability is a major constraint; in many cases, the land of marginal agricultural value in the proximity of the major cities has already been taken up. The long-term solution of the housing question in China's great cities is not, therefore, the procurement of further funds (either from public or private sources), but the limiting or even reduction of their core populations alongside the development of satellite towns.

Conclusions

Over most of the period between 1958 and 1976, urban housing received insufficient funds to keep pace with rising populations and the depreciation of the housing stock. This led to a steady dimunution of available living space per capita, and to a deterioration in urban housing conditions generally. In a brave effort to overcome these inherited problems, the post-Mao leadership has allocated resources to housing on an unprecedented scale. Yet the unexpected and steep climb in China's urban population of the late 1970s and early 1980s has absorbed the great bulk of the construction effort. The slight overall improvement between 1977 and 1982 was not shared by the largest centres, where the average per capita floorspace remained much below the national standard.

The inadequacy of funds for urban construction (and especially for housing) in the 1960s and early 1970s gave rise to a perception of over-urbanisation — strongest in relation to the larger cities. In the mid-1980s, the impulse to migrate to the cities remains, albeit in a less fierce form than previously. But the land resources of China's major metropolises are finite, and the flow of funds on a grand scale to non-productive capital projects places the economy under great strain. The awareness of these constraints is an important factor behind the continuing perception of 'over-urbanisation'. It accounts for the determination shared by most of China's urban planners that in the future, the larger cities should not be allowed to expand their populations further, and a vigorous small-towns programme should be implemented.

Notes

1. Fu Wenwei, JZXB, no. 4 (1983), p. 28.
2. Ibid., p. 28.
3. Shen Lang, RKYJJ, no. 4 (1982), p. 18.
4. Having travelled extensively in China during this period, I feel that this view is warranted.
5. This is also the Soviet way of reckoning housing space — it was passed on to the Chinese in the 1950s; the traditional Chinese method is by the number of rooms (*jian*), a fairly standard measure based on the number of roof-beams.
6. Derived from Kang Chao, 'Industrialisation and Urban Housing in Communist China', *Journal of Asian Studies*, vol. XXV, no. 3 (May 1966), Table 1, p. 382.
7. See also Table 6.3, which relates housing floorspace to population from 1977. In that year, the calculated average per capita space for all urban China is 5.2 square metres.
8. BR, no. 48, 30 November 1979, p. 21.
9. Su Xing, HQ, no. 2 (1980), p. 8.
10. BKNJ 1981, p. 540.
11. He Gongjian, JHLT, no. 6 (1980), p. 14.
12. Su Xing, HQ, no. 2 (1980), p. 8. Here the reference is to 300,000 households in Beijing.
13. Qian Lingjuan, RKYJ, no. 1 (1980), p. 41.
14. XHDR, 18 November 1979; these categories are not explained.
15. BR, no. 41, October 1982, pp. 26–7; this figure was for '200 municipalities' but it was probably in fact for all the then existing *shi*.
16. The worst urban housing is in the private sector, but that is not to say that all private housing is in poor shape. Where it is good, it is excellent (for example, in the small streets to the west of Zhongshan Beilu, Nanjing). But equally, where it is bad, it is really bad: the crumbling shacks overlooking the Yangzi at Chongqing are a case in point.
17. Rumour had it that the Tangshan earthquake (1976) caused 15,000 dwellings to collapse in Beijing, despite the relatively minor tremors that hit the capital.
18. The explanation of this calculation is extremely involved, and I will not trouble readers with it.

19. Interestingly, it has also been claimed — quite contrary to the record — that Stalin opposed 'production for production's sake'. See BR no. 5, 21 December 1979, pp. 9–13.
20. GMRB, 21 May 1980.
21. Sheng Lang, RKYJJ, no. 4 (1982), p. 17.
22. By 1984, the end of the readjustment period had still not been formally announced. It is likely that it will be dated retrospectively from 1978 to 1980.
23. XHDR, 1 October 1981.
24. The plan announced in December 1982 was to build an average of 62 million square metres during 6th FYP. (BR no. 51, 20 December 1982, p. 18.) This would leave 141 million square metres to be built in the three years 1983/5. The preliminary figure for 1983 is 45 million square metres, which is in fact about one third of the total outstanding in the Plan (see TKP, 23 February 1984).
25. RMRB, 18 June 1981.
26. ZXQJ 1978, and ZXQJ 1983; also, TKP, 1 March 1984.
27. See chapter 4, Table 4.9.
28. For the 15 'million' cities, see BKNJ 1981, p. 541; for all urban China (1979) see Table 6.3.
29. TKP, 1 March 1984, reported that the experiment was underway in Zhengzhou, Changzhou, Shashi, Siping (Jilin). The average apartment of 50 square metres was on the market for 9,000 *yuan* — equivalent to about 7 years' average household income. There was a discount for full cash payment of 20–30 per cent. Otherwise, a mortgage could be taken out over a period of 20 years.

7 MODERNISATION OF AGRICULTURE AND THE IMPACT ON THE AGRICULTURAL LABOUR FORCE

Emergence of Excess Labour in the Countryside

The Land Problem

For two decades and more, China remained impervious to the growing concern in the outside world about over-population in the developing nations. Though China's exceedingly stringent population planning policies of the 1980s can be traced back to at least the early 1970s, only after 1976 could the advocates of birth control policies be certain that they would not be condemned as Malthusian conspirators.

The post-Mao transformation has brought China to a late awareness of the constraints on nation-building imposed by a huge population and limited material resources. Paradoxically for a country of 9.6 million square kilometres, the most dire of these constraints is the shortage of agricultural land.

We now know, of course, that in the three decades after 1949 China's population increased by around 75 per cent, and by the mid-1980s it has practically doubled. At the same time, one of the most powerful images of Cultural Revolution China was of the massed ranks of the peasantry struggling with little more than their bare hands to terrace mountainsides, excavate irrigation canals, and fill in marshes. The overwhelming impression created by these huge capital projects was of an ever-increasing supply of farmland — at least sufficient to keep pace with rising population. However, a very different reality has now been revealed.

It is true that in the first years of the People's Republic, the area under cultivation had risen quite markedly. The main reason was the restoration of under-utilised or abandoned farmland after many years of war and chaos. In addition, easily reclaimable territory could be rapidly brought into production. The consequence was that between 1949 and 1957 the area of cultivated land rose by 14.3 per cent.

In the 22 years after 1957, an area greater than the entire province of Guangdong (214,000 square kilometres — more than

England and Scotland combined) was added to China's stock of farmland. Yet the astonishing fact is that over the same period the growth of cities, the building of roads, railways, canals and reservoirs, along with the expansion of villages to accommodate the rising rural population, have eaten up a far greater area. The gross loss in farmland between 1957 and 1979 came to 335,000 square kilometres — equivalent to one third of the total land available in 1957. As for the net loss, as Vice Premier Wan Li pointed out in a speech in 1980, at 12.1 million hectares it was equivalent to the combined farmland of the five provinces of the North-west region.[1] This 11 per cent net reduction brought the proportion of China's land area under cultivation down from 11.7 per cent in 1957 to just 10.4 per cent in 1979.[2] The overall outcome has been a halving of the per capita cultivated land in China since 1949 (Table 7.1), and a reduction in the land available to each rural labourer from 8.1 *mu* to only 5 *mu* between 1957 and 1979.[3]

Table 7.1: Decline in Cultivated Land Area, 1949–79

	Population	Cultivated land		Land per capita	
		mu	ha.	*mu*	ha.
	(m.)		(m.)		
1949	548.77	1,468.22	98.34	2.68	0.18
1957	656.63	1,677.45	112.45	2.55	0.17
1967	760.92	1,538.46	103.04	2.02	0.14
1979	970.92	1,490.84	99.86	1.55	0.10

Note: The population figures differ somewhat from those given elsewhere in this study. 1 *mu* = 0.067 ha.
Source: Yao Shimou, Wu Chucai, 'A Special Form of Urbanization of Rural Population: A comment on the Population of both Workers and Peasants', paper prepared in English for a Conference of the Association of American Geographers, May 1981.

China's agricultural economists are quick to point out that their nation's land/population ratios compare extremely unfavourably with prevailing international standards. According to one account, in the 26 nations which in 1981 had populations over 50 million, China ranked 24th in terms of arable land available per person. The ratio for all nations of the world and China in 1981 was 3.4:1. Comparisons are made between China and the nations which rank with it as having the greatest land masses: Canada's per capita cultivated land is 17 times that of China, the USA's is 8 times, and even the USSR has 7 times China's figure.[4]

The unfavourable situation is not confined to arable land availability. In 1981, the per capita ratios for China and the world as a whole were as follows:[5]

All land	1:3.4
Cultivated land	1:2.7
Afforested land	1:8.3
Pasture	1:2.3

China's extremely uneven distribution of population means that in certain regions population densities are over five times the national average. And in the eastern provinces of Jiangsu, Shandong and Henan, densities in 1982 were 658, 490 and 450 persons per square kilometre respectively (Appendix Table A5.5). Yet the figures for the great western expanses of Qinghai, Xinjiang and Tibet were just 5.5, 8 and 1.6. Even here there is often an uneven spread of population. For instance, almost 80 per cent of Qinghai's inhabitants are crowded into the agricultural region around the capital of Xining. In Xinjiang the density of population in the Shule corridor is over 300 per square kilometre compared with the average of 8 persons for the whole autonomous region.[6]

These macro-regional and sub-provincial disparities in population density greatly accentuate the inadequacy of China's land resources, and provide the backdrop for current concerns about rural over-population and the emergence of a 'surplus labour force' in China's countryside.

The Growing Perception of an Excess Labour Force

China's non-urban population in 1982 totalled 862.5 million, or 85 per cent of the nation's population. Approximately 40 million of these were non-agricultural persons living in places other than urban places, meaning that around 820 million people depended upon agriculture. Of these, 330 million (40 per cent) were counted in the agricultural workforce.[7]

The requirements of further industrialisation will further reduce the total arable land, and unless the scale of reclamation is dramatically raised, this loss will not be offset by the opening up of new agricultural tracts in provinces such as Heilongjiang. One official projection is that there will be a net reduction in arable land from 1979's 100.0 million to 90 million hectares in the year 2000. This would bring the land available to each member of the rural population down from 1.8 *mu* to 1.2 *mu*, and the ratio for each rural worker down from 5 to 3.7 *mu* (0.24 ha.). To China's agricultural planners, such prospects are quite horrendous.[8]

Even today's population-to-land ratios are considered untenable, though it is difficult to come by detailed estimates of the overall surplus labour force, the situation varying greatly from locality to locality. It is commonly asserted, however, that in the countryside of the early 1980s, five people were doing the work of three. By 1982, the *People's Daily* pronounced one third of the then 320-odd million members of the rural workforce surplus to the requirements of crop cultivation. Counting dependants, 270 million people could therefore be removed from the countryside without detriment to rural production.[9]

Writing in the journal *Renkou yanjiu* (*Population Research*) in 1983, Yang Chenggang presents a typology of the excess labour force in China's countryside. Firstly, there is the traditional *seasonal surplus*, reflecting the fluctuations imposed by the crop cycle: for most of the country this occurs in the months between the autumn planting and the spring harvest and replanting. Secondly, he identifies a *structural surplus* determined by specific changes in the structure of the rural economy such as the transfer to different kinds of crops. More important is the catch-all *common surplus* arising from steady transformation in the level of agricultural technique as well as steady population growth.[10]

Quite clearly, the enormous surplus population has not appeared out of the blue. Its origins lie in the falling ratios of arable land per capita outlined above, but also in the very gradual progress made over the years to mechanise agriculture. Some broad indicators of the scale of mechanisation are as follow: in 1957, the combined power of all agricultural machinery was 1.65 million h.p. By 1965, it had risen to 14.94 million h.p., and by 1978, to 181.92 million h.p.; as for the four years after 1978, they saw an increase amounting to 25 per cent. Further, between 1957 and 1982, the number of tractors (regardless of capacity) increased from a mere 14,674 to over 812,000, and the proportion of all cultivated land considered to be under basic mechanisation rose from around 2 per cent to over 42 per cent.[11]

In many areas, the combination of even still-low levels of mechanised processes with a growing rural population has been sufficient to cause serious difficulties:

In the Zhennan Brigade of Wuming County (Guangxi), comprehensive mechanisation has been achieved, thus releasing 17.7 per cent of the labour force. But because the surplus labour has nowhere to go [*meiyou chulu*], the effectiveness of mechanisation is severely limited. From now on in China, such contradictions will become more serious.[12]

In this over-populated area, once-welcomed innovations such as diesel-powered pumps for irrigation had been cast aside, the peasants reverting to traditional means. 'Lowering of the labour productivity rate [due to over-population] is the main cause of rural poverty,' noted the *People's Daily*.[13]

But why is it that the consciousness of 100 million excess farmhands has so suddenly dawned? The explanation lies in the fact that under the system of collective labour and distribution practised in the rural people's communes between 1958 and 1979, over-employment had become increasingly endemic. With the abandonment of these collective forms of rural organisation, the huge latent surplus rapidly became exposed. The new 'responsibility system' (introduced since 1978) emphasises individual and household effort, and removes much of the collective umbrella which both safeguarded the weak and less able and — by all accounts — held back those with greater strength and initiative. Confronted by the necessities of individual performance, the peasants are now obliged to put in more labour for potentially greater reward.

The heightened productive activity of the existing rural labour force has, therefore, been one factor in exposing the excess of labour over means of production — including that of land. The effect has been compounded by a sudden expansion in the rural workforce. Between 1970 and 1978, the maximum annual increase in the officially-registered rural labour force was around six million, and the minimum was just one million (between 1976 and 1979 the increases were particularly small, reflecting the mass returns to the cities). But suddenly in 1980 there was an 8 million increase in the rural labour force, followed by a 9 million increase in 1981 and a further rise — of 10 million — in 1982.[14]

There are a number of reasons for this spiral. Both the urban and rural labour markets after 1978 started to feel the pressures of the early-1960s birth boom. The return flow to the cities began to slow down. And most significantly, the sweeping changes in the organisation of rural production meant that suddenly there was a premium on household labour. Individuals who had previously not taken part in collective farmwork, or who had only been engaged part-time, now became full-time members of the labour force as far as the contract system was concerned. That is to say, where land was now distributed on contract according to the number of working people in a household, it was greatly to a family's advantage to register as many labourers as possible. Their numbers were boosted by up to three-quarters of a million demobilised members of the armed forces yearly, the majority of whom had previously entered the non-agricultural sector. Many rural administrators at brigade and team level also registered as full members of the agricultural workforce. In addition, and not figuring in the official statistics, was the *de facto* entry into the rural labour force of millions of people previously considered only partially economically-active. In the past, China's rural labour force had been reckoned by counting all women and all men outside the years of 18 to 55 as 'half labour powers'. Apart from at the height of the Cultural Revolution, when all were encouraged to take part in collective labour regardless of their physical attributes or of their other duties, this assessment probably more or less reflected the true situation. In the 1980s, many males outside the 18 to 55 age limits are full-time labourers, and millions of women are taking a full share in their households' farming tasks.

In its first stages, then, the dramatic changes in rural organisation increased the demand for labour. But since these changes occurred within a basically unaltered structure of agriculture — in which crop cultivation remained the dominant activity — they quickly came up against the limitation of a finite and shrinking cultivable area. It was in this situation that from 1982 on, the scale of the rural surplus population became a matter of intense official concern.

The Size of the Agricultural Surplus and Future Plans

A key reason for the introduction of the ongoing reforms in the rural sector after 1978 was the failure over the long term to raise productivity levels in the countryside. Indeed, they had actually fallen in the previous two decades. In 1955, agricultural output value produced by each rural labourer was 298 *yuan*, and in 1978 it was only 270 *yuan* (constant prices).[15]

Low productivity and an ever-rising rural population have acted to severely limit the amount of the rural product available to the state. With China being a staple food nation committed to the maximum possible self-reliance, the most crucial element of this product is grain. The figures show an extraordinarily stagnant situation: in 1955, the proportion of all output acquired by the state through purchase and tax means (what the Chinese call the 'commodification rate') was 24 per cent. By 1978, it had fallen away to just 15.4 per cent. The actual amounts had hardly changed in 23 years (44 million tonnes in 1955 and 47 million in 1978).[16]

Despite the low commodification rate, China's economists calculate that directly and indirectly, the agricultural sector supplies 85 per cent of the nation's consumables and consumer durables, and 40 per cent of all industries' immediate inputs. For light industry, the proportion stands much higher — at 70 per cent.[17] Thus agricultural productivity, and especially the surplus available to the non-farming sector, are issues fundamental to the success of future development plans. These plans envisage a situation in which agriculture can supply an ever-increasing surplus to meet the expanding needs of industry and the non-farming population. In the early 1950s, agricultural output value was about two-thirds of GVIAO, and industrial output value one third; by the 1980s this ratio had been reversed. The aim is that differential growth of the agricultural and industrial sectors, with the latter feeding off the former, will further diminish the overall role of agriculture in the economy as a whole. The Chinese government is determined in the last part of the twentieth century to transform the age-old situation of food production being the basic activity of its population. As one writer recently put it: 'The socialist system cannot be consolidated on the basis of a subsistence economy: and it cannot do without the development of commodity production.'[18]

The Move Towards Specialised and Diversified Cultivation

Post-1979 policies were designed to encourage the shift from subsistence agriculture in a number of ways. Most important is an emphasis on the more efficient and diverse use of the available cultivable land. Such an emphasis clearly exacerbates the problem of the rural surplus labour force. Another central method involves the transfer to agriculture-related activities (including small rural-based industries) which do not rest directly on the cultivation of land. Such transfers tend to release pressure on the land and ameliorate the surplus labour problem.

By the end of 1983, over 90 per cent of all rural households had come out of collective farming and distribution and were working instead by the very different rules of the contract or 'responsibility' system.[19] This new mode of organisation has brought with it increased specialisation in production, in terms both of households and of locality. From the early 1980s on, a growing proportion of contracting farmers have acquired the status of 'specialised households'. The shift to specialisation has been spearheaded by the better-educated peasantry: a survey in Yingxian County, Shanxi Province, showed that 85 per cent of the specialised households were those of rural cadres, of 'educated youth' (those with at least a junior middle-school background) and demobilised soldiers.[20] The development of specialisation has been greatly facilitated by the new policies which permit individual peasants to purchase agricultural equipment of all varieties (from tractors to light planes for crop spraying) as well as modern inputs such as fertilisers and pesticides.

Grain Cultivation. Here, the purpose of the state is to encourage a small number of highly skilled, highly capitalised and productive farmers to take over an increasing proportion of the land that is best suited to grain growing. By 1984, the success of this policy was being copiously illustrated in the Chinese media. Of the many models cited, the most extraordinary example is perhaps that of specialised grain growers in Yanbei Prefecture (Shanxi): they accounted for just 4 per cent of all the prefecture's households, yet their sales of grain to the state accounted for 75 per cent of the prefectural total.[21] Overall, the move towards specialisation in grain production has been highly effective. With a greatly reduced labour input, and a 2–3 per cent annual decline in the area devoted to grain, the early 1980s have seen a steady rise in the total grain crop, from 320 million tonnes in 1980 to over 380 million tonnes in 1983.[22]

Cash Crops. The decline in grain land has been accomplished by a dramatic rise in the area sown to industrial and cash crops, as well as similar orders of improvement in productivity to that experienced in grain growing. To illustrate some of the consequences: in the 1979 to 1983 period, cotton output more than doubled, and the production of oil-bearing crops increased by over

80 per cent.[23] Millions of peasants have transferred to specialist production of timber, vegetables, fruit, herbs, flowers, as well as livestock, fish, and other activities which require only small plots of agricultural land.

The trend towards specialisation and higher productivity in crop cultivation has reduced labour requirements, though, in a still fluid situation, to what degree remains unclear at the time of writing.

Diversification towards Activities not Directly Requiring Arable Land

Household 'Sidelines' and Services. While millions of peasant households have become specialised tillers of the soil, large numbers have shifted into production and service activities which do not directly depend on access to cultivable land. They have gone into fish-farming, poultry-breeding, pig-rearing, apiculture, silkworms and even the scientific breeding of snakes and earthworms. Some specialise in basket-weaving, furniture-making, and carpentry. Others provide services such as transportation, repair of machinery, and seed merchandising. While many of these specialised producers and suppliers are working under the contract system, by the end of 1982, 1.27 million private rural businesses were registered.[24]

Obviously, this proliferation of households engaged full-time in what were previously known as 'sideline' occupations, and the corresponding reduction in those concerned with crop cultivation, has acted to relieve the pressure on the land. Indeed, in certain regions large numbers of households have even abandoned the plots given over to them in contract in order to engage in more profitable non-cultivating undertakings. This occurred to such a degree in Mianyang County (Hubei) that the *People's Daily* found it necessary in 1983 to bring the matter to the attention of the nation.[25] The phenomenon of land abandonment is a symptom of the growing social and economic polarisation amongst China's rural population, as one of its causes is undoubtedly the inability of some households to afford the inputs which specialised cultivation demands. But perhaps more crucially, it is a symbol of the extraordinary success of rural diversification, and of the resurgence of a multitude of economic activities in the Chinese countryside that the collective system so long repressed.

Recent Development of Small Rural Enterprises. An essential element of China's rural policy during the Cultural Revolution was the fostering of small-scale industrial enterprises in the rural areas. The key plants — fertilisers, pesticides, agricultural machinery and primary processing of food and industrial crops — were usually operated under *xian* ownership. However, the practice of establishing small plants and specialised units at commune and brigade level was increasingly adopted from the early 1970s onwards. Between 1975 and 1979, their value of output increased on average by 24 per cent annually, compared with 9.2 per cent for industry as a whole.[26] The degree of development of these commune and brigade enterprises by 1978 was such that they already employed 28.8 million rural dwellers, making up 9.5 per cent of the entire agricultural workforce. And they contributed 29.7 per cent of total commune income.[27]

Far from abandoning these enterprises — as might have been expected from the general drift of post-Mao economics — in the late 1970s and early 1980s they were regarded as an indispensable part of both the agricultural and the industrial economies. Their value was — and is — considered all the greater because they provide yet another means of solving the growing problem of an excess rural labour force without actually adding to the nation's permanent urban population.

Since the early 1980s, the character of these small enterprises has become the subject of an increasing attention in China. Perhaps their most important feature lies in the transitional nature of their workforce. Most of the employees straddle both the farming and non-farming sectors. For this reason, they have become known as *yi gong yi nong renkou* (hereafter YGYN) — literally, 'population that is in both industry and agriculture'.

The YGYN system is no new idea. It operated in many of the small rural enterprises established in the Cultural Revolution and in the Great Leap Forward too. Its essential feature — the continued attachment of the employee to his or her original unit — was seen in the contract and temporary labour systems operated before the Cultural Revolution (revived on a grand scale in 1978). All these forms of employment rest on a ready, mobile and cheap supply of labour, for which the contracting unit has very little responsibility in terms of welfare. A key feature of the YGYN system is that the individual's grain supply must be found outside the state rationing system. And the total amount of foodgrains required by the YGYN workers comes to no small amount — in 1981, for instance, it was equivalent to around 15 per cent of all 'commodity grain' mobilised by the state.[28]

Though a variety of methods of remuneration for the YGYN workers has been used, depending on the locality and the kind of unit and its performance, the custom has been to pay most of the income in kind. In the early 1980s, work was evaluated according to the now-outmoded workpoint system of the rural collectives, and the brigade had to supply grain, vegetable oil and other items, the balance of earnings being paid out at the end of the financial year in cash. Where the YGYN worker was employed in a unit other than his native brigade, the latter received a cash payment from the employing unit, and in turn passed a part on to the worker as a monthly 'subsidy' (*buzhu*).

Since they maintained their membership of the rural unit, as well as rural household registration, the majority of YGYN workers could be called upon to return to the fields during harvest and planting seasons when there is generally a great shortage of labour in the countryside. According to a 1981 survey in Jiangsu, the ratio of enterprise employment to farmwork was generally 4:1.[29] A further great benefit to the state of the YGYN system is that it does not greatly increase the demand for quasi-urban facilities:

> They (the YGYN population) do not burden urban transport, and there is no great requirement to build new housing for them or for their family dependants; nor is there an increased demand for other installations serving the people's livelihood.[30]

In the early 1980s, the YGYN form became particularly well developed in the most densely populated rural areas of eastern China, and particularly in Zhejiang and Jiangsu. Most of the enterprises operating the system were located in townships within half an hour to one hour's walking distance from the villages of their employees.[31] In Jiangsu an almost equal number to that employed in the small commune- and brigade-run enterprises had been sent further afield, to provide the labour force for the great construction boom of the late 1970s and early 1980s. A city such as Nanjing in 1982 had a temporary population of YGYN-type workers equivalent to 10 per cent of its permanent population. Generally, those contract workers make few demands on the city facilities. They live on-site in makeshift dormitories, and work long hours. If a YGYN worker fell ill, responsibility lay with the native production brigade, and he would be sent back to the countryside.

Counting in the contract workers in the cities, in 1979 around 15 per cent of Jiangsu's rural workforce were classed as YGYN, the proportion being higher in the richer areas such as Suzhou prefecture and Wuxi *xian*. Nationally, the figure was rather lower: 9.5 per cent, totalling 29.09 million workers.[32]

The scale and structure of employment of the commune and brigade enterprises at the end of 1982 is illustrated in Table 7.2. It will be noted that, nationally, over half of these enterprises were

Table 7.2: Structure of Commune and Brigade Enterprises, 1982

	Enterprises		Employees	
	number (m.)	%	number (m.)	%
Agriculture-oriented	0.29	21.5	3.44	11.1
Industrial	0.75	55.0	20.73	66.6
Transport	0.10	7.0	1.13	3.6
Construction	0.05	4.0	4.21	13.5
Other	0.17	12.5	1.62	5.2
Total	1.36	100.0	31.13	100.0

Source: Adapted from TJNJ 1983, p. 206.

classed as industrial, accounting for two-thirds of the roughly 31 million workforce. Of the 1.36 million collectively-owned enterprises, 75 per cent were operated by communes and the remainder by the brigades. In the former, the average size of the workforce (44 persons) was some three times greater than that of the brigade businesses.

The very rapid expansion of the small rural-based plants in the 1970s meant that by the end of the decade, 98 per cent of all communes and 82 per cent of all brigades had diversified in this manner. They provided over 30 per cent of all commune income, and over 10 per cent of the nation's gross industrial output value.[33] In short:

They have become indispensable supplements and auxiliary producers to the big urban industries. In 1981, for instance, some rural industrial producers made up a substantial proportion of the total national output. They produced 19 per cent of the nation's coal, 80 per cent of its building materials (bricks, tiles, stone, lime, etc.) and 34 per cent of its gold. Rural industries also contributed 40 per cent of the garment industry's output, and produced a full 70 per cent of medium-sized and small farm implements and handicraft articles.[34]

As well as assuming an important place in overall national industrial production, the rural enterprises serve a local market, assist in the diversification of rural production, and provide employment for a significant proportion of the rural population without increasing the pressure on scarce land.

Rural Diversification's Impact — An Overview. By the end of 1983, 24.82 million rural households (13 per cent of the total) had turned to specialised production, selling between 70 and 90 per cent of their produce to the state.[35] A further 31 million peasants were employed in small commune- and brigade-run enterprises. The effect of the diversification policies has been to raise the overall level of *production for exchange* in the countryside from 40 per cent of all output (measured by value) in 1978 to 50 per cent in 1983.[36] This testifies to the increasing trend away from an agrarian subsistence economy in rural China of the 1980s.

To summarise, one aspect of specialisation has been the move towards capital-intensive and highly-productive crop cultivation. In as much as this has occurred, it has acted to heighten the population pressure on the land, and accelerated the emergence of surplus manpower. However, the main thrust of the specialisation process has been to open up new realms of production in the home, farm-yard, or in the small collectively-owned industries and services. These activities are not land-hungry, and their growing impact has been to reduce pressure on the soil. The way in which this has happened is decribed in numerous reports in the Chinese press and specialist journals. Take, for example, a large-scale survey of changes in nine production brigades in Jilin, Hubei and Jiangsu from 1976 on. Here, within a couple of years, an average of 33 per cent of the total labour force left crop cultivation for various locally-run industrial enterprises.[37] Elsewhere, a similar scale of transfers out of crop cultivation had actually caused localised labour shortages.[38]

Diversification's Future Prospects

Estimates of the Size of the Future Labour Surplus
While the immediate problem of a 100 million labour surplus may

have been eased by the measures to diversify the rural economy discussed above, China's strategic planners are agreed that in the long term the problem will get worse. Most accounts now speak of 200–225 million members of the existing and potential agricultural labour force having to be deployed out of agriculture, forestry and sidelines by the year 2000. The latest projections (1984) are that by the end of the century, only a third of the prospective rural-based workforce of just over 400 million will be cultivators of grain and other crops (the part of total arable land given over to grain having shrunk substantially), while 20 per cent will be engaged in subsidiary agricultural activities (forestry, animal husbandry, fisheries, and so on). As for the remaining 40-odd per cent (that is to say, around 180 million persons), 'they can only be employed in industry, construction, transportation and communications, commercial undertakings, and other service trades in rural towns.'[39]

Prospects for Further Rural Enterprise Development

The proposal mentioned above would have about 180 million people working in small rural enterprises by the year 2000. But will this sector, presently employing 31 million people, be able to accommodate over 150 million more workers over the coming 15 years or so? These enterprises are labour intensive and low in productivity. There is every indication that the liberalisation in economic policy, characterised by an emphasis on national markets and on the role of the law of value in regulating production and exchange, is likely to become more prominent in the late 1980s. In the absence of protective measures provided by the central state, the inefficient producers — including almost the entire rural industrial sector — will be confronted by irresistible forces of competition from the city-based plants. The effects of these forces have already become apparent, and they are reflected in recent years in the sluggish growth in the proportion of the agricultural workforce employed in the commune and brigade enterprises. In fact, between 1978 and the end of 1983, this figure actually declined somewhat (from 9.5 to around 9.2 per cent). Of course, in this period many peasants who otherwise would have leapt at the chance of joining a non-farming enterprise (thus getting one foot into the wage economy) found other more lucrative opportunities in sidelines. And still others were obliged to supplement their household's labour force because of lack of hands.

The chief cause of the relatively slow development of the small enterprises in the early 1980s, however, has been the increasing problem of competition from more efficient plants in the same sector. The figures show that in 1981, the commune and brigade enterprises' combined workforce remained more or less static, but the number of units declined from 1.43 million in 1980 to 1.34 million at the end of 1981.[40] In the same year, there was a fair degree of alarm at the fact that a number of large plants were unable to operate properly because they were being deprived of raw materials and of markets by small plants in the countryside. For example, in the cotton-growing province of Hubei numerous small collectively-owned textile mills were set up in the late 1970s:

> The question here is that in the consumption of raw materials, the quality of products or the cost of production, these small mills are all inferior to the large mills in Shanghai and other cities. Now that the raw materials are used up by these small mills, the larger mills in the cities often operate under capacity and are sometimes even forced to stop production.[41]

The position was considered serious enough in 1981 to warrant the intervention of the State Council in favour of the larger plants. A central directive called for 'readjustment' of the commune- and brigade-run industrial enterprises. They were strictly forbidden from operating textile mills, cigarette factories, and other locally-profitable ventures such as salt fields; in December 1981, additions to this list included oil refineries.[42] The small plants were ordered to confine their future processing activities to a limited range of agricultural raw materials. Rural units should endeavour to develop service trades which offered no threat to established economic centres, or to confine themselves to those productive enterprises more obviously related to agriculture (fish-farming, scientific poultry and pig-breeding, apiculture, even artifical-pearl culture).[43]

However, government intervention of this nature has not been effective. It is impossible to surpervise the activities of hundreds of thousands of small rural units, and there is every incentive for the communes and brigades to keep enterprises going as long as they are able. Furthermore, were the rural plants to be restricted to matters more closely associated with agriculture, then a very large proportion of them would have to close down. For in 1982, 67 per cent of the combined commune and brigade enterprise workforce was classified as industrial, and just 11 per cent agricultural.[44]

It is true that in the vicinity of the cities, many small plants are already operating as contracting subsidiaries to larger urban factories. To that extent they will be less threatened by growing domestic competition in a market that is becoming increasingly national-based than will the remoter rural enterprises. But as the forces of the market assume a greater role in regulating industrial production in China, they are bound to threaten the less efficient small-scale units. It is unthinkable that this sector could expand to absorb 150 million more excess rural labourers over the coming 15 years without its being afforded a powerful measure of protection through absorption into the central industrial planning system.[45]

In the meantime, it is likely that in the mid-1980s, the enterprises face further difficulties arising from the changes in agricultural organisation. To a hard-pressed central state, the chief virtue of the commune and brigade enterprise has been that they enable a transition to non-agricultural pursuits without increasing the state's burden in procuring and distributing staple foods. Yet with the universalisation of the contract system, rural units may not now have access to the grain they require to feed their YGYN population. The mechanisms whereby they can continue to be supplied with grain are not clear, though it seems likely that if grain has to be purchased from outside it will both threaten the viability of many enterprises, and place difficult demands on the central government.

Prospects for Exploitation of Untapped Natural Resources

As an alternative to further development of the small rural industries sector, some agronomists believe that efforts should be concentrated on opening up the country's untapped resources in agriculture, forestry and fisheries. This, they argue, would provide the most hopeful means of soaking up the growing excess of rural labour. For instance, China has round 270 million ha. of grasslands suitable for livestock farming, yet at present the utilisation rate is exceedingly low, only around 10 million sheep and cattle being raised. In sharp contrast, a similar area in the United States supports 130 million head of livestock. China has over 800,000 square kilometres of sea-surface suitable for the development of fisheries, but at present only one seventh is utilised. The 5 million ha. of fresh water suited to intensive fish-farming are a long way from their potential productivity. There are 73 million ha. of bare mountain wasteland, and even the present afforested area is not properly exploited, the replacement ratio being just 13 per cent. In the south, there are over 60 million ha. of mountainous grasslands which have hardly been touched — etc., etc.[46]

Thoughout the present century, there has been much discussion of the enormous potential offered by China's huge and varied territory. Yet even the sweeping powers over the direction of resources available since 1949 have made little mark on traditional patterns in which nature is exploited. Enormous obstacles lie in the way of opening up untapped resources. Quite substantial efforts have been made since 1978 to open up new territory and improve existing farmlands, but the price has been high. In Heilongjiang, for example, 200,000 hectares have been reclaimed for wheat, maize and soya beans. But within the financial constraints of the day this has only been possible through loans from the World Bank and the International Development Association. Here, it is estimated that the cost per hectare has been at least US$500.[47] The expense of reclaiming saline lands, of semi-deserts and uplands — as some experts propose — would be all the greater. In order to make any serious impact on the problem of a huge rural surplus workforce, it would be necessary to exploit most of the massive existing potential in forestry, fisheries and land outlined above. But China would not have committed itself to large-scale borrowing if such projects of agricultural improvement could easily be financed out of existing domestic resources. It is unlikely that the state budgetary situation will permit a substantial improvement in the coming years.

A further problem of any ambitious land-improvement plans lies in moving tens of millions of settlers into the remote regions where most of the potential lies, and in furnishing them with new skills. Given the difficulties encountered in past mass resettlements, transfers on the scale required could only be effected with the active consent of those involved. Such cooperation would necessitate enormous state expenditures in order to provide cultural, educational, and other amenities which approximated to those of the migrants' native areas. When the General Secretary of the Communist Party, Hu Yaobang, conducted an inspection tour of Qinghai Province in 1983, he called on volunteers to resettle and develop the plateaux and basins of this remote region. Within a few months, 17,000 people had flocked to the Qaidam Basin, but almost all were from the urban-industrial sector, and their assignments in Qinghai were in mineral extraction and refining, and in railway construction, rather than in agricultural or forestry.[48] While Chinese news reports of such events emphasise the pioneering spirit of those involved, in reality their motivation is rather less lofty: the fact is that non-agricultural wages in such regions are far higher than in the cities of the eastern seaboard. And construction assignments are often only temporary.

Apart from the huge costs in terms of equipment and materials which the opening up of land resources entails, the state has to consider the capital construction and consumption needs of the resettled population. Past experience has shown that enforced and ill-financed migrations often create more problems than they solve. If, therefore, a success is to be made of resettling tens of millions of peasants in remote and inhospitable parts of the country, the state will have to countenance truly massive spending on public infrastructure and wage subsidies. By their very nature, such projects of reclamation, improvement of pasture lands, afforestation, and so on, can take years to bear results. In the meantime, the central authorities will be obliged to shoulder the cost of means of production, of roads, housing, schools, hospitals, shops, cultural centres, as well as of most current expenditures — that is to say, the wage bill. In addition they will have to ensure a sufficient supply of foodstuffs to the new population. This will be particularly awkward in non-grain producing projects.

In the coming years, it seems likely that the state will only be able to take on those key land improvements that produce a moderately quick return, and do not require too much expenditure of a non-productive nature. In these terms, it is likely that the reclamation of large virgin tracts for cereal production in Heilongjiang and Inner Mongolia will be the most appealing options. The problem here is that, while the actual work of reclamation may require large labour inputs, the subsequent production activities do not promise to absorb a large workforce. With the introduction of large tractors, combine harvesters and the like, it is inconceivable that the government should contemplate an application of the standards of the 1950s, when land was reclaimed on the basis of one farmer per hectare. The purpose of reclamation is certainly not regarded as the re-creation of subsistence agriculture.[49]

In an assessment of China's capacity to utilise latent land resources of twenty years since, H. Y. Tien came to the following view:

Whatever their political, military, social and economic returns are, the conclusion is inescapable that the solutions to the Chinese population question must be found in programs other than land reclamation and organized population transfers.[50]

While there is a determination to continue with reclamation, all the issues of cost outlined above render it likely to be on a modest scale, and in projects which promise a reasonable return in the short term. The prospects of absorbing tens, or even hundreds of millions of displaced cultivators from the densely populated regions of eastern and central China seem as dim today as they did to Tien in the early 1960s.

Conclusion

We have considered in this chapter the decline in arable land of the past thirty years, and the emergence of a surplus agricultural labour force equivalent in the early 1980s to approximately one third of the total rural workforce. New forms of economic organisation established after 1978 in the countryside (likely to be further consolidated in coming years) has profound implications for the land/labour question. While in the initial stages of the reform, the labour demands of crop cultivation increased, the trend towards specialisation and high productivity in crop growing will mean a long-term contraction in the rural labour force engaged in this pursuit. Current estimates are that by the end of the century, only one third of the total rural labour force of around 400 million will be required in crop cultivation. On the other hand, it is hoped that the proportion of those engaged in forestry, in fish-farming, animal husbandry, and other similar activities will be increased to around 20 per cent of the rural workforce. On present performance this seems a reasonable target.

The real problem lies in the expectations placed on the small-scale rural enterprises at present run by communes and brigades. In present official plans, these are scheduled to absorb the lion's share of the peasant labourers thrust out of crop cultivation. Nothing in present proposals explains how their production will fit with an increasingly modernised and efficient state-sector industry located in the larger urban centres. In view of this contradiction, some Chinese agronomists believe that the surplus labour force could be absorbed in a much-extended programme of land reclamation, forestry, fisheries, and the like. The limitations here appear to be the extremely high cost to the state, as well as the problems involved in persuading millions of peasants to move to the often-distant regions where many of the latent resources are located.

One option for dealing with the excess labour force which we have not so far considered is, of course, to transfer it to the truly non-agricultural sector — that is, to substantially add to the existing urban population through mass rural-to-urban migration. As we shall see in the following chapter, this is an option which few of the Chinese specialists in the field are willing to consider.

Notes

1. Reported on Beijing Radio (domestic), 29 December 1981 (FBIS Daily Bulletin no. OW301420, 7 January 1982, pp. K2–3). The five provinces referred to are Shaanxi, Gansu, Ningxia, Qinghai and Xinjiang.
2. Zhou Xiantang, JWTS, no. 5 (1982), p. 38.
3. 1 *mu* = 0.067 ha.
4. *China Daily*, 31 January 1982.
5. Sun Jinghzhi *et al.*, ZRKL, pp. 63–4.
6. Ibid., p. 67.
7. TJNJ 1983, p. 120.
8. Zuo Xiantang, JWTS, no. 5 (1982), pp. 39–40.
9. RMRB, 5 February 1982; in RMRB 8 October 1980 it is stated that some areas already had a surplus rural workforce of over 30 per cent. The same figure is offered in Yang Chenggang, RKYJ, no. 3 (1983), p. 25.
10. Yang Chenggang, RKYJ, no. 3 (1983) p. 22, finds a distinct regional pattern of these three types, ranging from a common surplus in the south-east of the country, a seasonal surplus in the less densely packed central China, to a structural surplus in the provinces of Shaanxi, and eastern Gansu. In the remoter provinces of the north-west he finds an insufficiency of agricultural labour.
11. TJNJ 1983, pp. 186 and 197; note that since 1979, there has been a significant decline in this ratio — down from around 42 per cent to 35 per cent. The reason lies in the introduction of the new modes of rural organisation, broadly termed the 'responsibility system'.
12. Cai Yi, NDRZ (1981), p. 181.
13. RMRB, 5 February 1982.
14. TJNJ 1983, p. 120.
15. Zuo Xiantang, JWTS, no. 5 (1982), p. 40.
16. Ibid., p. 41. Here the figures are absolute ones, and I have worked them out according to the data on grain production in TJNJ 1983, p. 158. Note that some sources (eg, Jing Ping, HQ, no. 5 (1983), p. 32), give 14 per cent for 1978, not 15.4 per cent.
17. Zuo Xiantang, JWTS, no. 5 (1983), p. 41.
18. BR, no. 9, 27 February 1984, p. 4.
19. Vice Premier Wan Li, reported in BR no. 9, 27 February 1984, p. 16.
20. Ibid., p. 16.

21. Ibid., p. 21.
22. TJNJ 1983, p. 158, and BR, no. 8, 20 February 1984, p. 14.
23. In terms of physical volume of output; TJNJ 1983, p. 159, and BR, no. 8, 20 February 1984, p. 14.
24. TKP, 24 February 1983.
25. RMRB, 11 July 1983.
26. Ma Qingyu, JJDL, no. 2 (1983), p. 127.
27. TJNJ 1983, p. 120; also, Liu Qingxiang, 'Resolution of Excess Rural Population Problems Studied', *Liaoning daxue xuebao (Journal of Liaoning University)*, no. 2 (March 1983), reported in *China Report (Political, Sociological and Military)*, no. 427, JPRS 83605, p. 94.
28. Estimated at around 48 million tonnes of *shangpinliang*, on the basis of 20 kg monthly per person, and a grain commodification rate of 14.9 per cent for 1981.
29. Interview with Wu Chucai, Nanjing Institute of Geography, July 1982.
30. RMRB, 3 February 1981.
31. Interview, Wu Chucai, Nanjing Institute of Geography, July 1982.
32. Yang Chenggang, RKYJ, no. 5 (1983), p. 25.
33. Ibid., p. 25.
34. RMRB, 5 February 1982.
35. BR, no. 9, 27 February 1984, p. 4.
36. Ibid., p. 4.
37. Yang Chenggang, RKYJ, no. 5 (1983), p. 23.
38. Yang Jingying, RKYJJ, no. 4 (1982), p. 13.
39. BR, no. 16, 16 April 1984; here the figures are a little confusing, as 10 per cent of a total of '450 million able-bodied people' are earmarked in the projection as having gone to the cities. A report by Du Rusheng, Head of the Chinese Research Centre for Rural Development, estimates that by the year 2000, 30–40 per cent of the rural workforce will be in rural industries and in 'sideline occupations' (see BR, no. 18, 30 April 1984, p. 19).
40. Sun Jingzhi *et al.*, ZRKL, p. 66.
41. BR, no. 29, 20 July 1981, p. 7.
42. RMRB, 31 March, 1981.
43. Beijing Radio (domestic), 3 January 1981, reported in JPRS OWO 41039.
44. TJNJ 1983, p. 206.
45. This is recommended by a number of writers. See, for example, Wang Xinrong *et al.*, JZXB, no. 4 (1983), p. 37.
46. Yang Jingying, RKYJJ,no. 4 (1982), p. 14.
47. According to TKP, 28 April 1983, the World Bank and the IDA supplied US$35.3 million as loan and also a credit worth US$40 million. In BR, no. 8, 20 February 1984, p. 18, it is stated that foreign loans accounted for between 34 and 60 per cent of the total investment in such large-scale projects. I have estimated cautiously, assuming that in the Heilongjiang case the figure is 60 per cent. The total sum for agricultural development of foreign capital grants, technical aid and long-term interest-free or low-interest loans came to US$600 million between 1978 and early 1984.
48. BR, no. 11, 2 March 1984, p. 10.
49. H. Y. Tien, 'The Demographic Significance of Organized Population Transfers in Communist China', *Demography*, vol. 1 (1964), pp. 223–4.
50. Ibid., p. 226.

8 PROSPECTS FOR FUTURE URBANISATION: DEBATES AND POLICIES

Important changes in agricultural, industrial and local government organisation set in motion in 1979 have brought with them a rethinking of the spatial and regional elements of China's development strategy. These include the magnitude and form of future urbanisation. Whereas in 1980, the wisdom of a small-town-based strategy was unquestioned amongst urban specialists, by 1983 the consensus was no longer. The present chapter will consider this significant shift in the debate, and speculate on what the future may hold for China's urbanisation policy.

The Projected and Sustainable Urban Population

It was customary from 1981 to 1983 for Chinese academic writers to speak of a surplus rural labour force totalling 200 million before the end of the century.[1] By 1984, a higher figure (around 225 million) had been enshrined in official government proclamations.[2] The basis of such round estimates is never explained in the Chinese sources. In particular, it is not clear whether the meaning is that 200-odd million members of an enlarged rural workforce will actually be removed from active farming, or whether the global figure includes those reaching working age and going directly into the non-agricultural sector.

And what of the dependants of this workforce? The anticipated transformation of both crop production and small-scale agriculture-related activities which do not rest on tilling the land will, presumably, eventually squeeze out most of the rural dependants of urbanised (or quasi-urbanised) workers. So the 200 million surplus labourers amplifies to between 450 to 500 million footloose rural dwellers before the year 2000. Before considering the manner in which it is hoped that these huge numbers might be accommodated outside farming — that is, the implications for future urbanisation — we will examine some of the projections of Chinese experts regarding the size of China's urban population by the end of the century.

202 *Prospects for Future Urbanisation: Debates and Policies*

These projections fall into two broad groups. Firstly, there are the calculations based on per capita GNP studies, and secondly, the more traditional analyses of China's supportable non-agricultural population which rest on grain production targets. The GNP studies came into vogue in 1982, when the Chinese Academy of Social Sciences embarked on a major analysis of the data for 139 nations, resulting in three differing estimates for China's urban proportion at the end of the century. These were a high of 41 per cent, a low of 24 per cent, and a median figure of 30 per cent.[3]

Some provincial authorities conducted their own parallel studies in 1982. Social scientists in Jiangsu, for instance, made use of a complex amalgam of value of output data, national income statistics, and anticipated changes in industrial productivity in the province. From this they came with a 'necessary labour force' for industry, and a rise in non-agricultural urban population from 15.2 per cent in 1980 to 29.6 per cent in the year 2000.[4]

China's long-term plan, announced at the 12th Party Congress in September 1982, is to raise per capita GNP to around US$1,000 by the end of the century, and per capita 'national income' (a reckoning similar to GNP but excluding the tertiary sector) to US$800. These targets gave rise to a flurry of projections of China's future urban level — most based on the most dubious assumptions and extrapolations. Some examined the urbanisation experience of the industrially advanced nations, finding that France had an urban level of almost 60 per cent when the per capita GNP reached the $1,000 mark, Japan 68 per cent, and the Soviet Union 48 per cent.[5] Others concerned themselves with the supposed empirical evidence of a 9.6 per cent rise in urban level for every rise of US$100 in per capita GNP. If all went to plan with regard to the latter, this would leave China 70 per cent urbanised by 2000.[6] Rather more reasoned and cautious use of the international data led still others to conclude that China's level could be expected to rise from around 15 per cent in the early 1980s to 'between 37 and 41 per cent' in a couple of decades' time.[7]

Generally speaking, what such prognostications have in common is their mechanical transfer of foreign experience to China, resulting in a fairly crude form of trend planning. The total population target for the year 2000 is 1.2 billion,[8] and the various GNP-type projections examined by the present writer would give China an urban population in that year of anything from a low of 288 million to a high of 840 million. In other words, these exercises at their present state of sophistication are of little more than academic interest.

Less nebulous approaches to the question of future urban levels provided by such projections, or by the 'push from the land' models, are those which seek to identify the constraints upon future urban growth. In the first place, existing levels of congestion in the municipalities — and especially in the larger cities — is subjected to examination. Many of the Chinese discussions of urbanisation strategy begin by cataloguing the problems of housing, transportation, environment, and employment which plague the cities. Obviously the degree to which such factors act as constraints on future urbanisation is very much dependent upon the government's political and economic priorities. More people could be crowded into the cities without corresponding increases in non-productive capital expenditure, but there might eventually be a political price to pay. However, there is one factor which all commentators have long regarded as a relatively independent constraint — that of grain supply. Since the catastrophes following the Great Leap Forward, it has been universally accepted in China that transfers to the non-agricultural sector must keep in step with the expansion in the mobilisable grain surplus.

The underlying assumptions here are firstly, that China will remain basically self-sufficient in food grains and secondly, that the Chinese nation will, in the foreseeable future at least, continue to be a staple-food nation. As to the first point, it is true that China has since the early 1960s been an importer of grain, particularly of wheat. And in 1979, the decision was taken to substantially ease the burden on the farming population by bringing in up to 10 million tonnes annually — equal to around one fifth of all 'commodity grain' but less than 4 per cent of recent domestic production figures. Though the remarkable turn-around in China's foreign trade performance since 1980 has, in theory, provided the where-withal to increase imports of grain in the future, the Chinese government will almost certainly not do so in any substantial measure. The ensuring of adequate grain for the people has, over the centuries, taken on a powerful symbolic significance as a test of the rulers' legitimacy. The Communist Party is unlikely to go in for a policy of reliance on large food imports which — in its perception — could so easily threaten both its own mandate and the very basis of the nation's hard-won independence. Hence the supposed validity of models for sustainable future urban population which rest on growth in domestic grain production.

In this respect, the projections for China's sustainable non-agricultural and urban populations arrived at by Professor Wu Youren are worth considering here.[9] Wu firstly draws the link between national grain production and the pace of industrial-urban growth:

> After Liberation, our urbanisation experience testifies that whenever there is a bumper harvest, and grain is relatively abundant, in the ensuing year (or years), both industrial output and the global urban population have gone up. And the contrary case is, of course, true. Therefore, since Liberation, the increase in grain output has been more or less paralleled by the growth of China's urban population.[10]

Crucial to the model are the estimates for China's grain production over the two decades or so before the end of the century. For the 27 years from 1953 to 1980, grain output grew at a compound average annual rate of 2.2 per cent, but this figure is lowered by the 'man-made catastrophe' of the Great Leap period: both 1959 and 1960 saw annual reductions of 15 per cent.[11] For agriculture as a whole, the target is for a 5 to 5.5 per cent growth rate in the remaining years of this century.[12] Taking into consideration past performance, and the surge in grain output since the late 1970s, Professor Wu opts for three possible rates of growth in grain output — 3, 4 and 5 per cent per annum. He assumes a raising of the commodification rate from around 15 per cent to an average 20 per cent for the rest of the period. In view of the gradual diversification in the nation's diet, he allows for quite a generous increase in average grain consumption — from 324 kg in 1980 to 350 kg in 2000 (Table 8.1).

On the basis of all these assumptions, projections for the total non-agricultural population (*fei nongye renkou*) are derived, and these are converted into estimates for urban population (*chengzhen renkou*) using a ratio of 72.5 per cent. This compares with 1949's 61 per cent, and 1979's 81.7 per cent.[13]

Not unexpectedly, Professor Wu refers the median projection of an urban population of 282 million — that is to say, an absolute increase of almost 150 million over the twenty years from 1980 to 2000. This more-than-doubling of the urban population would mean that at the end of the century, one in four of China's population would be urban, compared with one in six today.

Table 8.1: Projections for Sustainable Urban Population, 2000 AD

Annual growth in grain (%)	Total output of grain (m. *jin*)	Commodity grain (m. *jin*)	Non-agricultural population (m.)	Urban population (m.)
5	17,367	3,463	490	355
4	13,704	2,740	390	282
3	11,306	2,260	320	232

Note: 1 *jin* = 0.5 kg.
Source: Wu Youren, ZRKL, Table 3, p. 98.

However, in view of present plans to place much of the surplus rural labour force in places at present lacking official urban status, the most important figures are for the projected supportable non-agricultural population. On the basis of the 4 per cent rate of increase in grain output, a further 80 million people could be absorbed by the commune seats and other townships. Thus we are speaking of a theoretical capability to support 230 million people more than in 1980 in the non-agricultural sector. This squares well with the customary figure of the early 1980s of a surplus agricultural workforce of 200 to 225 million, but it does not allow for the additional 280 to 315 million dependants of these excess labourers.

Since this question is never considered in the Chinese accounts, we can assume that the dependants of those who move to new avenues of employment in the city or in the local township will be expected to stay put in the villages. What is more, they will have to produce at least enough grain to feed themselves. How this can be achieved in an increasingly rationalised agriculture, in which (if all goes to plan) only 30 per cent of the rural workforce will be engaged in grain growing, is never explained. Thus, unless there is an agricultural miracle, or the state requisition rate is raised far above the 20 per cent mark of Professor Wu, it seems that there is a serious contradiction between the present plans for agricultural modernisation and the projected supportable level of non-agricultural population.

The 'Small-towns' Consensus of the Early 1980s

In so far as the politics of the Cultural Revolution had offered a model for China's urbanisation, it was that of the Daqing oilfield. Daqing's supposed merits were that it promoted a physical convergence of city and countryside, industry and agriculture. The oilfield was upheld as the living example of the new communist egalitarianism in which each family had one foot in agriculture and the other in industry, where no central city was allowed to dominate, and where the new spirit of selfless collectivism was the order of the day. Here, then, would be a true 'combination of agriculture and manufacturing industries [and the] gradual abolition of the distinction between town and country' demanded in *The Communist Manifesto*. Daqing also seemed to suit the orthodoxy of the time, for Mao himself had laid down that large enterprises 'should engage in agriculture, trade, education, and military training, as well as industry'.[14]

Daqing's lesson for the great cities — with their congested conditions and decaying urban fabric — was far from transparent. The only clear message to city planners was that as little as possible should be spent on urban housing and utilities, in order to free funds for more productive and socialistic ends. The obvious utility of Daqing was a model for entirely new industrial developments away from existing urban centres, where these developments by their very nature had to be scattered. Thus, when the new Guizhou coalfield was opened up in the early 1970s, an effort was made to emulate the Daqing arrangement. Here, a 'paper municipality' was cobbled together from around 50 dispersed mining communities. The greatest distance between the nodes of the new Liupanshui *shi* was 100 kilometres.

By the end of the 1970s, disenchantment with threadbare recipes for urbanisation of the Daqing variety was openly voiced. For the 300,000 citizens of Liupanshui, organisation into one municipal unit was now said to be the cause of 'much inconvenience in both production and daily life'. Rather than providing the means to a better existence, cities of the Daqing variety would merely ensure that urban conditions would be 'kept at the level of the countryside'.[15] Far from producing the 'city-like countryside' and the 'countryside-like city' of the communist future, they could only result in a hopeless mutation — an 'uncity-like city' and an 'uncountry-like countryside' (*cheng bu cheng, xiang bu xiang*).

The eschewing of the Maoist prescriptions for China's urbanisation left a vacuum which it was the task of the resuscitated urban planning organisations of the late 1970s to fill. To this end, a major national conference on city development was convened in Beijing in October 1980. A prominent theme of the conference was the pathetic state of the cities after many years of false models and denial of essential expenditures. A minister threatened popular impeachment on municipal leaders who neglected to improve the urban environment. But above all, the conference took on the task of formulating a grand strategy for urbanisation in the age of the 'four modernisations'. Henceforth, the major preoccupation of planners was not to be the re-creation of the countryside in the city, or the transformation of 'consumer cities' into 'producer cities', but the elaboration of policies which would provide the country with a balanced and rational network of thriving urban-industrial centres. The essence of the new urbanisation strategy was summarised in a new slogan: 'Strictly control the development of the large cities, rationally develop medium-sized cities, and vigorously promote the development of small cities and towns' (*yange kongzhi da chengshi, heli fazhan zhong deng chengshi, jiji jianshe xiao chengzhen*). We shall now consider the implications of the new strategy for the various classes of settlement to which it refers.[16]

The Large Cities — Renewal of Satellite-town Policies

At the end of 1979, China had 43 cities classed as 'large' (*da chengshi*), 15 of which were over 1 million and therefore in the 'extra-large' (*teda chengshi*) group. The big cities were to be greatly encouraged to expand their economic role without significant growth of their populations and areas. To this end, the slogan *wa qian, gexin, gaizao* ('prise out potential, innovate and transform') was much to the fore. The example of the Shanghai textile industry became commonly cited as an example to the big cities of what could be achieved if existing plant were modernised and better used. In the early 1950s, between 4,000 and 5,000 mills were producing in Shanghai, with a combined workforce of 500,000 to 600,000. By 1978, the industry employed fewer than 400,000 and the number of units had shrunk to one tenth of their original number, yet their production had risen almost ten-fold.[17] While the aim of strict control of big-city growth remained entirely consistent with strategies dating back to the 1950s, the old combination of exhortation and strict migration policies was now to be complemented by more positive measures of town planning. Chief amongst them was to be a reactivation of the satellite-town programme first seen in the late 1950s.

This meant a reappraisal of past experience in satellite development. On the whole, this is not held to be a happy one. Central planners identify the main reason as being an inability to match industrial growth with adequate 'municipal construction' — that is, housing, schools, hospitals, roads, parks, and so on. As we have already noted, Shanghai (where the satellite-town policy has been more vigorously applied than anywhere else), has thus been unable to attract a settled population; one consequence has been an enormous journey-to-work problem. Similar problems have dogged one of Beijing's fledgling satellites, the petrochemicals base at Fangshan, where in 1980 only 17 per cent of the inhabitants had moved from Beijing city proper. Sixty-five per cent had moved in from other parts. This situation frustrates the central purpose of satellite development, that is to say, the relief of population pressure on the core city districts.[18]

The *Jianzhu xuebao (Architectural Journal)* felt that several crucial points should be borne in mind when upgrading the existing satellites or building new ones.[19] The first concerned the employment situation in new towns. With a rigid gender division surviving in many avenues of work, even where the entire family is able to be rehoused in the satellite there is likely to be enforced unemployment resulting from the narrow mix of job opportunities. This causes serious hardship, as China's 'low-wage policy' is based on the notion of household rather than breadwinner's income. Thus the new programme of satellite construction should try to ensure that sufficient and varied job opportunities be provided to allow all members in a family to find suitable employment.

Secondly, medical, educational, and recreational services, as well as the provision of housing and public transportation, should be up to the levels found in the mother cities. The third point was that the location of a new satellite should be at a sufficient distance from the core city to establish a degree of independence and identity. In the past, the satellites and quasi-satellites had often been neither self-contained nor well connected to their core cities. Take, for example, Nanjing's industrial satellite of Dachangzhen situated 20 kilometres north-east of the mother city (and known to this present writer as he once worked there). In the mid-1970s, this place of over 50,000 inhabitants had all the appearance of a 'one-horse town': to travel into Nanjing for shopping, entertainment and family visits required no less than three changes of bus.[20]

After 1980, almost all the 'million cities', and a good number of the cities over half a million, began to lay out plans for satellites, or revive old plans that had never been implemented. Beijing, one report notes, has designated 40 satellite sites, 'but none has achieved the anticipated results for lack of overall planning'.[21]

Satellite Development in Beijing

While in the past it was Shanghai that had set the pace in satellite development, since 1980 Beijing has taken the lead. The capital had received more than its share of grand industrial projects during the three decades when a city's progress was measured almost solely by the growth in its production figures. For as an administrative and cultural centre before 1949 — in official terminology, the epitome of a 'consumer city' — Beijing had not merely to industrialise, but to become a showplace for heavy industry. The consequence was that in terms of the proportion of heavy industry in its economy, Beijing long ago overtook the old production centres of Tianjin and Shanghai.

After 1980, there emerged a powerful lobby aimed at preventing the further industrialisation of Beijing-proper. A prestige-conscious and more wordly-wise leadership in Beijing decided that the measure of a capital city's civilisation was not a high degree of industrialisation but, rather, the lack of it. Planners were sent to investigate the degree of capital city industrial employment, and they discovered that in Washington it was just 3 per cent, while Paris had one of the highest figures (30 per cent). In Beijing, however, 40 per cent of the working population were in industry.[22]

Hence, in July 1980, the *People's Daily* announced a decision taken at the highest level (the Secretariat of the Central Committee) to press for the decongestion and partial de-industrialisation of the capital. The aim would be to maintain Beijing's core population at 4.3 million, or even slightly reduce it. The means was to be a vigorous expansion of the various classes of urban node around the core city and within Beijing *shi*, to bring their combined population up from 800,000 to over 2 million by the end of the century. In the first phase, the key developments are in Fangshan, Tongxian, Changping and Huangcun. This last place would be expected by the end of the century to have grown to around four times its 1980 size of 50,000. A campaign to persuade enterprises and their workers of the great advantages of satellite location was launched, and various happy experiences advertised. For example, in its old premises in the inner city, Beijing's Number 6 Glassworks occupied a cramped and unsuitable site in a largely residential district. In Huangcun it now has a purpose-built factory situated away from housing areas, and there are no more complaints of pollution. But most important in its success story, the Glassworks managed to quadruple output within the first two years of operation on the new site.[23]

In an effort to overcome the resistance to moving to satellites, firms have offered a variety of tempting inducements to their workers. Extra flats have been offered to their unemployed offspring. Some enterprises have provided generous wage supplements as an inducement to move. Meanwhile planners have been entreated to give sufficient thought to the housing and infrastructure of the satellite towns, and to the securing of the necessary construction funds. This is where the rub comes, for in approving plans for satellites, it seems that civic leaders in Beijing and elsewhere may have been unaware of the very high costs of new town development.[24]

The Medium-sized Cities

In the strategic urbanisation formula put forward at the 1980 city planning conference, China's 'medium-sized' cities (defined as between 200,000 and 500,000, and numbering about 70) were singled out for 'rational development'. Perhaps the vagueness of this prescription was designed to leave maximum room for flexibility and manoeuvre. As in the case of the larger centres, the intention was, as far as possible, to limit the population growth of such cities, while taking maximum advantage of their present economic structures in order to increase production. Further industrial development should emphasise the technological reform of existing plants, though completely new large-scale enterprises could be built where local conditions were appropriate. The Chinese sources have not, since 1980, offered any outstanding cases of 'rational development' of the medium-sized cities, this suggesting that their role in overall urbanisation strategy is seen as limited. As one writer remarks, 'Some medium-sized cities having big industry can expand and build new industrial areas; but this will not be the main strand in our country's urbanisation.'[25]

The Small Municipalities

A far richer literature has developed around the smaller class of municipalities of under or around 200,000, which in 1979 accounted for almost half total *shi*. By their nature — being at the lowest of the three levels of the *shi* hierarchy — they are the most dynamic and rapidly developing group. In the slogans of 1980, the small cities were specifically marked out for vigorous growth. Unlike the larger centres (including most of the medium-sized cities), they do not generally suffer from poor housing, crowded buses and high unemployment. They are noted for their distinct role in the space-economy, and for their strong economic links to their respective provincial capitals. Despite their scale, they may already be the location of large industrial plants.

A loose classification of these *xiao chengshi* is offered by one eminent geographer:[26]

i. Those small cities which have already developed to the point of having their own special economic integrity. Such places as Zhuhai in Hubei, and Yantai (Shandong) are said to have a well-balanced and 'rational' economic base, and offer their inhabitants a pleasant environment. Such municipalities would be thrust into disequilibrium if future growth were too vigorous.

ii. Mining and heavy industrial centres based on local raw materials. Dukou in Sichuan province, and Ma'anshan in Anhui are said to be typical of this group, where in the past the economy has been dominated by a single heavy industrial sector. In small cities of this type, some further growth can be countenanced, preferably in the direction of diversification of the economic base. Because the problem of lack of non-productive capital investment has been particularly associated with heavy industry, the service sector in such places can be vigorously expanded from its present 'incomplete' (*bu peitao*) state.

iii. Small cities that are on a tide of rapid growth, because of certain special local factors. The impetus can be continued, to make such places 'sub-provincial centres' (*sheng nei jingji qu*). A prime example here is Shashi in Hubei province (a core city population of 188,000 in 1982).[27] Shashi's rapid growth in recent years is due to the modernity of its textile industry, but it also has much to do with its role as a servicing centre for the great Gezhouba Dam project on the Yangzi. Future extension of Gezhouba will ensure Shashi's continuing growth.

iv. Small cities that play a special role in the national transportation network. With the constant expansion and modernisation of the railway system, of river and sea ports (and to a lesser degree, of long distance highways), a large number of small transport nodes can be expected to flourish and grow.

One could add to the second category in this list the limited number of cities which can be expected to experience dynamic growth because of their location at sites of newly exploited primary resources. A case in point is the settlement of Jinchang, elevated to *shi* status by the State Council in 1981. Jinchang owes its existence to a brand-new nickel and platinum refining industry based on huge local deposits of nickel sulphide. It achieved its promotion to *shi* despite a relatively small population of 60,000: in the waste-lands of the Gansu corridor, Jinchang no doubt looms as a major metropolitan centre.

The expansion of energy resources is a key priority of the present planning era, and coal-mining activities will give rise to a number of rapidly growing small cities in Shanxi, Inner Mongolia, Henan and Shandong. For instance, the new municipality of Yima has recently appeared in Henan; the burgeoning county seat of Yanzhou in southern Shandong — site of a massive new coal-mining venture — will doubtless continue to recruit large numbers from the countryside, and it may thus be expected to qualify for municipal status.[28]

Though the Chinese literature on small municipalities remains rather sketchy in its presentation of their generic features, it continues to provide a strong line in the description of various models for emulation. In the early 1980s, a number of small municipalities were singled out by the Chinese press and dutifully reported in the specialist journals. They included Weihai and Yantai in Shandong, Changzhou and Nantong in Jiangsu, and Foshan in Guangdong. The chief reason for their being presented as models is, every time, their strong economic performance. This emphasis is an expression of the ongoing divergence of interests between China's geographers and spatial planners on the one hand, and central and provincial economic and industrial planners on the other. The message which the former group are so keen to convey to the latter is that small cities are marvellous places to locate new plant — not primarily on account of their better urban conditions, but because they can guarantee tangible economic returns which are comparable to those of the great industrial centres. Let us, for example, summarise the evidence as it is presented for one such model small city — Nantong, situated on the estuary of the Yangzi in Jiangsu not far from Shanghai.[29]

The location of China's earliest native-owned mechanised textile industry, Nantong's industrial performance has been spectacular; by 1981, its average urban per capita output value was over 50 per cent greater than the national average.[30] The process of reforming Nantong's textile industry began in the 1950s. Gradually, automated printing and dyeing mills were grafted on, and key technologies imported from Europe using locally-derived export earnings. In the 1970s, diversification into other light industrial sectors was strongly promoted, care being taken to select those industries 'which consume little energy but yield quick returns'.[31] The early 1970s was a time when most urban managers felt they had to prove their socialist credentials by encouraging the growth of heavy industries, with their high costs of investment and slow rates of return. But Nantong bravely rose above this dogmatism and opted for light industries. This decision was to stand it in very good stead at the end of the 1970s, when most cities were experiencing increasing levels of unemployment: light industry absorbs more labour per unit of fixed assets than does heavy industry. With an urban population of around 200,000 in 1981, over the four years starting in 1978 the city managed to add almost 27,000 to its industrial payroll, over half being in light industry and textiles.[32] By 1981, the city's employment participation rate had climbed from 27 per cent (1949) to over 70 per cent — a figure well above the national average for the urban areas.[33] The consequence was that Nantong became in the early 1980s one of the few cities which could claim insignificant unemployment. Indeed, if the experience of the similarly-dynamic nearby city of Changzhou is anything to go by, recent years have probably found Nantong with a labour shortage which it has had to make good by extra-plan recruitment direct from the villages.[34]

In most Chinese accounts of successful economic performance, the final section catalogues the material rewards which have accrued to those involved — the producers. The statistics for Nantong show that per capita industrial income has risen at a far greater rate than the national average; there have been numerous additional benefits for Nantong's citizens. Particularly noteworthy is that between 1979 and 1981 alone, sufficient new housing floorspace was added in the city to accommodate 45,000 people at current standards of allocation.[35]

To summarise then, the urbanisation strategy developed in the early 1980s was to restrict population growth of the big cities, principally by building satellites in their hinterlands, to encourage selective growth of the medium-sized cities, and to put no barriers in the way of all-out expansion of small cities such as Nantong. But will the municipalities alone be able to cope with the huge rural surplus which we have earlier described? As a very rough means of estimation, let us suppose that the number of small municipalities (planned to bear the brunt of all municipal growth) were to increase from the 100-odd of 1980 to the 300 or so anticipated as the total for the year 2000. Were they each to add 100,000 to their populations in this period, the most they could jointly absorb of a rural surplus of hundreds of millions would be 30 million people.[36] Even with the several tens of millions which the larger cities might absorb, we can see that the order of discrepancy between the demands imposed on China's municipalities and their capacity to satisfy that demand is enormous. It is precisely in recognition of this ominous discrepancy that the slogan of the 1980 planning conference incorporated an active role for the sub-municipal centres — the *xian* seats and the countless smaller townships.

The Nature and Proposed Role of the Sub-municipal Centres

The unchallenged assumption of the 1980 to 1982 period was that since it will be impossible to concentrate the huge numbers of rural dwellers to be thrust off the land in a more conventionally urban setting, China's myriad small towns will play a huge role in future urbanisation. These places were unanimously regarded as the *central* means of anchoring the footloose peasantry to their native rural areas. Hence the small towns have been enthusiastically described as potential 'storage reservoirs', preventing 'torrents of surplus agricultural labourers from flowing into the large and medium-sized cities'.[37]

While in the short space of a couple of years, some of the initial enthusiasm regarding the potential of the small towns has become muted (we will consider the reasons later), the stark circumstances of a growing excess rural population mean that they will continue to be regarded as the only viable means of preventing a devastating deluge of the cities.

The small towns are not undifferentiated in their present role and future potential. At the top of the hierarchy are the county towns, the *xian* seats, numbering around 2,130 in the early 1980s. Of these county towns, roughly 1,760 are designated as towns (*zhen*), the balance of 370 being denied this status merely for reasons of administrative anomaly.

Next come the approximately 1,100 *zhen* which are not county seats, and are administratively subordinate to the counties. Smaller than these places are the almost 50,000 rural townships (*nongcun jizhen*) which for the most part are headquarters of commune administrations, a proportion of them now being the loci of the newly restored 'township' (*xiang*) governments. And finally, at the base of this attenuated network of settlements are the 5 million 'natural villages'. We shall now consider in greater detail the nature of these different groups of settlements, and the potential claimed for them.

County Seats. The total number of *xian* has increased slightly since 1949, mostly as a response to changing population distribution in border provinces such as Heilongjiang. But in heartland China (broadly the coastal and inland regions of our earlier definition), the number of *xian* and, in many cases, the location of both their seats and their borders, have changed very little over the centuries. But there is a lack of overall descriptive information regarding the size and generic features of these places. We are told that the majority of them lie in the 10,000–50,000 group; all those county seats indicated as over 100,000 in a 1977 atlas have since been elevated to *shi* status, and it is reasonable to assume that the 40 county capitals which followed suit in 1983 were generally the larger ones.[38]

Visitors to the typical county town will find the prominent edifices of the county court, the education department, a plethora of industrial bureaux, the county guest-house for visiting officials, a main department store, Xinhua bookshop, middle school, and perhaps a theatre. There will also be a busy bus station from which routes radiate over the whole county. Many *xian* seats are also distinguished by their small industrial plants, producing fertilisers, pesticides, agricultural implements and simple machinery.

The county seats preside over quite varying rural populations. While the crude average for the nation as a whole is around 480,000, in remote regions the figure could be as low as 100,000 and in a coastal province it might be over 1 million. Even the contrast between neighbouring *xian* seats can be striking. In south-eastern Shandong, for example, the railway town and new coal-mining centre of Yanzhou is a sprawling settlement of wide, dusty avenues lined with two- and three-storey buildings of brick and concrete. Just a few miles down the road, Qufu, birthplace of Confucius, retains the atmosphere of antiquity. This is despite the present passion for 'modernisation' which brought the demolition of some of the last surviving town walls in China. Unprepossessing office buildings now stand on the site of the old walls, but Qufu has yet to attract any industries beyond the traditional noodle-making and blacksmiths' shops. The town's intimate links with the surrounding countryside are everywhere visible: in the harvest seasons, its narrow streets are transformed into drying grounds for maize and wheat. The housing is mostly the single-storey and brick-and-tile variety of the villages. There is no mistaking the fact that most of Qufu's residents depend directly on agriculture, yet in common with most county seats, the population of its rural hinterland no doubt regard it as the first and most important rung on the scale of true urbanness.[39]

It is recognised that most county town plants will continue to be closely linked to agriculture, and as such will — in the slogan of the Cultural Revolution coined by the late Zhou Enlai — 'strengthen the unity of industry and agriculture and town and countryside' (*gong nong jiehe, cheng xiang jiehe*). But apart from certain county seats such as Qufu, which should be designated as tourist centres and depend in the future on 'smokeless industries' (*wuyan gongye*), the message of the early 1980s was that most should develop 'in the direction of the small cities'. Industry should thus become the 'leading factor' in their development, and it should not be confined to small county-owned plants. Exponents of the small-town strategy are keen to emphasise that large-scale industries can do very well in small centres; a fine example is said to be the Hanjiang Iron and Steel Company located in Mian *xian* in Shaanxi Province, in the county town of just 20,000 people.[40]

Sub-County zhen. Around 1,100 of those places designated as towns (*zhen*) are not county seats, but are administratively subordinate to the county authorities (*xian shu zhen*). The great majority are in the 3,000 to 10,000 size group, though a small number are as large as 30,000 in population. Generally, around 70 per cent of their settled inhabitants are registered as non-agricultural persons. They are described as the 'political, economic, cultural, and transportation centres for small regions', their influence extending to a radius of around 10 kilometres.[41] Since 1958, most have also been the sites of commune administrations, and many will now play host to the newly-restored *xiang* or 'township' governments. While the small-town strategists see the *xian* seats following in the footsteps of the small municipalities, the sub-county *zhen* are expected to develop in the image of the county towns. In so doing, they will also develop small industrial enterprises and service units fuelled by surplus rural labour power organised on the YGYN basis. In the period shortly after the 1980 city planning conference, the Chinese media chose to extol the potential of such places. Luoshe Zhen, in Wuxi *Xian*, Jiangsu Province, gained particular mention in the local and national press accounts.[42]

Luoshe Zhen lies between the *shi* of Changzhou and Wuxi. This is a particularly densely populated part of China, where the average per capita arable land is just one twentieth of a hectare. It is also an area where the level of farm mechanisation is much above the average, and this has aggravated the common problem of an excess rural labour force. Traditionally, the population pushed from the land has been obliged to move to the nearby cities, and many of Shanghai's citizens have their roots in the area.

By 1980, Luoshe Zhen's population had risen from around 1,000 in the early 1950s to 18,000. Accounts of Luoshe's success identify the key reason as being vigorous growth of small industrial, commercial and service enterprises, which in 1980 numbered 76, employing 40 per cent of the town's residents. The control of these units varied, though well over half could be classified as collectively owned — that is by the rural communes and brigades. The most noteworthy productive enterprises were as follows:

xian-run units — a diesel engine plant, chemical fertiliser plant, and paper mill;

zhen-run units — a factory producing steam boilers, and one turning out parts for lasers;

gongshe (commune)-run units — an electric-fan factory, a manufacturer of agricultural equipment, and a printing works.

As might be anticipated, Luoshe Zhen's well-developed enterprise-base provides considerable funds both for the coffers of the state, and for local reinvestment and consumption. The aid to the agricultural sector is many-sided: first, the agriculture-related products and services are, in the main, utilised by nearby farming communities. In Luoshe Zhen, the demand for small tractors, electric motors for threshers and pumps, crop sprayers, cement boats (a local speciality in this timber-starved region of lakes and canals), and medium-sized tools and equipment is said to have been 'basically met'. Second, some of the enterprise profits are used to aid the rural community directly. Nationally in 1982, 14 per cent of all commune and brigade enterprise profits were given over to the purchase of farm equipment, to the improvement of the land, and to financial subsidies to poor production teams.[43] Third, as we have seen earlier, the development of the enterprises can be a very useful way of absorbing large numbers of people who are no longer needed in crop cultivation.

The long-term ability of a small town to act as a 'storage reservoir' for the rural population depends on the kind of living conditions it can offer. This is recognised as central to the purported failure of the small-town strategy to date. 'Water flows down to lower places, but people flow up to richer places', goes a Chinese saying[44], and China's planners well understand today that whatever the juridical and physical barriers to migration, in the long term the old adage will prevail. For this reason, locally-financed health, education and welfare facilities in places like Luoshe Zhen are seen to be vitally important. Luoshe itself has a combined middle school and teachers' college with 1,700 students in all, two primary schools, a 100-bed hospital capable of performing complex operations. The town has a cinema, good shops, and planned housing developments. All in all, its facilities serve not only the resident population but they also attract peasants from as many as eleven of the surrounding communes.

The accuracy and truthfulness of such glowing reports is not questioned. But it must always be borne in mind that by definition a model is far from typical. Indeed, recent history has shown that many emulation models have enjoyed an unfair advantage at an early stage of their development; this places them on the cumulative spiral of success — often at the expense of their peers. It is not known if Luoshe Zhen has benefited from such favouritism; but that apart, Luoshe (as in the case of most other *zhen* models) is in one of the best agricultural regions of China. Astride both the Grand Canal and the Nanjing–Shanghai railway, it enjoys excellent communications. And even in 1949 it was unusual in having several non-agricultural enterprises: 300 of the town's then 1,000 inhabitants were employed in an oil-extracting factory, a grain mill, and a porcelain factory. The more typical state of things in small towns will be considered presently.

Smaller Rural Townships. At the bottom of the hierarchy of places considered as important to future urbanisation strategy are the *nongcun jizhen* (NCJZ — literally, 'rural market towns') which are said to number about 50,000.[45] Of these places, something over 40,000 feature as the sites of rural people's communes, and the balance are non-commune market centres. Though one report suggests that a significant number of the NCJZ are between 4,000 and 5,000 in population, while in provinces such as Liaoning one seventh are over 10,000, most observers agree that the great majority lie in the 1,000 to 2,000 size group.[46] This seems to fit with this writer's own first-hand observation: the NCJZ are over-whelmingly oriented to agriculture, their non-farming populations rarely exceeding 20 per cent.[47]

The degree of development of these smallest 'urban' nodes varies very considerably between and within regions. The most advanced are almost up to *zhen* standard in their economies and in the public facilities they are endowed with. For example, this writer worked for a period in Molingguan in Jiangning *xian*, Jiangsu.[48] Here, the one-street settlement was more than a village yet less than a town. In the mid-1970s, it could boast a small machinery factory, equipped with its own 'backyard furnace' for smelting iron ore, with lathes and steam-hammers. The only other productive enter-prise was a mill where the commune members took their grain for dehusking. But Molingguan did at the time have a comparatively well-equipped middle school and a primitive hospital, as well as the various buildings of Moling commune administration. Then there were the usual general-store, post-office, and barber's shop. Standing back from the road and merging with the surrounding fields were the village-style huts of Moling's inhabitants — single-storey but connected to mains electricity and — unusually — to a piped water supply fed from an imposing concrete water tower. Doubtless the past few years have seen a considerable expansion of small enterprise, private stalls and shops, and peasant-run markets in Molingguan, for it is in a rich area and has the added advantage of a large mountain of iron ore within the commune boundary. The fact that a foreigner was allowed to observe conditions there closely in the mid-1970s proves that it was an advanced and atypical commune town; even today, most of these rural market towns are probably in a far less advanced state of development.

Not unexpectedly, the optimistic projections of the small-town lobbyists have the NCJZ developing along the lines of the ordinary *zhen*, with more and more of their population becoming partly enterprise employees and partly farmers — that is to say YGYN (*yi gong yi nong*) workers. Substantial growth of these small rural marketing centres is expected to be stimulated by the ongoing expansion of private enterprise and petty trading in the countryside.

Game Plans for Absorption of Population by Small Settlements

No proponent of the small-town strategy as a solution to China's surplus rural labour question can resist speculation regarding the supposed potential growth of the various categories of small settlement considered above. If, for example, the *xian* seats and other *zhen* grew to an average 50,000 from their present (notional) 15,000, they could jointly accommodate over 110 million additional people.[49] Add to such figures the possibilities offered by the over 50,000 *nongcun jizhen* — the commune seats and other small rural marketing centres — and the permutations of the numbers game seem almost unlimited. To mention just a few of the enthusiastic projections of different authors, in order of their extravagance.[50]

i. If each commune seat were to add just 1,000 to 3,000 new residents, then 53–159 million extra persons could be accommodated;
ii. If only 20,000 of the 53,000 commune seats absorbed 10,000 people, over 200 million new residents could be accounted for;
iii. Were each to add 5,000 people, the total would be 250 million;
iv. If all the present commune seats grew to 10,000 by the end of this century, they would then hold 500 million of China projected 1.2 billion people. Along with the 110 million accounted for by the *xian* seats and *zhen*, over half of the population could thus be accommodated by the sub-municipal places, compared with just 6 to 7 per cent today.

While game plans such as these seem to hold a fascination for most Chinese scholars of the great urbanisation dilemma, a minority have begun now to wonder whether they are rooted in reality. This reappraisal coincides with certain developments in official thinking on the regional and metropolitan questions which we will now review.

New Trends in Urban and Regional Strategy

A subtle change in emphasis is detected in the Chinese writings on urbanisation after 1982. The notion of a 'Chinese road to urbanisation' (distinguished from other national experiences principally by its small-town basis) has not been abandoned. But it is now less assuredly stated, and a surprising number of writers have begun to express a view which only a few years ago would certainly have been regarded as at best superfluous, and at worst 'revisionist'. It has almost become *de rigeur* to preface a discussion of China's urbanisation strategy with a declaration of the 'universality' and 'inexorability' of the urbanisation process. The following are typical:

> Urbanisation is a necessary consequence of the economic development of society, whatever the country, whatever its societal system, admitting absolutely no exception.[51]

> Urbanisation is an objective law in the development of the commodity economy, and is a trend which cannot be obstructed.[52]

This new perspective chooses to highlight not the evils of urbanisation, but rather its inevitability and even its desirability. It is the sea-changes which have swept the Chinese economy since 1979 which have brought this alteration in mood. The more rigorous accounting procedures, and the reforms in enterprise management and industrial planning, have served to underline the enormous importance of China's larger-scale industry in national economic development.

At the end of 1982, there were 388,600 industrial enterprises nationwide classified as state- and collectively-owned (the latter category includes both urban enterprises and rural ones at the commune level). Of this grand total, just 1.4 per cent (5,400 plants) were classed as 'large' and 'medium-sized', and they accounted for over 44 per cent of global industrial output value.[53] The crucial point here is that the great majority of such plants are located in the existing municipalities, and they are concentrated particularly in the larger settlements, the 'million cities'. The figures for 17 of the total of 20 such places in 1982 show that they contributed as much as 36 per cent of China's GVIO.[54] As for all the 50 cities of over half a million in their non-agricultural populations, they accounted for well over 60 per cent of GVIO.

We must distinguish from this point on between those who are unambiguously committed to the economistic arguments, with their unhesitant promotion of the existing centres of excellence, and those who continue to feel that the inevitable and unacceptable price of efficiency is less equality. The protagonists in this debate can be loosely divided between the political/economic/industrial planners on the one hand, and the spatial planners on the other. (It is important always to remember that the former group is more snugly integrated into the political power base than is the latter.) To marshal the new official enthusiasm for the great cities, in the spring of 1981 the State Council launched a vigorous campaign to popularise the experience of Shanghai, the nation's pre-eminent metropolitan centre. With around 1 per cent of China's total population, Shanghai *shi* produces over one tenth of the nation's industrial output value. And by every possible measure of industrial performance — value of output per worker, per capita national income, energy utilisation ratios, and so on — the city's record stands high above the average for the nation as a whole.[55]

The Notion of Key Cities

Following a lapse of twenty years, the late 1970s saw the restoration of the 'key-point city' (*zhongdian chengshi*) system. In 1981 there were 15 such places, and by the end of 1982, 17. The purpose of key-point status is to systemise preferential access to resources, and to increase autonomy in decision-making over and above the ordinary municipalities.[56] That all the key-point cities to date are also 'million cities' rather than medium-sized or small municipalities reflects both their weight in the national economy and a new determination to use their scale economies to maximum advantage.

In mid-1981, further affirmation of the increasingly positive role planned for the big cities was demonstrated in a campaign for the expansion of the influence of regional metropolitan centres. Specifically, it was proposed that Shanghai should develop its influence in eastern and central China, while Tianjin should take care of the north, and Guangzhou the south.[57] Lesser 'million cities' such as Qingdao, Dalian, Shenyang, Wuhan and Chongqing should also be encouraged to look beyond their traditional regional confines. For this purpose, more joint ventures or 'trans-provincial corporations' should be set up — along the lines, as one writer explains, of multinationals in the capitalist world.[58]

August 1982 saw the publication by the *People's Daily* of a major exposition of the advantages of inter-regional cooperation.[59] But the theme was only enshrined in government doctrine at the fifth session of the 5th National People's Congress held in December 1982. In his report to the Congress, Premier Zhao Ziyang outlined '10 great principles' for the development of the economy, one of which was to 'rely on the big cities, create economic centres (*jingji zhongxin*) at every level, and rationalise the economic network'.[60] This idea was taken up with some enthusiasm by the specialist economics publications. Articles appeared which extolled the virtues of the great cities, while lamenting that they had been held back by an ultra-left preference for spatial 'evenisation' (*junhenghua*). Shanghai, for example, had seen its nationwide economic network 'disintegrated' (*jieti*) by the strait-jacket of post-1949 administrative divisions. One dire consequence (as it was somewhat tendentiously claimed) was that by 1958, Shanghai had been overtaken in its volume of foreign trade by Hong Kong.[61] Similarly, for Wuhan, the key city of the central China region, which had had its economic links with other regions 'severed' by insensitive and constraining administrative delineation.[62]

The school of economic thought dominant in the mid-1980s holds that the economically-advanced cities and regions should 'break through the administrative fetters' imposed upon them by arbitrary fiat, thus restoring the supposed 'natural economic intercourse' (*ziran jingji lianxi*) of a past era. The present administrative divisions of the People's Republic are considered to be a grave hindrance to further rapid development. So are the majority of the existing planning mechanisms, not only in the restrictions they impose through over-verticality but also in those flowing from the wrong form of horizontal attenuation (the *tiao tiao kuai kuai* problem). The post-Mao reform of the regional planning system through the restoration of the six great regions is regarded as utterly irrelevant.[63]

These moves towards an unambiguous promotion of urbanism on the grand scale have an ideological rationalisation. Their defence rests in the catch-all justification for sweeping economic reform of the post-1978 period, that is to say, the need during Marx's 'lower phase' of communism to tolerate — indeed nurture — the 'commodity economy'. Hence, state planning must as far as possible be indicative and liberal, encouraging a form of commodity production and exchange not far removed from that of capitalism. Such reasoning is applied in almost every corner of the economy, whether it be to encourage price competition between enterprises, or 'commodification' (that is, selling off) of the state-owned urban housing stock to anyone rich enough to buy. In just four years, China has moved far closer to a fetishisation of market forces than have the Eastern European nations in two decades of liberalisation. The new perspective is also brought to bear on the urbanisation issue: the large cities remain a 'necessary feature of commodity production and of the socialist division of labour', and if this fact is recognised, they can become a 'tremendous force' in the economy.[64] Certain places can, therefore, 'turn their face to the whole nation', and become 'central cities' (*zhongxin chengshi*). To quote one writer on the subject:

> The question now confronting us is this: does socialist society need economic centres of gravity? [*jingji zhongxin* — this refers to the big cities]. The answer is in the affirmative. Because our country's socialist economy remains at the stage of a commodity economy, central cities are still economically pivotal [*jingji shuniu*].[65]

Further, it is asserted that in a nation just embarked on the socialist transition, the great cities can assume an even more crucial role than they do in the process of capitalist accumulation.

In 1983, various arrangements were proposed whereby 'central cities' can consolidate their links with far-flung parts of the country, while numerous successful cases of inter-regional cooperation were described in the newspapers. The ventures undertaken between Shanghai and units in the interior and border provinces, for example, fall into five main groups: united marketing of goods, compensation trade, technical cooperation, united investment and management, and 'cooperation companies'. Of these, the latter two are said to be more closely-knit and longer-term. From 1979 to 1982, the city established over 200 various cooperative relationships in 17 provinces and autonomous regions, involving over 900 separate contract items.[66]

A minority of the new inter-regional agreements are between interior and border provinces; for instance, Hebei badly requires phospherous, while Guizhou had a superfluity of the mineral. A compensation venture was thus established, Hebei providing the expertise and capital of 5 to 10 million *yuan* annually. The great majority, though, are between the advanced (coastal) regions and the backward interior areas. Some accounts of these inter-regional agreements emphasise mutual benefit. Others highlight the advantages to the recipients of capital and skills:

> There is fear in some quarters that for more advanced areas to invest in backward areas would impoverish the latter. Actually, the contrary is true because this can only result in narrowing the disparity between the different areas. It would mean that the more advanced areas would use their expertise and material and financial resources to help the backward areas develop their economy.[67]

The textile industry in Yichang (Hubei), for instance, was able to increase its profits per spindle four-fold within two years of signing a technical cooperation agreement with Shanghai.[68]

But in the specialist economics publications such as *Jingji yanji (Economic Research)*, a different interpretation has begun to be placed on these relationships. Though there have been considerable efforts to industrialise parts of the interior, it is felt that in general the results have been less than adequate. In the new scheme of things, interior and border provinces should be regarded as primarily the providers of raw materials and energy resources needed by coastal industry. In so far as they maintain and develop a manufacturing capacity, it should mainly be on the basis of the second-hand technologies off-loaded by the 'central cities'. As one writer has it, this will 'benefit the unity between the coastal region which has relatively advanced manufacturing technology, and the interior which is rich in raw materials'.[69]

The city of Shanghai has been particularly active in transferring equipment (accompanied in many cases by sub-contracting assignments) to other areas. When, for instance, the Shanghai Wool and Flax Company imported some high-technology spindles, it packed off its obsolete plant to commune enterprises in nearby Nanhui *xian*.[70] This process — it is argued — should be generalised, so that the coastal areas are re-equipped with advanced (and mainly imported) production equipment; a 'stepped system' of production technique should be developed, with the eastern and/or larger cities having the most modern technology; these gradations should be mirrored at the sub-regional scale. There is no reluctance to admit that the chief purpose of this arrangement would be to strengthen the hierarchy of cities and regions. The prevailing view amongst China's economists today is that the institutionalising of such inequalities will accelerate national economic growth, increase the capacity for national self-reliance, and guarantee an eventual all-round regional development.[71]

Implementation of the Key-city Idea. The notion of key cities has developed swiftly, and has already been translated into action on a number of fronts. First, there are the four Special Economic Zones (SEZs) designated in 1980 at Shenzhen, Zhuhai and Shantou in Guangdong and Xiamen in Fujian.[72]

Although the volume of foreign manufacturing investment the SEZs have attracted falls below expectations, these places neverthe-less powerfully symbolise the new policy of promoting rapid urban-industrial growth in China's coastal region. In 1981, SEZ-type privileges were granted to the city of Guangzhou, the aim being to strengthen high-technology light industry and get away from the heavy-industrial priorities of the past thirty years. Guangzhou had developed as a steel, coal, motor-vehicles and heavy-engineering base, but the outcome was 'a big lag in light industries and other sectors of the economy vitally important to the people's liveli-hood'. The municipal authorities now intended to promote 29 light-industrial items including watches, bicycles, sewing machines, electric fans and garments by opening up to foreign capital and skills.[73] At the same time, the State Council made a number of concessions to Shanghai, allowing the city to increase its autonomy in the national planning system, and permitting it more say over the generation of exports and the signing of foreign contracts agree-ments.[74] In 1984, the SEZ programme was greatly reinforced by the addition of fourteen coastal cities to the original list of four.[74]

A second element of the new urban and regional policy has been the move to establish macro-regions, their boundaries being func-tionally, rather than administratively defined. The first such unit to be designated was the Shanghai Economic Zone, extending over 74,000 square kilometres of the Yangzi delta.[76] The explanation offered for this innovation was that it would provide the means of overcoming bureaucratic obstacles to a fuller resource utilisation. A commonly cited case of under-utilisation was that of the port of Ningbo *shi* lying just to the south of Shanghai. Here, the 20 berths only handled 13 per cent of their actual capacity, while Shanghai port was stretched to its limits. In the new Shanghai Economic Zone this kind of difficulty could be more easily overcome, coordinated planning laying the basis for a great powerhouse of industry and agriculture, the force of which will be felt nation-wide. The existing basis for this growth-pole strategy is robust. With a mere 0.8 per cent of China's territory, and 5 per cent of national population, the Zone accounts for 20 per cent of GVIO, with 27 per cent of chemical industry output, 38 per cent of textiles, and 50 per cent of shipbuilding. It incorporates 10 cities, and straddles the three provincial-level units of Shanghai itself, the extreme eastern part of Jiangsu, and the north of Zhejiang province.[77] The hope is that the new unit of planning will stimulate growth of the main cities within its boundaries. At this sub-regional scale, a growth-pole or 'centres of excellence' strategy is explicitly proposed, as it is at the macro-regional level: ultimately, 'the thriving Shanghai economic zone will also promote the economic growth of the whole country'.[78]

Other new regional planning authorities are under consideration: preliminary study has been made of the viability of a northern region embracing the cities of Beijing, Tianjin and Tangshan (the Bohai Gulf Zone). In the North-east (the Shenyang, Anshan, Benxi and Changchun industrial belt), the Songliao Plain Zone may be established. And in the south-western provinces of Fujian and Guangdong — often known to Chinese as the 'Gold Coast' — there is also talk of formalising a great planning region. And in May 1984, a southwestern great planning region was established with its administrative headquarters in the 'central city' of Chongqing, taking in 1.376 million square kilometres of Sichuan, Guizhou, Yunnan and Guangxi.[79] This region contains over 200 million people, and a chief objective of the new authority is to promote the rapid exploitation of energy resources — water power and coal.

A third strand of policy which will heighten the centrifugal polarity of the existing municipalities — though not so much the coastal/interior dichotomy — is the move to abolish the prefectural (*diqu*) tier of China's administrative field system. The intention is to transfer all the *xian* currently under the prefectures to the municipalities. The model for this local government reform is Liaoning Province, where the process of county annexation being in 1958 and was almost total by the end of the 1970s.[80] As in the case of the 'central city' notion, the abolition of the *diqu* and the extension of *shi* boundaries trace back to the fifth session of the 5th National People's Congress held in December 1982. The reform is closely associated with the Prime Minister, Zhao Ziyang, and like the introduction of the greater economic zones, it is said to be aimed at the 'unified guidance' of commodity production and circulation. A further similarity is the emphasis placed on polar growth: 'the economically more developed cities [will act] as centres to bring on the surrounding rural areas'.[81]

In early 1983, the Liaoning experience was analysed at a nation-wide conference in Shenyang, and the decision was taken to introduce the system experimentally in Jiangsu Province. In March 1983, all the counties in Jiangsu were shared out by the province's 11 *shi*.[82] The experiment was evidently considered highly successful, for by the end of 1983 it had been greatly extended, with 35 pre-fectures abolished and their 390 counties handed out to the cities. With the pre-existing number, around one quarter of all the *xian* were now directly under 121 municipalities.[82]

While these changes are intended to assist rural development, there is no doubt that their chief purpose is to benefit industrial development of the central municipality by establishing unified authority and doing away with competing and overlapping responsibilities. This again recalls the differentiated nature of China's bureaucratic system, and the extraordinary impediments to planning created by over-verticality. As one observer candidly explains, before these administrative reforms were introduced, 'cities were not guaranteed agricultural or sideline products, nor raw materials for their industries', and these problems can only be solved under 'unified planning'.[84]

Implications for Urbanisation Strategy. In the long term, the successful promotion of 'central cities', of metropolitan regions like the Shanghai Economic Zone, and of city-led regionalism at the sub-provincial level, is bound to have a profound impact on China's space-economy. As a result of protective policies of state planning, large differentials now exist in inter-regional and intra-sectoral productivity. In one discussion concerning the benefits which the new regional economic links will bring to industrial output figures, the case of China's sewing machine industry is considered. The differentials in productivity between the country's 51 plants are enormous, with those in the East and in the larger cities having several times the output per worker as those in the smaller centres and the West. Comparable contrasts exist for bicycles, watches, and many other goods. By exposing the less-efficient plants to the forces of the market, it is hoped to even out these differentials, even if that should mean their closure.

That inter-regional cooperation should be biased in favour of the stronger areas is implied by this criticism of past relationships:

> By means of 'cooperation', small undertakings marked by high consumption rates in production, by low-quality products and unmarketable goods that were in excess supply, literally fought with big plants for basic resources and markets. The small therefore forced out the big, while the inferior goods squeezed out the better ones. As a result, 'good steel could not be used to make the blade of the knife' and this was to the serious disbenefit of society as a whole.[85]

As eastern cities are encouraged to extend their economic tentacles, the production units of the interior seem likely to feel a chill wind; the logical outcome of present developments is that they will at best take on a subordinate role in the division of labour to be imposed on them, and at worst be pushed out of business. Within provinces, the power of the existing municipalities will be augmented through an enlargement of their hinterlands, and this seems likely to be at the expense of the smaller settlements. There is no sign yet that the central authorities recognise that the new policies are likely to have a dual impact: on the one hand, they seem certain to enhance industrial output, but on the other, they threaten to imperil regional development plans and to undermine the economic wherewithal of small towns. So the course seems set for a reinforcement of municipal power in general, and of (eastern) metropolitan prowess in particular.

The agglomerative tendencies of production will not, of course, necessarily be matched by an increasing concentration (both spatially and aspatially) of China's urban population. But they will certainly enhance the polar attraction of the larger cities; if their magnetism is to be countered, present controls over migration and personal mobility will have to be strengthened accordingly. More crucially, the proposed relationship between the advanced and backward areas (both inter- and intra-provincially) is one which threatens to inhibit the growth of small-town economies. And the current plans for the *zhen* and rural market towns to absorb up to hundreds of millions of surplus rural dwellers over the coming fifteen years demand the maximum possible consolidation and expansion of their employment base.

In their defence of a small-town-based urbanisation strategy,

China's spatial planning fraternity habitually resort to quotation from the classics, and particularly from Engels' later writings in which he calls for an even spread of industrial development. It is ironic that those who favour a growth-efficient strategy resting on economies of scale are also able to recruit Engels to their cause, this time choosing passages where the master unreservedly applauds the vast economic power of modern industrial agglomerations.[86]

Re-evaluation of the 'Chinese Road to Urbanisation'

> The emphasis for the present . . . should be placed on the construction of big and medium-sized cities. This is because . . . the cities cannot truly fulfil their functions if they are too small. Implementation of the policy of building small cities and towns in China over the years has proved that there were more failures than successes. So only when big cities are developed is it [*sic*] possible to support the construction of small towns and cities.[87]

Thus spoke the final communiqué of a conference on the urban economy and population growth held in 1980. The particular view represented here is that of the more hard-line 'economic results' lobbyists who, even as early as 1980, had little time for the small-town schemes of the urban planning fraternity. Generally, China'a urbanists assume a subordinate role in the process of economic development planning, and it was not unexpected that their consensual position in the urbanisation debate was to undergo a subtle transformation from that of the 1980 city planning conference. The shift in the debate has been hastened by subsequent rapid developments in economic policy, and by the official affirmation in 1982 of a 'central-city-based' regional planning strategy.

At a major conference on the urbanisation question held at Nanjing in 1982, three distinct positions were expressed.[88] The first was a more extreme form of the small-towns policy put forward in 1980: now *only* small towns should be allowed to develop, and no growth should be permitted in the larger cities (including the medium-sized ones) even where the conditions were excellent. A second perspective endorsed the economic arguments for concentrating development in the larger (and eastern) cities, but was eager not to add to their present problems of congestion. The solution would therefore be an accelerated satellite and small-town programme in the immediate vicinity of these cities.

But an entirely new element in the debate — so far, that is, as geographers and urban planners were concerned — was represented by a third group of participants at the Nanjing conference. Taking their cue from the rapid and ongoing developments in regional planning described earlier in this chapter, this group put forward the following opinion:

> Our country's urbanisation process is at its early stages, and the economic base is relatively fragile. Therefore we will encounter many problems if we try to energetically develop the small towns and cities. If we wish to develop our economy as rapidly as possible to a higher stage, then we must give full play to the economic centres represented by the large and medium-sized cities. Their industrial base is relatively strong, and the external economies of their firms are strong [literally, 'production cooperation conditions are good']. Their level of techniques in production is high, and their returns from investment are better than those of the small towns.[89]

Thus, development of the larger classes of cities (and especially the medium-sized centres of 200,000 to 500,000) should be fostered, while the small rural townships could ony be granted selective attention. Furthermore, it was maintained that the less developed the region, the more likely that small-town development would be precluded altogether because of the weakness of the economic base.

An even more strident justification for such views appeared shortly after in the journal *Economic Geography*.[90] In an article tellingly entitled 'Is the Development of Small Cities China's Sole Correct Road to Urbanisation?', the main premise of the geographer-author, Feng Yufeng, is that national economic development and urbanisation are inextricably linked, and it is therefore essential to promote the latter. This line of argument is worthy of summary, for it is one which seems likely to be increasingly voiced.

Feng adopts a crude 'stages' theory of economic and urban development. In their pre-industrial era, cities are described as being essentially centres for agricultural marketing and administration. As in the experience of Europe and North America, the growth of manufacturing industry brings a spatial concentration of the new means of production. Therefore, this second stage is characterised by a close association between the growth of per capita manufacturing output and urbanisation. Countries in which industrial production may be very high, but manufacturing insignificant, have correspondingly low urban levels. Typical here are those economies based on mineral extraction — epitomised by the oil-rich countries of the Middle East. Only in the third phase, when the tertiary sector becomes more prominent in a nation's economy than primary and secondary activities, is there a move away from centralised urban concentrations:

> In this period, people begin to seek improvements in the quality of life because of economic advances. The degree of economic development allows them to abandon — where conditions permit — the past reliance on spatially-concentrated and large-scale industrial production, which is no longer (necessarily) the most efficient means of obtaining good economic results.[91]

This process of dispersal is, of course, facilitated by well developed modern communications.

The universal path of city development proposed here is, therefore, spatial dispersal of population, followed by concentration, which in turn leads to a new form of dispersed urbanism. Feng does not consider it surprising that the advanced capitalist countries are pursuing an active policy of new town development. But for Chinese planners to slavishly copy this experience at the nation's present level of development would be foolhardy and wasteful; it would mean jumping over a necessary stage of development.

The kernel of this particular argument lies in its appraisal of the economic characteristics of China's small towns. They are seen as unambiguously *agricultural* places — that is, belonging to the first stage of development. This is even true of a minority of the smallest category of municipality. For instance, in a gross population of several hundred thousand, Shaoxing *shi*'s non-agricultural population amounts to only about 10 per cent. Such rural bias is, of course, more generally the rule for the population profiles of county seats. Despite the development of commune and brigade enterprises, many county seats can be found where the income from agricultural production amounts to 70 to 80 per cent of the total population's income. Commerce may be more or less developed in such places, but is a commerce based on the exchange of agricultural commodities. These places are, then, hardly even *incipient* urban nodes; as for the less tangible quality of 'urban life-style', he finds them devoid of this ingredient.[92]

The charge here is that those who opt for an urbanisation strategy resting on China's myriad small towns are guilty of self-deception and idealism. They overlook a fundamental material point: China's capital resources are extremely limited, and a road to urbanisation which constrained the big and medium-sized cities would also constrain capital accumulation, for it would forego their high productivity. Furthermore, the capital costs of both developing industry in the thousands of small settlements, and providing them with essential urban-style infrastructure, are regarded as completely unsupportable.

A Re-appraisal of Small-town Strategy

The reasoned hostility towards a small-town-based strategy reviewed above is an important element in the continuing discussion regarding China's path to urbanisation. Such contributions to the grand debate raise fundamental questions about the economic viability of the 1980 city planning conference formula. But they fail to address other vital questions which weigh heavily on the minds of most spatial planners. While the point is clearly made that the Chinese economy cannot modernise and make the 'great leap' into the twenty-first century on the basis of petty production in the small towns, we are also left in no doubt that neither can it progress on the backs of petty agricultural producers. Therefore modernisation of agriculture is still demanded, and this process will certainly release tens and hundreds of millions from the soil. The 'big city' polemicists barely indicate how and where they will be absorbed. Certainly, they fall short of openly advocating that the existing municipalities should inflate not merely their economic role but also their populations. But their *laissez-faire* attitude to the problem of the surplus rural population suggests no alternative.

Nevertheless, the historical and economic approach to the small-town model's potential does take the debate one step on from the crude numbers games of the urban planners. It promotes a closer examination of small-town characteristics and potentialities; the urgent need to be better informed in this area was recognised in an inter-ministry decision in 1981 to conduct a 9-province survey of the economic and demographic features of commune seats.[93] Closer empirical study of small towns has made their enthusiasts realise that more is required than the simplistic game plans which dwell optimistically on their potential powers of absorption of population. By the end of 1982, the attention of the planners had begun to focus on the practical problems to be overcome if the small-towns strategy were to be realised. The chief areas of difficulty identified in these more sober accounts are now described.

Poor Living Conditions in the Small Towns. The advocates of a small-town strategy hope for a cumulative spiral of development:

> The more the small towns develop, the more their power to attract will increase, and the more the number of people moving to the cities will decrease and the growth of the big and medium-sized cities will thus be better controlled.[94]

But at present, many small towns are said to be primitive places, with 'old and broken-down housing, dirty streets, lacking drainage or running water'.[95] One survey concluded that four-fifths of the rural market towns (*nongcun jizhen*) have none of the recognisable attributes of 'local political, economic, cultural and livelihood centres'. Even the *zhen* and many county seats are without basic facilities such as cinemas and over two-thirds of them do not possess cultural installations of any description. Poor conditions make most of them unattractive places to live; without great improvement, they will be unable to play the part of 'storage reservoirs' for the rural population.[96]

Another aspect of their lack of appeal to rural migrants is the discrimination which urban residents of small towns suffer in terms of welfare and the provision of rationed goods. Wage standards in such places are also generally lower than in the cities, including in plants of a similar scale. Surprisingly, in the ordinary *zhen*, even official market prices for vegetables are said to be set a higher level than in the county seats.[97] Numerous irrational stipulations of this nature weigh against the rural townships.

Chaos in Small-town Management. Many writers pinpoint the lack of clear administrative responsibilities for coordinated development and planning. The average county seat contains enterprises and units which have nothing in common with each other except for their proximity. Some may be owned by the county, some by communes and production brigades, others by the prefecture, the province, and even the central ministries. There are no mechanisms for a coordinated approach to problems of water and electricity supply, sewerage, and land use. There is usually no town plan, and no town planners. As for the sub-county *zhen*, things are even more chaotic here. The *zhen* administrations are powerless to control construction projects, and the county land use office (*xian tudi bangongshi*) gives out land indiscriminately to the communes to build housing and factories.[98] The situation is no better in the tens of thousands of smaller townships, some of which are affiliated to communes and some to brigades. In short, 'most small towns have no overall construction and development plan, and there is no overall consideration and arrangement for the use of land and construction funds'.[99] Some effort is now being put into the streamlining of economic and spatial planning in the small towns. Every *xian* has its 'basic capital construction bureau' (*xian jiben jianshe ju*). Hitherto, the chief concerns of this body have been economic (output achievement) rather than spatial (town planning). Recognising this inadequacy, some counties have recently set up 'urban construction offices' (*cheng jianshe ju*).[100] In addition, many provincial governments in the early 1980s set up departments responsible for researching into the structure and problems of small towns and promoting their development.[101]

The re-introduction of the old *xiang* ('township') tier of rural government — abolished in 1958 with the formation of the people's communes — is seen as an important means of unifying local administration and promoting development of the small marketing centres.[102] The declared purpose is to draw clear lines of demarcation between the spheres of production and administration. By the end of 1983, 22,000 township governments had been set up in around half of the nation's counties, charged with 'making all-round plans . . . for culture, education, public health and other public affairs' in the countryside.[103] Further down the scale, the 5 million or so villages under the new township administrations are being encouraged to set up village committees to coordinate construction and public services.[104]

Shortage of Capital for Small-town Development. The deficiencies in coordination of small-town management aggravate the shortage of capital which they require for healthy growth. As the *People's Daily* put it:

The masses demand that the higher authorities establish guidelines to encourage the development of small towns. They want
concrete stipulations and policies, involving control of
investment.[105]

The situation is bad enough in the county seats, but it is far worse
in the *zhen* under the counties; whatever funds are available are
dominated by the county towns. As for the tens of thousands of
rural market towns (the *nongcun jizhen*), 'they get even less'.[106]
Funds will be needed not simply for the productive enterprises in
the small towns, but for 'urban construction'. A number of
positive recommendations have been made regarding the raising of
revenue for this purpose:[107]

i. Taxes on the profits of commune and county industry and
commerce located in the county seat to be used to assist all small
towns in the area.
ii. The extraction of a percentage of capital construction funds
from enterprises newly locating in small towns, this to be used for
public utilities and urban management.
iii. Appropriations from the county budget; one writer suggests
that 20 to 30 per cent of all *xian* tax revenue should be granted to
small-town construction.
iv. County seats in particular should introduce a land-use tax on all
land uses.
v. The mobilisation of voluntary construction labour from
amongst the local residents.

Additionally, those small towns within the jurisdiction of municipalities should be allocated construction and management funds by
the *shi*. Specifically, it is proposed that 5 per cent of their industrial
and commercial profits, and 5 to 10 per cent of their urban support
funds (*chengshi weihu fei* — a state budgetary allocation) should be
made available to the small settlements.[108]

Problems of Small-town Enterprise Viability. We have earlier had
occasion to examine the key issue of the viability of small-town
enterprises in the context of an increasingly competition-oriented
economy. As one analysis of the situation points out, even under
the relatively protected operating conditions of the past, 'competition has moved production from the backward areas to the large

state-run factories.[109] Already by 1981, restrictions in the supply of raw materials to large city plants had forced many of them to slow down, or even suspend production. The problem arose because of the expansion of the rural small-enterprise sector; commune and brigade plants were castigated for not only depriving modern sector industry of its wherewithal, but for turning out low-quality end-products at high cost, and ruining established marketing networks. The Ministry of Agriculture called a national conference in October 1981 to try to work out a means of reconciling the needs of commune and brigade enterprises with those of large-scale industry. However, by 1984 there were still no signs of a comprehensive and integrated approach to this strategic issue.[110]

In so far as a solution to the competition problem is offered by China's spatial planners, it is to persuade large-scale industry to locate in small rural centres:

> Departments in charge of state and local industry should arrange in a planned way certain large and medium-sized industrial construction projects in small towns. Through various forms, large industry in cities can carry out joint management and cooperation, or the processing or ordering of goods, with industry in small towns, so as to give energetic support to small towns.[111]

In the present era, with the emphasis on the benefits of agglomeration and central cities, the likelihood of this occurring on a large scale is extremely limited. Where large plants do go to small places, it will most likely be to those townships and newly-designated satellites within the boundaries of the municipalities.

Thus the various practical impediments to the small-town-based urbanisation strategy have greatly reduced its appeal to Chinese planners. However, there remains one sphere in which it still appears a credible policy: all the objections on the grounds of lack of management structure, of capital, and of industrial viability seem to be met in those new urban-rural integration models of the 1980s which rest on the relationship between a core city and its tributary townships. We shall now describe the practical basis of such relationships as seen in the case of Weihai.

Restricted Applicability of the Small-towns Strategy

The Model of Weihai. Weihai *shi* is a small coastal municipality, situated in the Jiadong peninsula of east Shandong. In 1979, the city was singled out for special praise in the provincial newspaper. Soon the central news media had elevated Weihai to the status of national model for small-town development. The particular utility of Weihai's experience would seem to this writer to be the way in which the surplus rural labour force has been absorbed by the non-agricultural sector without mass migrations to the true urban areas; at the same time, the problem of lack of competitiveness of small-town enterprises seems to have been avoided. This has been so because of the strict subordination of the small-town economy to that of the municipality as a whole.

The Party journal, *Hongqi*, described the importance of Weihai's urban-rural development process in the following terms:

> In Weihai municipality . . . there is an average of just over one *mu* of land per person. Since agricultural mechanisation is proceeding quite quickly in this area, the problem of surplus rural labour is becoming more and more serious here. And there is another aspect: because China's agricultural base remains weak, it cannot meet the requirements placed on it by the swift development of industry and the increase in the urban population. While industry must be developed further, urban population growth must be controlled. This means that the surplus rural labour cannot be allowed to move rapidly into the towns and cities. Herein lies a contradiction, and Weihai *shi*'s introduction of 'product diffusion' has resolved this contradiction rather successfully.[112]

Though Weihai (as a sub-prefectural municipality) has no annexed counties, in 1979 a mere 32,000 of the total *shi* population were resident in the three square kilometres of the urban core. The remaining 166,000 citizens of Weihai inhabited the 120 square kilometres of surrounding rural tract as members of seven rural people's communes.

Concerned to push forward agricultural production, in the early 1970s the city authorities had considered alternative strategies. The first was to invest heavily in field improvement and advanced equipment, creating a highly efficient agriculture. Large numbers would be pushed out of the villages, and would have no choice but to go to the city proper. The second was to utilise the limited funds in a gradual diversification of agriculture towards animal husbandry, cash crops and commune- and brigade-run enterprises.

The exigencies of national policy of the early 1970s did not, when it came to it, permit anything but the second path. Weihai was thus set on a course which encouraged maximum rural diversification, while discouraging further industrial and population growth within the three square kilometres of built-up area. The method chosen was that of dispersal, or 'diffusion', of core city production to Weihai's rural areas. This process began when a carpet factory secured a large export order, and was unable to expand production because of space limitations of its urban site. In 1974, the factory established 18 production workshops in nearby rural centres, taking on 1,000 ex-peasants and thereby quadrupling output. By 1979 it was fourteen times greater, and the rural workforce in 41 sites amounted to 2,000.

The pattern was soon copied by other units. At the end of the 1970s, of the 83 enterprises run by Weihai *shi*, 49 operated a dispersed production system, and over half of the almost 200 rural production brigades had entered into a production relationship with a core-city parent company. The ownership and control over this new rural industry lay with the municipality. While a large proportion involved textiles (an obvious candidate for dispersed production), a number of other sectors are involved, including cement, glass products, chemical fertilisers, light-bulbs, batteries, explosives, chemicals and electrical equipment.

The intrusion of municipal (state-owned) enterprises was a stimulus to the development of small industries controlled under the collective banner by rural communes and brigades. Back in the 1960s, the simple forges in the villages had been able only to produce basic hand-tools — hoes, mattocks, sickles and spades. As elsewhere in rural China, the other chief non-agricultural occupation was the production of lime and bricks for local construction needs. By the end of the 1970s, however, the communes had under them 58 non-agricultural enterprises, and the brigades almost 400, making a very wide variety of products in addition to those turned out for the municipal units.

In the 1960s the division of labour between urban and rural Weihai was straightforward (urban = industry, commerce, services; rural = agriculture). Today the situation is far more complicated. Firstly, on the industrial side, there are the units owned by the municipality on the one hand, and those 'collective' units run by the communes and brigades on the other. The workforce of the former group subdivides into full- and part-time, while the latter group is basically of the *yi gong yi nong* (that is, part-time) type. Secondly, on the agricultural side there are those who work part-time in industry (both state and collective units) and those who are considered fully engaged in farmwork. The complexity of rural employment after 'production diffusion' is indicated in Figure 8.1. Accounts of Weihai's industrialisation model emphasise its relatively low capital costs. Much of the machinery in the dispersed rural factories is obsolete plant from parent companies in the city proper. For urban industry as a whole, the estimated cost of adding every new worker (including housing) is around 10,000 *yuan*, whereas in Weihai's case it is just 4,000 *yuan*.

Figure 8.1: Industrial and Agricultural Employment, Weihai Municipality, 1979

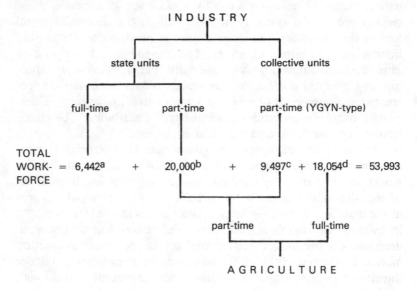

Notes: a. 12 per cent of the rural workforce. This figure refers to the ex-peasants permanently engaged in industrial production in the 287 small plants established by Wehai (state) industries. b. 37 per cent of the rural workforce. These people are almost exclusively female peasants who do outwork (mainly embroidery work) in their homes for state factories. c. 17 per cent of the workforce. From the figures available it is not clear whether all are of the *yi gong yi nong* type. Probably a small number were employed on a full-time basis. They were in 58 commune-run and 380 brigade-run units. d. only 34 per cent of the rural workforce fully engaged in agricultural tasks.
Source: DZRB, 12 September 1979, and Gu Shutang *et al.*, HQ, no. 23 (December 1980), pp. 21–5.

Had all the more than 6,000 new workers added to Weihai's state industrial payroll been accommodated in the built-up area of the city, a major housing and industrial building programme would have been required.[113]

There are also a number of other savings — in services, health, education, and so on. The city's new workforce 'do not live or eat in the city or present any burden, but their manpower directly supports the city's production'. In particular, the state has not had to greatly increase its allocation of rationed grain to the area.

An important extra benefit has been the aid to agriculture from the growing rural industrial sector. By 1979, the numbers of tractors and other agricultural machines available to the 195 production brigades far exceeded the national average. Grain output in rural Weihai more than doubled in the 1970s, and per capita income of the city's rural-based population rose to over twice the national average. Not only have funds been generated locally for small-town development, but the city authorities have insisted that the growth of rural industry be accompanied by improvements in their planning. Many of the small towns expanding on the sites of commune seats now have running water, electricity, and new roads.

As for the urban-core population, they have not seen a degradation of general environmental standards which might otherwise have taken place had industry and population expanded in a more conventional manner. Inevitably, a part of the original urban workforce has been required to move out of the city proper as part of the diffusion process. Normally this would present difficulties, as it would necessitate a change in household registration and thus in living standards. Weihai anticipated this problem by an early decision allowing those who were moved out to retain urban *hukou*, entitling them to the same rations and wage standards as in the city proper. This applies also to their offspring.

As we have seen, the viability of a small-town-based urbanisation strategy has been increasingly challenged since 1980. Criticism has centred on the lack of cohesive management structure in most small towns, on the shortage of funds for public utilities, and, above all, on the fragility of their economic base. All these points are adequately met in the model provided by Weihai; it is especially important to note that far from offering a threat to urban industry, the development of small-town-based enterprises has served to complement it.

The Impact of Further xian *Annexation.* Some of Weihai's success in production diffusion is due the labour-intensive nature of the industries involved (carpet making, embroidery, and so on). Nevertheless, the mutually-beneficial process whereby plant and expertise are dispersed from city factories to a constellation of rural settlements seems to be catching on in many areas. In 1983, the abolition of the prefectural tier of administration gathered pace. Previously, this reform had been presented as necessary to establishing a clear line of municipal command over the surrounding rural resources. Now, however, it was promoted mainly in terms of its utility in assisting rural development, and particularly the growth of the economy of small towns. Once again, the government chose the familiar method of popularising a reform through use of a model: in this case, the steel city of Anshan (Liaoning) and its two subsidiary *xian* were chosen for national emulation.[114]

The Anshan municipal government helps Haicheng and Tai'an counties by supplying equipment for their enterprises, by sending out hundreds of retired workers to lend their skills, by supplying raw materials such as scrap iron, and by setting up subsidiary factories along the lines of Weihai's production diffusion model. They have also run a great many training classes in the rural townships to teach basic industrial and management skills. The establishment of diverse cultural activities has been encouraged by the municipal cultural bureau. And the city has helped small towns to electrify, and to improve their urban amenities. In short, the benefits to those rural areas directly under municipalities are presented as being endless.

The reality is that such relationships are not so one-sided, and even that the core city stands to gain more materially than does the countryside and its townships. This is intrinsic to a situation in which there are such great disparities in the levels of production technique. However, the exploitation of the rural areas by core cities must be seen in its rightful context: rural conditions have until recently been so impoverished that any transitional mechanism which radically raises basic standards is a great boon to the peasantry. This is so even if, on balance, the parent city gains more from the relationship, and the relative differences between city and countryside widen. (In fact this is not occurring, as rural policies post-1979 have offered the peasants so many new and practicable ways of bettering themselves economically.)

Conclusion

This chapter began by reiterating Chinese claims that the coming years would see an excess in the rural labour force running into hundreds of millions. Quite apart from the question of whether the state will be able to supply the hugely inflated non-agricultural population with grain, the central problem for China's spatial planners is where to accommodate the vast numbers no longer needed on the land. The accounts of 1979 and 1980 were wildly optimistic regarding the absorption-potential of China's tens of thousands of small towns. But soon it became clear that the sweeping national economic and administrative changes, and especially the promotion from on high of key cities and their inter-regional networks, did not augur well for a small-towns-based urbanisation strategy. These developments brought a more sober assessment of the possibilities of the small towns. They were found to be generally deficient — in management, in capital resources, and above all in the buoyancy of their non-agricultural economies.

The grand debate on China's future urbanisation has elicited extreme positions. For some, the small-towns strategy is the only correct route for China; others entirely discount it in favour of a policy of active agglomeration. But a more middle-of-the-road solution seems likely to prevail. The compromise of a 'dual system' of urbanism is likely to gain more support in the coming period. One branch will be the large cities founded on modern industry, and the other — consciously and deliberately — small rural townships based on unsophisticated technologies.

A more elaborate variant would aim for better economic integration of the total urban network, creating an ordered but hierarchical system of large, medium-sized and small cities with the rural townships forming the broad base. As ever, the system is encapsulated in an appropriate slogan: 'The big cities as the nucleus (*hexin*), the medium-sized cities as the link (*niudai*) and the rural market towns as the cell (*xi bao*)'.[115] But in common with so many of the fond schemes of geographers which speak of 'integration' and 'balance', the actual mechanisms and divisions of economic and political responsibility necessary to the workings of such a system are left unstated.

The central problem here is that with the further introduction of market regulation of China's industrial planning system, it seems inevitable that conflicts between the more and the less efficient producers will be increasingly resolved at the expense of the latter. Thus, unless measures are brought in to protect small industries from overbearing competitive forces, there will be further pressure on the township enterprises to restrict their operations to commerce, the service trades and to productive activities (for example, factory farming) which do not compete with urban industry.[116]

The prospects for development of the small-town economy do seem bright, however, where it gains its essential protection through an integration with, and a subordination to, the modern-sector enterprises of the cities. As the cases of Weihai and Anshan illustrate, the conditions are most favourable in the immediate hinterlands of the municipalities. The current programme of abolition of the prefectures and the sharing out of all rural China amongst the municipalities should, therefore, improve the ability of many small towns to absorb the excess rural population.

The Chinese government appears to hope that a combination of bright local initiatives and spontaneous, market-led developments will provide the solution to the formidable question of what to do with the growing rural surplus labour force. The central state is inclined to limit its own role to exhortation and the publicising of models for emulation. If this almost non-interventionist position is adequate for the time being, it is because of the exceptional features of the present period. The rationalisation of agriculture of the early 1980s has certainly fomented a large surplus workforce, but at the same time the sudden liberalisation of the rural economy has opened up a great number of new avenues for its re-absorption. The urbanisation debate has, therefore, been robbed of its initial urgency. However, the lull can only be temporary. Firstly, the numbers squeezed out of crop cultivation will increase, as will the rural population of working age. Secondly, after two decades of politically-inspired limitation of the rural services, construction industry and commercial sectors, their growth in employment in the early 1980s was extremely rapid. Their capacity to absorb new labour will, however, be increasingly restricted. If a dual system of urbanism is to be the solution to China's urbanisation quandary, the central authorities will have to go beyond their present *ad hoc* and passive approach. They will need to develop an effective admix of economic and spatial planning policies which actively protect and enhance the environmental and economic interests of both the municipalities and the rural townships.

Notes

1. For example, Li Mengbai, CXJS, no. 12 (1983), p. 18.
2. BR, no. 16, 16 April 1984, p. 7; here the figure is adjusted to take account of the fact that, of the 450 million rural workforce projected for the year 2000, 10 per cent would have gone — or would go — to the towns.
3. Discussions with personnel from the Jiangsu Branch of the Chinese Academy of Social Sciences, who hosted my research visit in June and July, 1983.
4. Ibid.
5. Ma Qingyu, JJDL, no. 2 (1983), p. 130.
6. SJDB, 25 January 1982.
7. Li Bianren, CSGH, no. 2 (1983), p. 27.
8. Considered on the low side by various international agencies, but justified by the Chinese specialists. See, for example, BR, no. 14, 2 April 1984, pp. 1–2.
9. Professor of Geography at Nanjing University; ZRKL, pp. 99–101.
10. Ibid., p. 99; in reality it is hard to correlate the data in a close manner, for at certain times annual grain output has fluctuated wildly.
11. TJNJ 1983, p. 158; also, BR, no. 9, 28 February 1983, p. 20.
12. BR, no. 9, 28 February 1983, p. 20.
13. See chapter 3, Table 3.2.
14. BR, no. 22, 27 May, 1982, p. 26.
15. Discussions with geographers at Nanjing University, June 1982, and BR, no. 45, 10 November 1980, p. 6.
16. Reported in RMRB, 16 and 17 October 1980.
17. Chen Weibang, JJYJ, no. 11 (1979), p. 55.
18. Bai Demao, JZXB, no. 4 (1981), p. 26.
19. Ibid., p. 20.
20. Now that Dachangzhen is officially designated as a satellite town for Nanjing, its infrastructure has been much improved compared with that of 1976 when I worked in the giant chemical fertiliser plant there (the name of the settlement actually means 'big plant town'). By 1982, an impressive multi-lane highway had been constructed to link Dachangzhen with the mother city.
21. XHDR, 27 August 1980, p. 5.
22. RMRB, 11 June 1981.
23. XHDR, 27 August 1980, p. 5 and *China Daily*, 25 June 1982.
24. Gleaned from discussions with Beijing planners, 1979–82.
25. Cai Yi, NDRZ, p. 82.
26. Professor Wu Youren: ZRKL, pp. 103–4.
27. Shashi had a total municipal size of 229,000 in 120 square kilometres. Dimensions from RMRB, 13 February 1982 and BR, no. 25, 21 June 1982.
28. TKP, 6 August 1981.
29. RMRB, 15 January 1982.
30. Ibid. 6,000 *yuan* is the national figure, and 10,740 *yuan* for Nantong.
31. BR, no. 1, 4 June 1982, pp. 7–8.
32. In Chinese sources, textiles and light industry are usually tabulated separately.
33. National average in 1981: 56 per cent (XHDR, 18 January 1982).
34. Ma Qingyu, JJDL, no. 2 (1983), p. 131, reports that Changzhou has had to take this step. Nationally, 4 million were recruited from the villages 'extra-plan'.
35. That is, 540,000 square metres: RMRB, 15 January 1982.
36. Li Mengbai, CXJS, no. 12 (1983), p. 18. Li anticipates 170–200 more *shi* in this period, so 300 is a generous estimate (it assumes that none had been promoted to the next category up — the medium-sized cities).
37. RMRB, 13 April 1983, and RMRB, 27 April 1983.

38. Atlas: ZFDJ 1977; note that when there is promotion, the county administration often moves to another township.

39. The significance of the *xian* as an economic planning unit has not in the past been granted due recognition by foreign scholars — see Y. Y. Kueh, 'Economic reform in China at "Xian" Level', *China Quarterly*, no. 96 (December 1983), pp. 665–88.

40. Wang Xinrong *et al.*, JZXB, no. 4 (1983), p. 36.

41. Ibid., p. 37.

42. The information on Luoshe Zhen is from RMRB, 3 February 1981, and interviews with staff of the Jiangsu Branch of the Chinese Academy of Social Sciences, June/July 1982.

43. TJNJ 1983, p. 207.

44. Zuo Xiantang, JWTS, no. 5 (1982), p. 38. In Chinese, *Ren wang gao chuzou, shui wang di chuliu.*

45. Wang Xinrong *et al.*, JZXB, no. 4 (1983), p. 37.

46. TKP, 9 February 1981, states that these places are in the 4,000 to 5,000 range, only one being over 10,000 nationally. Yet Bu Juecha, CXJS, no. 12 (1983), p. 21, claims that of the 700 rural market towns in Liaoning Province, 100 are over 10,000; Wang Xinrong *et al.*, JZXB, no. 4 (1983), p. 37, agrees that the 1,000 to 2,000 range is typical.

47. This is the estimate of Wang Xinrong *et al.*, JZXB, no. 4 (1983), p. 37.

48. During this period in the later part of the Cultural Revolution, students and college staff frequently spent periods in the countryside or in factories, doing 'open-door schooling' (*kaimen banxue*).

49. Cai Yi, NRDZ, p. 82.

50. Points i–iv respectively can be found in the following sources: Wu Youren, ZRKL, p. 104; TKP, 9 February 1981; Shen Daoqi *et al.*, 'The Development of Minor Cities and Towns in China', manuscript in English presented to the author at interview at Nanjing Institute of Geography, July 1982; Cai Yi, NDRZ, p. 82. The final point in iv. regarding the potential capacity of the *xian* seats and the *zhen* is from (respectively) RMRB, 13 April 1983, and RMRB, 27 April 1983. The former are said to have a potential capacity of 60 million and the latter, of 70 million.

51. Li Bianren, CSGH, no. 2 (1983), p. 27.

52. *'Renkou chengshihua'* ('Urbanisation'), SJDB, 25 January 1982. Such attitudes inform many other studies of 1982 and 1983: for instance, Feng Yufeng, JJDL, no. 2 (1983), pp. 136–40; Ma Qingyu, JJDL, no. 2 (1983), pp. 126–31.

53. TJNJ 1983, pp. 313 and 215; the exact criteria used for this classification today are not known.

54. TJNJ 1983, pp. 35–102, and p. 215.

55. The Shanghai campaign reported in TKP, 23 April 1981; also, BR, no. 33, 16 August 1982. For an explanation of the Chinese economic category 'national income', see Xu Dixin *et al.*, *China's Search for Economic Growth: The Chinese Economy Since 1949* (New World Press, Beijing, 1982), pp. 199–200.

56. The actual details of such preferential treatment (financial allocations from the central state, and so on) are not known.

57. See editorials in RMRB, 31 March 1981, and 17 January 1981 for statements on the importance of the coastal region in future development strategy.

58. See the article by the leading economist Xue Muqiao in SJDB, 22 June 1981.

59. RMRB, 2 August 1982.

60. *'Jingji xuejia lun zhongxin chengshi he jingji zhongxin'* ('Economists Discuss Central Cities and Economic Centres'), SJDB, 25 January 1982, p. 4. This is a report of a conference held in Dalian.

61. *'Zhongxin chengshi de hengxiang jingji lianxi zenneng geduan'* ('How is it

Possible to Sever the Transverse Economic Relationship Between Central Cities?'), SJDB, 25 January 1982, p. 4.

62. RMRB, 18 June 1983.

63. 'How is it Possible to Sever the Transverse Economic Relationships Between Central Cities?' SJDB, 25 January 1982, p. 4.

64. Ibid.

65. 'Economists Discuss Central Cities and Economic Centres', SJDB, 25 January 1982, p. 4.

66. Huang Daming *et al.*, JJYJ, no. 2 (1983), p. 51.

67. Xue Muqiao, SJDB, 22 June 1981.

68. RMRB, 2 August 1982, p. 5.

69. Huang Daming *et al.*, JJYJ, no. 2 (1983), pp. 52–3.

70. BR, no. 30, 28 July 1980, p. 16; Shanghai signed 32 such agreements between 1979 and 1980.

71. Huang Daming *et al.*, JJYJ, no. 2 (1983), p. 53.

72. Approved by the 5th National People's Congress in August and in October 1980. In March 1984, the Xiamen SEZ was extended to the area of the whole city (TKP, 22 March 1984).

73. TKP, 14 May 1981.

74. *Jiefang ribao* (*Liberation Daily*), 3 May 1983, and BR, no. 22, 3 May 1983, p. 8.

75. The fourteen cities are Qinhuangdao, Tianjin, Dalian, Yantai, Qingdao, Lianyungang, Nantong, Shanghai, Ningbo, Wenzhou, Fuzhou, Guangzhou, Zhanjiang and Beihai. See BR, no. 16, 16 April 1984, p. 6.

76. RMRB, 8 April 1983, and TKP, 14 April 1983.

77. BR, no. 16, 16 April 1984, pp. 16–23.

78. Ibid., p. 17.

79. BR, no. 22, 28 May 1984, p. 11.

80. For a description of the process in Liaoning Province, see chapter 3.

81. TKP, 1 March 1984.

82. It is not clear whether Jiangsu's third-order *shi* of 1982 (Yangzhou, Zhanjiang and Qingjiang) were permitted to annex counties, or whether they were first promoted to third-order status as an enabling measure (see chapter 3).

83. TKP, 1 March 1984; of the 390 counties, 368 have retained their county status, and 22 have been dissolved into municipal *shiqu*.

84. BR, no. 14, 4 April 1983.

85. RMRB, 2 August 1982.

86. 'Economists Discuss Central Cities and Economic Centres', SJDB, 25 January 1982.

87. BR, no. 11, 17 March 1980, p. 6.

88. The conference was held at Nanjing University, and was organised by the Chinese Architectural Association's Urban Planning Academic Council's Regional Planning and Urban Economy Study Group. (Li Bianren, CSGH, no. (1983), pp. 27–8/26.)

89. Ibid., p. 28.

90. Feng Yufeng, JJDL, no. 2 (1983), pp. 136–40.

91. Ibid., p. 138.

92. Feng Yufeng provides the results of a 1982 study of small-town economies in Wuyi and Jiangshan *xian*, Shaoxing prefecture, Zhejiang.

93. The study is under the State Agricultural Commission and the State Planning Commission (private communication).

94. The comments of Wu Chucai, a leading exponent of small-town development in Jiangsu (interview, Nanjing Institute of Geography, June 1982).

95. Jin Daqin, JJGL, no. 5 (1981), p. V–33.

96. RMRB, 27 April 1983.

97. Ibid.

98. Ibid.

99. Ibid.

100. Information from the newly established Ministry (of Urban-Rural Construction and Environmental Protection), June 1982.

101. They have, at least, been established in Jiangsu Province (interview with personnel from this department, Nanjing, July 1982).

102. Geographers at Nanjing University were of the view that the restoration of the *xiang* will certainly facilitate better physical planning at township level (discussions, July 1982, Nanjing).

103. BR, no. 11, 12 March 1984, p. 9.

104. Ibid. Progress has been slower here: at the end of 1983, only 170,000 village committees had been established nationwide.

105. RMRB, 3 February 1981.

106. RMRB, 27 April 1983.

107. Wang Xinrong *et al.*, JZXB, no. 4 (1983), p. 38.

108. Ibid., and RMRB, 27 April 1983.

109. Wu Chucai, interview, Nanjing Institute of Geography, July 1982.

110. Reported in RMRB, 22 October 1981.

111. RMRB, 27 April 1983.

112. Most of the information concerning Weihai is from Gu Shutang *et al.*, 'A Good Form of Cooperation Between Town and Country — An Investigation of "Factory-Team Links" and "Product Diffusion" in Weihai Municipality', HQ, no. 23 (December 1980), and DZRB, 12 September 1979.

113. 68,000 square metres, at a cost of 5 million *yuan*.

114. Bao Hui *et al.*, JJGL, no. 3 (1983), pp. 15–18, and Sun Hongzhi, JJGL, no. 2 (1983), pp. 37–8.

115. Li Mengbai, CXJS, no. 12 (1983), p. 16.

116. Beijing Radio (domestic), 3 January 1981, reported in JPRS OWO 41039.

9 AFTERWORD

Amongst the re-emerging Marxist currents in Europe and North America of the late 1960s and early 1970s, a widespread disillusion with the Soviet Union seemed to be amply compensated by a new-found optimism in the Chinese experiment. This mood was shared by the minority of Western urbanists who had concluded that any real solution to the crisis of the cities was impossible within the given political and economic framework. As Manuel Castells eagerly informed us in 1977, in contrast to the Soviet experience, the Chinese revolution was set on a course of robust industrial growth which would avoid the horrors of capitalist urbanisation by maintaining all the advantages of village life. Such a novel departure had its origins, it was supposed, in the peasant ante-cedents of the revolution and in the role of mass mobilisation and heightened political consciousness of China under Mao. This had not only brought an end to the age-old political, economic and cultural distinctions between city and countryside, but it had swept away the very division of labour intrinsic to class society. Castells grand verdict leaves no room for uncertainty:

> The example of China . . . show[s] clearly that accelerated, uncontrolled urbanization is not a necessary evolution deter-mined by the level of development, and indicate[s] how a new structuring of the productive forces and the relations of produc-tion transforms the logic of the organization of space.[1]

This typically 'commonsense' interpretation of the Chinese urban experience under the Communist Party was one which I myself carried to China some ten years ago. An opportunity to live in that country over several years — both in Cultural Revolution and post-Mao times — brought me to a perception of Chinese urbanism which was less sanguine. Far from creating the arcadian society of the Western imagination, the Chinese Communist revolution observed at close quarters loomed as a great *industrial* revolution. In truth, whatever nuggets of wisdom might be mined from Mao's numerous utterances on the peasantry and the 'anti-urban' theme, an equal number can be found which reflect an attachment to the conventional industrialisation model. Fascination with the 'Chinese road' as it was presented to the world ten years ago led us, conveniently, to exult in the former and overlook the latter. A predilection for utopias was — it must be said — buttressed by the official Chinese self-descriptions of the time, which few outside observers were able to place in their correct context.

Amongst these were many quotations from the classic writings of Marxism, selected in order to 'prove' China's socialist rectitude in following — ostensibly at least — a de-urbanist course. As I have attempted to show in my first chapter, what Marx and Engels had to say on this subject was not intended as any prescription for a backward peasant nation — either of the nineteenth or the twentieth centuries. In as much as 'anti-urbanism' *was* the outward face of Maoism, it was a mask for other ends. Where spatial egalitarianism did appear manifest at the regional and sub-regional levels (for example, in the decanting of the towns and cities or the transfer of population and productive means to the under-endowed interior) the real motivation was rather more prosaic. It was not so much to serve any grand socialistic ambition as to maintain *urban manageability* in a situation of constrained grain supplies and stubborn unwillingness to invest in non-productive urban infrastructure. Equally significant as a real purpose was that of military preparedness; the influence of strategic thinking on Chinese space economy over the Mao years bears much closer examination than it has previously been accorded.

It is true that during the 1960s and early 1970s, the outsiders' elevation of anti-urbanism to a prime position in Chinese urban policy did seem justified by the facts as they were then available. But as the series for urban growth presented in chapter 4 unambiguously demonstrates, the enforced evacuation of the cities during this period was required by the massive 'over-urbanisation' of the first decade of the People's Republic. Again, strident Maoist rationalisation — ever eager to make a socialistic virtue of a stark material necessity — obscured the pragmatism which informed China's city-restricting policies. The grand purpose of 'anti-urbanism' (if that is the right term) was to *guarantee* the new urban-centred industrial system rather than to undermine or dissolve it. The three cycles of urbanisation which I have identified demonstrate the dangers in relying for our evaluation of the Chinese model on the Cultural Revolution image. Just as the second cycle of mass deportations from the urban areas was an unavoidable response to the first, the third and current phase is the consequence of the second phase, and the actors in the process — the recent migrants to the cities — are in many cases the self-same individuals who were earlier ejected.

A word in passing on chapters 3 and 4, which form the data-core of this study on urbanisation. Any quantification of China's aggregate urban proportions would be meaningless without a close analysis of what is meant by 'urban'. I hope that the definition of urbanness which has been provided here, and all the ambiguities and confusions which have beset students of China's urbanism — both within and outside China — have now been laid to rest.

The analysis of chapter 5 shows that the great programme of social engineering which removed millions from the overcrowded coastal cities to the interior and border lands has had a dramatic impact on the latter's population and economic profiles. Yet such were the spatial differentials at the outset of this rebalancing exercise that the *overall* effect on China's locational form hardly registers. Nevertheless, Chinese planners take some satisfaction in the multiplying of populations and of industrial output in the remoter provinces. They are far less comfortable with the record on vertical redistribution of the urban population and industrial productive forces. The reason for this lies mainly in the steady decline of conditions in the great cities of the east from the mid-1950s on.

This fact has given added impetus to the great urbanisation debate which has emerged since the late 1970s. The bias against the primacy of cities expressed in the well-known spatial planning goal of promotion of small towns arises not so much from a perception of under-performance in terms of vague 'diffusionist' goals. Rather, it comes from a recognition of the enormity of big city problems. Unhappily, the commendable efforts of the present government to solve the most obvious problem of urban congestion — that of housing — have been all but offset by the spectacular rise in urban populations since 1977.

Ironically, no sooner had the urban planners begun to articulate their small-towns strategy (promoting small and medium-sized centres and rural townships, building self-contained satellites, and so on) and invest it with some empirical detail, than a shift in the contextual economic framework appeared. The economic policies introduced after 1979 explicitly favour agglomerative tendencies and virtuous regional spirals, thus threatening the fond schemes of the physical planners. The small-towners seem incapable of producing definite proposals whereby the small-town economy can be protected and developed. Without a strong economic foundation for the smaller settlements (and especially the rural townships earmarked to take the bulk of the surplus rural dwellers), the small-towns strategy remains an idle dream. Similarly, the prevailing economic climate holds little promise for a successful implementation of optimal size standards in the existing metropolises. All this is nothing new — for the failure to prevent the growth of unwanted conurbations in the Soviet Union in the post-war period has shown that a developing post- or non-capitalist economy is not autarkic, and the productivist ethos arising from the intense need to accumulate capital remains all-powerful. Under Mao, the strategic aim was to turn 'consumer cities' into 'producer cities', and in the post-Mao era the pressures to continue along such lines are just as powerful as ever. In a poor nation bent on socialist collectivism, the bottom line is always what suits rapid economic growth. As one commentator on the Soviet failure to implement an optimal size-based urbanisation strategy bluntly puts it, at the end of the day, 'the optimal city . . . is one in which the disparity between the urban resident consumes and what he produces is the greatest'.[2]

With the renewed pressure to increase output and achieve 'socialist modernisation' by the end of this century, the small-town lobby in China has been thrown into disarray. Taking their cue from on high, a small but significant minority of participants to the debate have broken with the long-established consensus. The call is for a reassessment of the old and tired demands for 'spatial balance', 'evenisation' and an 'integrated and rational' urban network. Following from this, the small-town-based urbanisation strategy is considered quite inappropriate to the present level of development of China's productive forces.

This partial retreat from the universal platitudes of spatial planning is most welcome. Yet it does not hold within it any specific solutions to the great question confronting China: what to do with the hundreds of millions of rural dwellers whose labour will not be required in traditional agriculture. The small-towns solution is decried for its lack of economic viability and shunning of economies of scale and linkage. Further, in an era of increased competition between producing units, the big-city plants are bound to win out over those situated in the smaller places, and their economic wherewithal undercut. But not even the wildest pro-urbanist would truly contemplate adding hundreds of millions to the existing municipal populations. There is a failure to explain how even a modest expansion of the cities will be coped with, and a lack of recognition of the real social costs which further growth of many large places would entail.

While the arguments go back and forth, China's large cities continue to add to their populations and expand outwards at an alarming rate. Not long since, I made a tour around the entire perimeter of Beijing on the new outer ring road, the *san huan lu*. The visual evidence of untrammelled growth is striking — where there were until recently cabbages and aubergines, now there are new factories, peasant homes and even multi-storey luxury hotels for urban bureaucrats. Under the guise of 'leases', many peasant collectives have lost one third of their farmland in the past few years. The richness of vegetable lands on the urban periphery has been built up over many centuries, and their destruction for ephemeral gain is unjustifiable. If optimal-size-targeting is to be abandoned as abstract and counter to economic rationality, then at least China needs to rapidly introduce mechanisms of development control which will prevent the loss of one of the most valuable urban assets.[3]

However, despite the vast scale of the problems under discussion, examples such as Weihai *shi* do seem to offer some ray of hope for China's future urbanisation. Here, the method adopted appears to overcome the contradictions between differing elements of the industrial system. At the same time, the conflict between the town planners (objective — liveable places) and the economic planners (objective — productive places) is satisfactorily resolved. The result is a good measure of economic and spatial integration within a framework — it should be said — of institutionalised exploitation of the new industrial producers in the subsidiary and satellitic plants. But such a compromise is to the general satisfaction of those exploited, for it provides a bridge between the uncertain farming existence and the security of the industrial wage-economy. In other words, it is a useful transitional form which appears to suit China's present economic stage.

What this study has shown to its author — and hopefully to his readers too — is that China shares many of the difficulties of development faced by the so-called developing nations. Where China's experience of urbanisation is unique, it is not because the distinction between the rural and urban worlds has been overcome. That will be left to the distant future. China's claim to a special place in the annals of urbanisation must rest on two pillars of political and social policy peculiar to its culture and polity. The first is an uncompromising and often painful command over human resources which has allowed over-urbanisation to be temporarily overcome. The second is the achievement of substantial industrial growth without the urban misery which we commonly associate with industrial revolutions in their early stages. In this new era of development, it remains to be seen whether these special qualities of China's urbanisation process can be preserved.

Notes

1. M. Castells, *The Urban Question* (Edward Arnold, London, 1977), p. 71.
2. A. J. DiMiao Jnr., *Soviet Urban Housing* (Praeger, New York, 1974), p. 49, citing the Soviet planner V. Perevedentsev.
3. This part of Beijing visited in the company of central planners in June 1982; the worst unplanned growth seemed to be in the southern Fengtai District of the city.

APPENDICES

Table A3.1: Urban Population by Province, 1982 Census

	Total population 1	Urban population 2	Urban % 3	*shi* no. 4	*shi* population 5	*zhen* no. 6	*zhen* population 7
Beijing	9.23	5.97	64.7	1	5.60	14	0.37
Tianjin	7.76	5.33	68.7	1	5.14	7	0.19
Hebei	53.01	7.27	13.7	11	6.05	50	1.22
Shanxi	25.29	5.31	21.0	7	4.25	48	1.06
Nei Mongol	19.27	5.56	28.9	10	3.19	102	2.37
Liaoning	35.72	15.13	42.4	13	11.88	93	3.25
Jilin	22.56	8.94	39.6	9	5.52	101	3.43
Heilongjiang	32.67	13.24	40.5	12	8.53	101	4.71
Shanghai	11.86	6.98	58.8	1	6.32	33	0.65
Jiangsu	60.52	9.57	15.8	11	6.75	114	2.83
Zhejiang	38.88	10.00	25.7	9	6.86	165	3.14
Anhui	49.67	7.08	14.3	12	4.89	118	2.20
Fujian	25.87	5.48	21.2	7	3.31	119	2.17
Jiangxi	33.18	6.45	19.4	10	4.22	106	2.23
Shandong	74.42	14.19	19.1	10	8.69	97	5.50
Henan	74.42	10.51	14.1	17	6.92	109	3.59
Hubei	47.80	8.28	17.3	11	5.47	127	2.80
Hunan	54.01	7.77	14.4	15	5.07	186	2.69
Guangdong	59.30	11.08	18.7	14	7.12	132	3.96
Guangxi	36.42	4.31	11.8	7	2.48	92	1.83
Sichuan	99.71	14.25	14.3	13	9.88	309	4.37
Guizhou	28.55	5.63	19.7	5	4.06	93	1.57
Yunnan	32.55	4.19	12.9	6	2.43	128	1.75
Xizang	1.89	0.18	9.5	1	0.11	9	0.07
Shaanxi	28.90	5.49	19.0	6	4.06	81	1.43
Gansu	19.57	3.00	15.3	5	1.97	45	1.03
Qinghai	3.90	0.80	20.5	2	0.63	7	0.17
Ningxia	3.90	0.88	22.5	2	0.67	14	0.21
Xinjiang	13.08	3.72	28.4	8	2.62	64	1.10
Total	1,003.94	206.588		236	144.68	2,664	61.91

Note: Urban population in the census is 'municipal and urban' (*shizhen*) population. It thus incorporates substantial numbers of agricultural population (*nongye renkou*) though not the inhabitants of *xian* under municipal control.

All absolute numbers in millions and corrected to the nearest 10,000.
Columns:

1: Total population by provincial-level unit, excluding those in the armed forces, at 1982 census time (1 July 1982).

2: Total urban (*shizhen*) population by provincial-level unit.

3: Proportion of provincial-level unit's population accounted for by its *shizhen* population. This measure is only an approximate guide to urbanness in the preferred definition of the present study (see chapter 3).

4: Number of designated municipalities (*shi*) in each provincial-level unit.

5: Aggregate population of the *shi* in each provincial-level unit counted as part of urban population.

6: Number of designated towns (*zhen*) counted by the census in each provincial-level unit (not all towns included in the count).

7: Aggregate population of the *zhen* in each provincial-level unit counted as part of urban population.

Source: State Statistical Bureau, Department of Population Statistics, *The 1982 Population Census of China (Major Figures)* (Economic Information and Agency, Hong Kong, 1982), pp. 16—17.

Table A3.2: Two Contrasting Series for Urban Population, Illustrated by Three Major Regions

	TJNJ 1981			CENSUS 1982		
	number (m.)	urban (%)	rank (1–26)	number (m.)	urban (%)	rank (1–26)
I. COASTAL						
Beijing	5.00	55.4	—	5.97	64.7	—
Tianjin	3.94	51.6	—	5.33	68.7	—
Hebei	4.90	9.3	19	7.27	13.7	23
Liaoning	11.85	33.5	1	15.13	42.4	1
Shanghai	6.71	57.7	—	6.98	58.8	—
Jiangsu	7.39	12.3	12	9.57	15.8	17
Zhejiang	4.18	10.8	16	10.00	25.7	6
Fujian	3.12	12.2	13	5.48	21.2	8
Shandong	5.73	7.8	26	14.9	19.1	13
Guangdong	7.48	12.7	10	11.08	18.7	15
Guangxi	2.96	8.2	24	4.31	11.8	25
Total	63.26	45.6		95.31	46.1	
II. INLAND						
Shanxi	3.49	13.9	8	5.31	21.0	9
Jilin	6.61	29.6	3	8.94	39.6	3
Heilongjiang	10.29	31.8	2	13.24	40.5	2
Anhui	4.74	9.6	18	7.08	14.3	20
Jiangxi	3.97	12.0	14	6.45	19.4	12
Henan	5.81	7.9	25	10.51	14.1	22
Hubei	6.33	13.4	9	8.28	17.3	16
Hunan	5.21	9.7	17	7.77	14.4	19
Sichuan	9.19	9.3	20	14.25	14.3	20
Guizhou	2.54	9.0	21	5.63	19.7	11
Yunnan	2.67	8.3	23	4.19	12.9	24
Shaanxi	3.61	12.6	11	5.49	19.0	14
Total	64.46	46.5		97.14	47.0	
III. BORDER						
Nei Mongol	4.45	23.4	4	5.56	28.9	4
Xizang	0.16	8.6	22	0.18	9.5	26
Gansu	2.22	11.4	15	3.00	15.3	18
Qinghai	0.65	17.0	6	0.80	20.5	10
Ningxia	0.58	15.0	7	0.88	22.5	7
Xinjiang	2.92	22.4	5	3.72	28.4	5
Total	10.98	7.9		14.13	6.8	
Grand Total	138.70	100.0		206.58	100.0	

Appendices

Sources: State Statistical Bureau, Department of Population Statistics (*The Population Census of China (Major Figures)*), pp. 16–17, and for the 1981 year-end data, TJNJ 1982, p. 90.

Note: In Henan, the 1982 figure is almost double the 1981 figure. In Zhejiang and Guizhou it is more than double. In Shandong it is almost treble. These gross inflations of the urban data reflect the extremely eccentric morphologies of *shi* in these provinces. For example, in Shandong places like Zibo are hundreds of square kilometres, but the rural territory is not divided into counties. The same has happened in Guizhou, and the bias is particularly due to the influence of Liupanshui here (a coal-mining 'municipality' covering an enormous region).

Table A4.1: Differing Chinese Estimates of the Contribution of Net Migration to the Growth of Aggregate Urban Population, Various Periods

	Aggregate urban growth due to net migration		Period
	%	no. (m.)	
i.	20	14.2	1949–79
ii.	22	14.5	1952–81
iii.	23	17.6	1949–81
iv.	33	25.0	1949–80
v.	17–35	12–25.0	1949–79
vi.	42	30.0	1949–79

Note: The present author's calculation is 34.6 per cent (32.9 m.) for the period 1949–82.
Sources:
i: Cai Yi, ZRKL, p. 80; ii: DGB, 8 May 1982; iii: BR, no. 28, 12 July 1982, p. 3; iv: Wu Youren, ZRKL, p. 97; v: Zhu Zhuo, RKYJ, no. 3 (1980), p. 12; vi: Zhu Zhuo, interview in Beijing, June 1982: this was 'the opinion of some colleagues'.

Figure A5.1: The Aihui-Tengchong Division of China's Territory

The Aihui-Tengchong division is a straight line between Aihui *xian* in Heilongjiang and Tengchong *xian* in Yunnan. On the left-hand side of this line there are 6 provincial-level divisions, and on the right, 23. The six provincial divisions account for over 60 per cent of China's land area, and in 1982 contained 6.1 per cent of the nation's population.

Table A5.2: Gross Value of Industrial Output by Province and Region, 1952 and 1982

| | Percentage of GVIO | | Change |
	1952	1982	(%)
I. COASTAL			
Beijing	2.4	4.1	69
Tianjin	5.4	3.8	42
Hebei	3.9	4.1	4
Liaoning	13.3	8.5	−36
Shanghai	19.1	11.4	−40
Jiangsu	7.6	9.0	19
Zhejiang	3.2	4.1	27
Fujian	1.2	1.6	31
Shandong	6.4	6.6	7
Guangdong	5.1	4.9	−4
Guangxi	1.0	1.6	58
Total	68.5	59.7	−13
II. INLAND			
Shanxi	1.9	2.4	27
Jilin	3.2	2.6	−20
Heilongjiang	5.6	4.8	−14
Anhui	1.9	2.6	40
Jiangxi	1.7	1.8	7
Henan	2.6	3.9	51
Hubei	2.8	4.9	74
Hunan	2.3	3.5	55
Sichuan	4.9	5.4	11
Guizhou	0.8	0.9	14
Yunnan	1.0	1.4	43
Shaanxi	1.1	2.0	79
Total	29.6	36.2	22
III. BORDER			
Nei Mongol	0.6	1.2	114
Xizang	—	—	—
Gansu	0.7	1.5	121
Qinghai	0.1	0.3	150
Ningxia	0.03	0.3	900
Xinjiang	0.5	0.8	57
Total	1.9	4.1	116

Sources: For 1982: TJNJ 1983, p. 234; for 1952: adapted from N. Lardy, *Economic Growth and Distribution in China* (Cambridge University Press, Cambridge, 1978), Tables A1 and A2, pp. 197–8.

Table A5.3: Total Population by Province and Region, 1953 and 1982

	1953 (m.)	1982 (m.)	Change (%)
I. COASTAL			
Beijing Tianjin Hebei }	42.00	70.53	29
Liaoning	20.57	35.92	75
Shanghai Jiangsu }	47.13	72.70	54
Zhejiang	22.87	39.24	72
Fujian	13.14	26.04	98
Shandong	50.14	74.94	49
Guangdong	34.77	59.81	72
Guangxi	19.56	36.84	88
Total	250.18 = 42.9%	416.02 = 41.1%	66
II. INLAND			
Shanxi	14.31	25.46	79
Jilin	11.29	22.58	100
Heilongjiang	11.90	32.81	176
Anhui	30.66	50.16	64
Jiangxi	16.77	33.48	97
Henan	43.91	75.20	71
Hubei	27.79	48.01	73
Hunan	33.23	54.52	64
Sichuan	65.69	100.22	53
Guizhou	15.04	28.75	91
Yunnan	17.47	32.83	88
Shaanxi	15.88	29.04	83
Total	303.94 = 52.2%	533.06 = 52.7%	75
III. BORDER			
Nei Mongol	7.74	19.37	150
Xizang	1.27	1.89	48
Gansu	11.29	19.75	75
Qinghai	1.68	3.93	134
Ningxia	1.64	3.93	140
Xinjiang	4.87	13.16	170
Total	28.49 = 4.9%	62.03 = 6.1%	118
GRAND TOTAL	582.61	1,011.11	73

Note: i. For the sake of comparability, Tianjin and Beijing are included in Hebei, and Shanghai is included in Jiangsu; ii. Percentage figures in totals for each region are of the national total (except for third column).

Sources: 1953: from the census of that year, as presented by J. S. Aird, 'Recent Provincial Population Figures', *China Quarterly*, no. 73 (1978), Tables 1 and 2, pp. 3 and 24. Aird's figures in Table 2 are adjusted for later boundary changes. The most important of these was the loss by Inner Mongolia (Nei Mongol) of large parts of its territory to Heilongjiang, Liaoning and Jilin. These were restored in 1979, so the data in Table A5.3 do not include Aird's adjustments. Other slight changes in provincial boundaries, such as that between Ningxia and Gansu in 1976, are ignored for present purposes.

1982: TJNJ 1983, p. 106; these figures exclude the armed forces.

Table A5.4: Urban Population by Province and Region, 1953 and
1981

	1953 (m.)	1981 (m.)	Change (%)
I. COASTAL			
Beijing			
Tianjin	10.11	13.84	37
Hebei			
Liaoning	8.65	11.85	37
Shanghai			
Jiangsu	13.73	14.10	3
Zhejiang	2.23	4.18	87
Fujian	1.58	3.12	97
Shandong	3.36	5.73	71
Guangdong	4.49	7.48	67
Guangxi	0.85	2.96	248
Total	45.08 = 57.8%	63.26 = 45.6%	40
II. INLAND			
Shanxi	1.85	3.49	89
Jilin	3.27	6.61	102
Heilongjiang	3.70	10.29	178
Anhui	2.05	4.74	131
Jiangxi	1.27	3.97	213
Henan	2.89	5.81	101
Hubei	2.39	6.33	165
Hunan	2.34	5.21	123
Sichuan	6.39	9.19	44
Guizhou	0.59	2.54	331
Yunnan	1.29	2.67	107
Shaanxi	1.57	3.61	130
Total	29.65 = 38.0%	64.46 = 46.5%	117
III. BORDER			
Nei Mongol	0.78	4.45	471
Xizang	0.16	0.16	—
Gansu	0.97	2.22	129
Qinghai	0.12	0.65	442
Ningxia	0.14	0.58	314
Xinjiang	0.53	2.92	451
Total	3.31 = 4.2%	10.98 = 7.9%	232
GRAND TOTAL	77.26	138.70	80

Note: To aid comparison, Beijing and Tianjin have been tabulated with Hebei, and Shanghai with Jiangsu. Percentage figures in the regional totals are of all national urban population.

Sources: 1953: Adapted from L. Orleans, *Every Fifth Child* (Eyre Methuen, London, 1972), Table 7, p. 71. Orleans derives these data from E. Ni, *Distribution of Urban and Rural Population of Mainland China: 1953 and 1958* (US Bureau of the Census, International Population Reports, Series P-95, no. 56, October 1960). Note the evaluation of Ni's data in E. Onoye, 'Regional Distribution of Urban Population in China', *The Developing Economies*, no. 8 (1971), pp. 112–19.

1981: TJNJ 1982, p. 90.

Table A5.5: Population Density by Province and Region, 1953 and 1982

	Persons per square kilometre	
	1953	1982
I. COASTAL		
Beijing ⎫		
Tianjin ⎬	194	327
Hebei ⎭		
Liaoning	141	247
Shanghai ⎫	435	658
Jiangsu ⎭		
Zhejiang	224	385
Fujian	109	215
Shandong	328	490
Guangdong	164	282
Guangxi	85	160
Average	194	323 (increase of 66%)
II. INLAND		
Shanxi	92	163
Jilin	60	120
Heilongjiang	25	70
Anhui	220	360
Jiangxi	101	201
Henan	263	450
Hubei	148	256
Hunan	158	260
Sichuan	116	177
Guizhou	86	163
Yunnan	44	83
Shaanxi	77	141
Average	100	176 (increase of 76%)
III. BORDER		
Nei Mongol	6.4	16.0
Xizang	1.1	1.6
Gansu	24.6	43.0
Qinghai	2.3	5.5
Ningxia	24.6	59.0
Xinjiang	3.0	8.0
Average	5.4	11.7 (increase of 118%)

Sources: Provincial population figures: see Table A5.3; areas of provinces: various Chinese atlases.

Table A5.6: Number of Designated Municipalities by Province and Region, 1953 and 1982

	1953	1982	
I. COASTAL			
Beijing	1	1	
Tianjin	1	1	
Hebei	12	12	
Liaoning	11	13	
Shanghai	1	1	
Jiangsu	12	11	
Zhejiang	7	9	
Fujian	4	7	
Shandong	9	13	
Guangdong	10	14	
Guangxi	4	7	
Total	72 (43%)	89 (36%)	(increase of 24%)
II. INLAND			
Shanxi	4	7	
Jilin	6	9	
Heilongjiang	5	14	
Anhui	7	14	
Jiangxi	6	10	
Henan	12	17	
Hubei	5	11	
Hunan	9	16	
Sichuan	11	13	
Guizhou	2	5	
Yunnan	3	6	
Shaanxi	5	6	
Total	75 (45%)	128 (52%)	(increase of 71%)
III. BORDER			
Nei Mongol	7	10	
Xizang	1	1	
Gansu	4	5	
Qinghai	1	2	
Ningxia	2	2	
Xinjiang	4	8	
Total	19 (11%)	28 (11%)	(increase of 47%)

Note: The percentage figures show the share of each region in total municipalities (166 for 1953 and 245 for 1982).
Sources: 1953: M. B. Ullman, 'Cities of Mainland China: 1953 and 1958' in G. Breese (ed.), *The City in Newly Developing Countries* (Prentice Hall, London, 1972), Table 1, p. 86; 1982: ZXQJ, 1983, pp. 1–3.

Table A5.7: Number of Cities Over 500,000 by Province and Region, 1953 and 1982

	500,000–999,999		Over 1 million		Over 500,000	
	1953	1982	1953	1982	1953	1982
I. COASTAL						
Beijing	—	—	1	1	1	1
Tianjin	—	—	1	1	1	1
Hebei	1	3	—	—	1	3
Liaoning	3	3	1	4	4	7
Shanghai	—	—	1	1	1	1
Jiangsu	1	3	1	1	2	4
Zhejiang	1	1	—	—	1	1
Fujian	1	1	—	—	1	1
Shandong	2	1	—	2	2	3
Guangdong	—	—	1	1	1	1
Guangxi	—	1	—	—	—	1
Total	9	13	6	11	15 (60%)	24 (50%)
II. INLAND						
Shanxi	1	1	—	1	1	2
Jilin	1	1	0	1	1	2
Heilongjiang	—	3	1	1	1	4
Anhui	—	2	—	—	—	2
Jiangxi	—	1	—	—	—	1
Henan	1	2	—	—	1	2
Hubei	—	—	1	1	1	1
Hunan	1	1	—	—	1	1
Sichuan	1	—	1	2	2	2
Guizhou	—	1	—	—	—	1
Yunnan	1	—	—	1	1	1
Shaanxi	1	—	—	1	1	1
Total	7	12	3	8	10 (40%)	20 (42%)
III. BORDER						
Nei Mongol	—	2	—	—	—	2
Xizang	—	—	—	—	—	—
Gansu	—	—	—	1	—	1
Qinghai	—	—	—	—	—	—
Ningxia	—	—	—	—	—	—
Xinjiang	—	1	—	—	—	1
Total	—	3	—	1	— (0%)	4 (8%)
Grand Total	16	28	9	20	25	48

Note: Percentage figures under regional totals are of grand totals in respective columns.
Sources: 1953: L. Orleans, *Every Fifth Child* (Eyre Methuen, London, 1972), Table 5, p. 61; 1982: TJNJ 1983, p. 165.

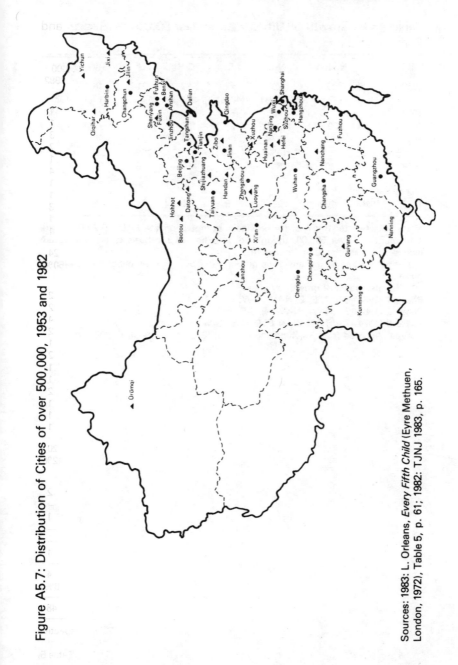

Figure A5.7: Distribution of Cities of over 500,000, 1953 and 1982

Sources: 1983: L. Orleans, *Every Fifth Child* (Eyre Methuen, London, 1972), Table 5, p. 61; 1982: TJNJ 1983, p. 165.

Table A5.8: Growth of Urban Places Over 50,000 by Region and Phase

	National	N-E	E	C-S	N	S-W	N-W
1953	151	20	42	37	21	16	13
	(39%)	(100%)	(40%)	(30%)	(14%)	(31%)	(38%)
1963	210	40	59	48	24	21	18
	(29%)	(19%)	(12%)	(19%)	(29%)	(67%)	(39%)
1973	271	57	66	57	31	35	25
	(11%)	(14%)	(14%)	(11%)	(16%)	(3%)	(16%)
1978	302	65	75	63	36	36	29
Increase							
1953−78 (%)	100	225	79	70	71	125	123

Notes: Six Greater Regions: for provincial composition see Figure 5.2. These are settlements of over 50,000, though no definition of the basis whereby they are judged urban is offered in the source.

The percentage figures are crude growth rates over the entirety of the respective phase.

Differential rates of growth by phase:

Phase 1 (1954−63): N-E, E, N-W, S-W, C-S, N

Phase 2 (1964−73): S-W, N-W, N, C-S, N-E, E

Phase 3 (1974−78): N, N-W, N-E, E, C-S, S-W

Source: Adapted from Xu Xueqiang *et al.*, JJDL, no. 3 (1983), p. 209.

Table A5.9: China's Settlements Over 50,000 in Population: Distribution by Size-class, 1953 and 1979

	NUMBER OF PLACES						POPULATION								
	all places		municipalities		non-*shi*		all places		municipalities				non-*shi* places		
	no.	%	no.	%	no.	%	no.	%	no.	%	%	%	no.	%	%
1953 Totals	**173**	**100.0**	**152**	**100.0**	**21**	**100.0**	**44.47**	**100.0**	**43.16**	**97.1**	**100.0**	**55.7**	**1.31**	**2.9**	**100.0**
Over 1 million	9	5.2	9	5.9	—	—	17.47	39.3	17.47	39.3	40.5	22.6	—	—	—
500,000–999,999	16	9.3	16	10.5	—	—	9.38	21.1	9.38	21.1	21.7	12.1	—	—	—
200,000–499,999	28	16.1	28	18.4	—	—	7.06	15.9	7.06	15.9	16.4	9.1	—	—	—
100,000–199,999	49	28.3	49	32.2	—	—	5.99	13.5	5.99	13.5	13.9	7.7	—	—	—
50,000– 99,999	71	41.0	50	32.9	21	100.0	4.57	10.3	3.26	7.3	7.6	4.2	1.31	2.9	100.0
Column	1	2	3	4	5	6	7	8	9	10	11	12	13	14	15
1979 Totals	**330**	**100.0**	**205**	**100.0**	**125**	**100.0**	**92.91**	**100.0**	**86.48**	**93.1**	**100.0**	**67.1**	**6.43**	**6.9**	**100.0**
Over 1 million	15	4.6	15	7.3	—	—	33.94	36.5	33.94	36.5	39.2	26.3	—	—	—
500,000–999,999	28	8.5	28	13.7	—	—	20.57	22.1	20.57	22.1	23.8	16.0	—	—	—
200,000–499,999	68	20.1	68	33.2	—	—	20.75	22.3	20.75	22.3	24.0	16.1	—	—	—
100,000–199,999	72	21.8	63	30.7	9	7.2	10.05	10.8	8.85	9.5	10.2	6.9	1.20	1.3	18.7
50,000– 99,999	147	44.6	31	15.1	116	92.8	7.60	8.2	2.37	2.6	2.7	1.8	5.23	5.6	81.3

Note: Urban populations in this table comprise non-agricultural population of places over 50,000. All absolute population figures in millions.

Columns:

10: Percentages of aggregate urban population of the places over 50,000.

11: Percentages of all municipal population.

12: Percentages of all registered urban population (1953 = 77.257m., 1979 = 128.86m.).

14: Percentages of aggregate urban population of the places over 50,000.

15: Percentages of all non-*shi* population included.

Sources: 1953: Adapted from M. B. Ullman, 'Cities of Mainland China: 1953–1959' in G. Breese (ed.), *The City in Newly Developing Countries* (Prentice Hall, London, 1972), Table 3, p. 91, and Table 4, p. 93; 1979: A wide variety of official but unpublished Chinese sources. The last three figures in columns 6 and 9 are estimates based on proportionate mid-size-class calculations.

Table A5.10: China's Cities of Over 500,000 and Over 1 Million in Their Non-agricultural Populations

i. 500,000–999,999

		Total *shiqu* population 1	*shiqu* Non-agricultural only 2	1/2 %
1.	Hangzhou	1.180	0.927	79
2.	Qiqihar	1.222	0.920	75
3.	Urumqi	0.947	0.899	94
4.	Zhengzhou	1.424	0.895	63
5.	Tangshan	1.333	0.887	67
6.	Changsha	1.072	0.859	80
7.	Baotou	1.042	0.853	82
8.	Shijiazhuang	1.070	0.845	79
9.	Guiyang	1.314	0.838	64
10.	Jilin	1.071	0.837	78
11.	Nanchang	1.046	0.837	80
12.	Yichun	0.803	0.748	93
13.	Fuzhou	1.122	0.709	63
14.	Handan	0.920	0.676	73
15.	Xuzhou	0.773	0.668	86
16.	Benxi	0.788	0.654	83
17.	Zibo	2.234	0.643	29
18.	Wuxi	0.799	0.637	80
19.	Jixi	0.793	0.613	77
20.	Datong	0.896	0.605	68
21.	Luoyang	0.978	0.582	60
22.	Suzhou	0.670	0.568	85
23.	Hefei	0.815	0.555	68
24.	Jinzhou	0.712	0.552	78
25.	Huainan	1.036	0.550	53
26.	Fuxin	0.636	0.534	84
27.	Nanning	0.866	0.525	61
28.	Hohhot	0.747	0.515	69
Total		28.309	19.929	average = 70%

Table A5.10 — continued

ii. Over 1 million

	Total *shiqu* population 1	*shiqu* Non-agricultural only 2	1/2 %
1. Shanghai	6.27	6.22	99
2. Beijing	5.55	4.77	86
3. Tianjin	5.13	3.92	76
4. Shenyang	4.02	3.03	75
5. Wuhan	3.23	2.73	85
6. Guangzhou	3.12	2.38	76
7. Harbin	2.55	2.15	76
8. Chongqing	2.65	1.94	73
9. Nanjing	2.13	1.74	82
10. Xi'an	2.18	1.61	74
11. Chengdu	2.47	1.41	84
12. Changchun	1.74	1.34	77
13. Taiyuan	1.75	1.28	73
14. Dalian	1.48	1.24	84
15. Lanzhou	1.43	1.08	76
16. Qingdao	1.18	1.08	92
17. Jinan	1.32	1.04	79
18. Fushun	1.19	1.04	87
19. Anshan	1.21	1.03	85
20. Kunming	1.43	1.02	71
Total	52.03	42.05	average = 81%

Notes: All absolute figures in millions. The designation in the two size-classes is based on non-agricultural population size. See chapter 3 for explanation of '*shiqu* population'.
Source: TJNJ 1983, p. 108.

Table A5.11: The Significance of Small-scale Industry to China's
Industrial Economy in the 1970s

Industry	Share of total output (per cent)	Description
Fertiliser		
(nitrogenous)	60	'locally-run'
(phosphorous)	80	'small'
Cement	57	'small'
Iron ore	28	'small mines'
Pig iron	28	'medium and small'
Crude steel	13	'medium and small'
Agricultural machinery	67	'local, small, medium'
Hydro-electricity generation capacity	34	'small'
Coal	28	'small'

Note: Data are reported as from various years between 1966 and 1975.
Source: C. Howe, *China's Economy — A Basic Guide* (Paul Elek, Granada
Publishing, London, 1978), Table 47, p. 128.

Table A6.1: Keypoint Cities (1982−end) — *shiqu* Populations and
Amount of Living Space per Person

City	Population of city districts (millions)	Average living space per head (square metres)
Beijing	5.55	5.3
Tianjin	5.13	2.9
Shanghai	6.27	4.3
Chongqing	2.65	2.5
Changchun	1.74	3.3
Guangzhou	3.12	3.4
Shenyang	4.02	2.6
Dalian	1.48	3.5
Qingdao	1.18	4.0
Wuhan	3.23	4.1
Chengdu	2.47	2.5
Nanjing	2.13	4.4
Jinan	1.32	3.6
Xi'an	2.18	3.0
Harbin	2.55	2.8
Lanzhou	1.43	2.9
Taiyuan	1.75	3.2

Notes: The population figures in millions refer to total populations of city districts
(*shiqu*), these including numbers of agricultural persons. The average per capita
living space from these figures (calculated from the gross floorspace and population
figures) is 3.6 square metres. If the agricultural population in the *shiqu* were
excluded, the available space would be somewhat less.
Source: TJNJ 1983, pp. 35−102.

Table A6.2: Cumulative State Housing Floorspace Constructed in Urban Areas, and Cumulative Rise in the Urban Population, 1949–82

Period	Cumulative increase in floorspace (million metre^2)	Cumulative increase in urban population (millions)	Average new floorspace available per capita (metre^2)
Restoration, 1950–2	13.4	13.98	1.0
1st FYP, 1953–7	108.0	41.84	2.6
2nd FYP, 1958–62	218.1	58.94	3.7
Readjustment, 1963–5	260.8	44.05	5.9
3rd FYP, 1966–70	314.8	48.89	6.4
4th FYP, 1971–5	440.5	54.06	8.2
5th FYP, 1976–80	675.4	82.63	8.2

Note: The cumulative total of urban housing living space built between 1949 and 1980 is 675.4 million square metres. If the figure depreciation is subtracted, the net cumulative total is just 470.4 million square metres. The per capita space availability on the basis of this net total is 5.7 square metres per person in 1980.
Source: TJNJ 1983, p. 357; for the urban population figures, see chapter 4, Tables 4.2, 4.6 and 4.9.

Table A6.3: Three Major Regions — Growth of Designated Municipalities, 1977–82

	1977 1	2	3	1982 1	2	3
I. COASTAL						
Beijing						
Tianjin						
Hebei	0	9	9	12	2	10
Liaoning	10	0	10	13	10	3
Shanghai						
Jiangsu	7	4	11	11	7	4
Zhejiang	3	0	3	9	3	6
Fujian	2	4	6	7	2	5
Shandong	4	5	9	13	5	8
Guangdong	8	2	10	14	10	4
Guangxi	4	2	6	7	4	3
Total	38	26	64 (34.2%)	86 (35.5%)	43	43
II. INLAND						
Shanxi	4	3	7	7	4	3
Jilin	2	7	9	9	2	7
Heilongjiang	6	5	11	14	7	7
Anhui	7	3	10	14	8	6
Jiangxi	3	5	8	10	4	6
Henan	4	10	14	17	6	11
Hubei	3	3	6	11	6	5
Hunan	3	7	10	16	5	11
Sichuan	4	7	11	13	4	9
Guizhou	1	3	4	5	2	3
Yunnan	2	2	4	6	2	4
Shaanxi	3	2	5	6	3	3
Total	42	57	99 (52.9%)	128 (52.9%)	53	75
III. BORDER						
Nei Mongol	3	6	9	10	3	7
Xizang	1	0	1	1	1	0
Gansu	2	2	4	5	3	2
Qinghai	1	0	1	2	1	1
Ningxia	2	0	2	2	2	0
Xinjiang	2	5	7	8	3	5
Total	11	13	24 (12.8%)	28 (11.6%)	13	15
Grand Total	91 (48.7%)	96 (51.3%)	187	242	109 (45.0%)	133 (55.0%)

Notes continued on next page

Notes: 1977: 1 — number of municipalities directly under provincial-level units; 2 — number of municipalities under prefectural-level units; 3 — total municipalities.

1982: 1 — total municipalities; 2 — number under provincial-level units; 3 — number under prefectural-level units.

Source: ZXQJ 1978 and ZXQJ 1983.

Analysis:

i. Changes 1977–82

Coastal	22 new municipalities	(33% increase)
Inland	29 new municipalities	(29% increase)
Border	4 new municipalities	(17% increase)

ii. Changes in proportions of total shi *in each region*

	1977	1982
Coastal	35.3	36.3
Inland	52.1	52.2
Border	12.6	11.5
	100.0	100.0

iii. Total increase in shi

In the five years 1977–82, the number of municipalities went up by 55 (29 per cent). In the 23 years between 1953 and 1976, there was a net increase of just 21 municipalities (from 164 to 185) — or 12 per cent.

iv. A note on the mode of designation

Of the 55 new *shi* created between the beginning of 1977 and the end of 1982, the majority (24) were previously seats of both county (*xian*) and prefectural (*diqu*) administrations. Fourteen were previously seats of county government alone, and 2 were seats of prefectures alone. The remaining 15 had no status in the administrative field system.

Almost all of the new *shi* followed the customary route of first becoming third-order (sub-prefectural) *shi*. The exceptions were the Special Economic Zones (*jingji tequ*) of Shenzhen and Zhuhai in Guangdong, which on their designation as *shi* directly became second-order; Dongying in Shandong, Liupanshui in Guizhou, and Jinchang (the new nickel mining and refining centre in Gansu) also rose directly to second-order status.

GLOSSARY

Chinese Journals in Chinese

CSGH   *Chengshi guihua* (*City Planning*), published by Chinese Architectural Association Urban Planning Academic Committee, Beijing.

CXJS   *Cheng xiang jianshe* (*Urban-Rural Construction*), published by Ministry for Urban-Rural Construction and Environmental Protection, Beijing.

HQ   *Hongqi* (*Red Flag*), theoretical journal of the Central Committee of the Chinese Communist Party.

JHLT   *Jianghan luntan* (*Jianghan Review*), (Wuhan).

JJDL   *Jingji dili* (*Economic Geography*), published jointly by the Chinese Geographical Association's Economic Geography Commission and Hunan Province's Economic Geography Research Institute.

JJGL   *Jingji guanli* (*Economic Management*).

JJYJ   *Jingji yanjiu* (*Economic Research*).

JWTS   *Jingji wenti tansuo* (*Exploration of Economic Problems*).

JZXB   *Jianzhu xuebao* (*Architectural Journal*), published by the Chinese Architectural Association, Beijing.

RKYJ   *Renkou yanjiu* (*Population Research*), published by the People's University, Beijing.

RKYJJ   *Renkou yu jingji* (*Population and Economy*), published by the Population Research Institute of the Beijing College of Economics.

ZGSK   *Zhongguo shehui kexue* (*Social Sciences in China*), published by the Chinese Academy of Sciences, Beijing.

Chinese Newspapers in Chinese

DGB   *Dagong bao,* published in Hong Kong and reflecting official Beijing opinion.

DZRB   *Dazhong ribao,* provincial daily newspaper of Shandong.

GMRB *Guangming ribao*, published daily in Beijing, and known as the 'intellectuals' newspaper'.

RMRB *Renmin ribao* (*People's Daily*), the official newspaper of the Chinese Communist Party, published in Beijing.

SJDB *Shijie jingji daobao* (*World Economic Reporter*), published in Shanghai.

ZGQB *Zhongguo qingnian bao* (*China Youth Daily*), published in Beijing.

Books in Chinese

BKNJ 1980 *Zhongguo baike nianjian 1980* (*The Encyclopaedic Yearbook of China, 1980*) (Zhongguo da baike quanshu, Beijing and Shanghai, August 1980). This volume uses 1979 year-end data.

BKNJ 1981 As above, but published in July 1981, with 1980 year-end data.

JJNJ 1982 *Zhongguo jingji nianjian 1981* (*The Economic Yearbook of China, 1981*), (Jingji guanli zazhi chubanshe, Beijing, 1982). This volume uses 1981 year-end data.

NDRZ *Renkou zhuanji* (*Special Issue on Population*), *Nanjing daxue xuebao, zhexue shehui kexue* (*Journal of Nanjing University, Philosophy and Social Sciences Edition*), *1981*.

TJNJ 1982 *Zhongguo tongji nianjian 1981* (*Statistical Yearbook of China*), compiled by the State Statistical Bureau, Beijing, and published in overseas edition by Jingji daobanshe (Hong Kong), October 1982. All series end with 1981 year-end data.

TJNJ 1983 *Zhonghua tongji nianjian 1983*, as above, except that all series end with 1982 year-end data.

ZFDJ *Zhongguo Renmin Gongheguo fensheng dituji (hanyu pinyin ban)* (*Atlas of the People's Republic of China, Chinese Romanization Edition*), (Ditu chubanshe, Beijing, 1977).

ZRKL *Zhongguo renkou kexue lunji* (*Symposium of Chinese Population Science* [sic]), *edited by the Beijing jingji xueyuan renkou jingji yanjiusuo* (Zhongguo xueshu chubanshe, Beijing, 1981).

ZXQJ   *Zhonghua renmin gongheguo xingzheng quhua jiance*
(1977–83) (*Administrative Divisions of the People's Republic of China*), published annually by the Ditu chubanshe, Beijing. The data are all of the previous year-end.

Chinese Newspapers and Magazines in English

BR   *Beijing Review* (called *Peking Review* before 1980). A weekly Chinese current affairs magazine.
CR   *China Reconstructs* — a monthly current affairs magazine.
TKP   *Ta Kung Pao* — weekly English edition of the Chinese daily *Dagong bao*.
XHDR *Xinhua Daily Report*, bulletin of news items produced by the official Xinhua (New China) Newsagency, Beijing (reprinted in Hong Kong, London, etc.).

Other

GCPP *Glossary of Chinese Political Phrases*, by Lau Yee-fui, Ho Wan-yee, Yeung Sai-cheung (Union Research Institute, Hong Kong, 1977).

BIBLIOGRAPHY

Articles in Chinese Journals

Anon., 'Guoji renkou xuejia Beijing yuanzhuohuiyi dabiao faxin zhaiya' ('Summary of the Statements of the International Beijing Round-Circle Conference on Demography'), RKYJ, no. 1 (1981), pp. 2–13.

Bai Demao, 'Weixing cheng nengqi kongzhi shiqu guimo de zuoyong ma?' ('Are Satellite Towns a Useful Means of Controlling the Population in Urban Districts?'), JZXB, no. 4 (1981), pp. 24–7.

Bao Hui, Zhao Changxin, ' "Shi guan xian" tuidong le nongcun jingji de quanmian fanrong' ('The System of "Cities Governing Counties" Promotes All-round Prosperity'), JJGL, no. 3 (1983), pp. 15–18.

Bu Juecha, 'Xianzhen he nongcun jizhen jianshe tanlun' ('An Enquiry into the Construction of County Seats and Rural Market Towns'), CXJS, no. 12 (1983), pp. 21–2.

Chen Weibang, 'Jiaqiang chengshi jianshe de jige wenti' ('Some questions concerning the strengthening of urban construction work'), JJYJ, no. 11 (1979), pp. 53–9.

Chou Weizhi, 'Dui jianguo yilai renkou qianyi de chubu yanjiu' ('A Preliminary Analysis of Migration Since the Founding of the People's Republic of China'), RKYJJ, no. 4 (1981), pp. 8–13/55.

Dong Liming, 'Tan chengshi de kongzhi fu fazhan' ('On the Control and Development of Cities'), CXJS, no. 12 (1983), pp. 19–20.

Feng Lanrui, Zhao Lukuan, 'Dangqian wo guo chengzhen laodongzhe jiuye wenti' ('On the Question of the Present Situation Regarding the Employment of China's Urban Workforce'), ZGSK, no. 6 (1981), pp. 189–200.

Feng Yufeng, 'Fazhan xiao chengshi shi wo guo chengshihua weiyi zhengque de daolu ma?' ('Is the Development of Small Cities China's Sole Correct Road to Urbanisation?'), JJDL, no. 2 (1983), pp. 136–40.

Fu Wenwei, 'Shijie chengshihua he Zhongguo chengshihua de daolu' ('World Urbanisation and China's Road to Urbanisation'), JZXB, no. 4 (1983), pp. 25–9.

Gu Shutang, Chang Xiuze, 'Weihai shi "changduigua gou, chanpin kuosan" de diaocha' ('A Good Form of Cooperation Between Town and Country — An Investigation of "Factory-Team Links" and "Product Diffusion" in Weihai Municipality'), HQ, no. 23 (December 1980), pp. 21–5.

He Gongjian, 'Zhuzai wenti de xianshi he jiejue wenti de shexiang' ('The Reality of the Housing Question and Ideas on its Solution'), JHLT, no. 6 (1980), pp. 13–16.

Hu Huanyong, 'Wo guo renkou dili fenbu gaishu' ('The General State of China's Population Distribution'), RKYJ, no. 4 (1982), pp. 25–9/46.

Hu Xuwei, 'Dui wo guo chengzhenhua shuiping de pouxi' ('A Close Analysis of China's Urbanisation Level'), CSGH, no. 2 (1983), pp. 27–8/26.

Huang Daming, Hu Runsong, Jin Zhi, 'Kaizhan jingji jishu xiezuo, fahui yanhai

282

chengshi zuoyong' ('Establish Economic and Technical Cooperation, Give Full Play to the Coastal Cities'), JJYJ, no. 2 (1983), pp. 51–5/67.

Jin Daqin, '"Renkou chengshihua" yu jianshe xiao chengzhen' ('"Urbanisation" and the Development of Small Cities and Towns'), JJGL, no. 5 (1981), pp. V3–V35/V11.

Jing Ping, 'Yao wending liangshi bozhong mianji' ('It is Necessary to Stabilise the Area Under Grain'), HQ, no. 5 (March 1983), pp. 32–3.

Li Bianren, 'Wo guo chengzhenhua daolu wenti de taolun' ('A Discussion on China's Road to Urbanisation'), CSGH, no. 2 (1983), pp. 27–8/26.

Li Mengbai, 'Wo guo chengzhen fazhan de zhanwang' ('China's Urban Development and Its Future Prospects'), CXJS, no. 12 (1983), pp. 16–18.

Lin Gang, 'Nongye luohou shi wo guo renkou xunzeng de genben yuanyin' ('The Backwardness of Agriculture is the Fundamental Reason for China's Rapid Increase in Population'), RKYJ, no. 1 (1981), pp. 17–22.

Ma Qingyu, 'Wo guo chengzhenhua de tedian ji fazhan qushi de chubu fensan' ('A Preliminary Analysis of Characteristics and Development Trends of China's Urbanisation'), JJDL, no. 2 (1983), pp. 126–31.

Qian Lingjuan, Xu Bing, 'Beijing shi de renkou fazhan qingkuang he dangqian de renwu' ('The Situation Regarding the Growth of Population in Beijing, and Our Present Tasks'), RKYJ, no. 1 (1980), pp. 39–44.

Qin Renshan, 'Guanyu renkou chengshihua de wenti' ('On the Question of Urbanisation'), RKYJ, no. 3 (1981), pp. 12–17.

Shen Lang, 'Beijing shi de renkou zengzhang yu huanjing baohu' ('Population Increase and Environmental Protection in Beijing Municipality'), RKYJJ, no. 4 (1982), pp. 17–19.

Sun Jingzhi, 'Guanyu Zhongguo renkou fenbu wenti' ('Concerning the Question of the Distribution of China's Population'), RKYJ, no.2 (1982), pp. 10–11.

Su Xing, 'Zenyang shi zhuzai wenti jiejue de kuai xie?' ('How to Solve the Urban Housing Problem More Quickly?'), HQ, no. 2 (January 1980), pp. 8–11.

Sun Hongzhi, 'Zhongxin chengshi lingdao nongcun you hen da de youyuexing' ('There are Very Great Advantages in the System of Central Cities Ruling the Countryside'), JJGL, no. 2 (1983), pp. 37–9.

Wang Xiangming, 'Lun laodong guoli yu zijin buzu de maodun' ('On the Contradiction Between the Excess of Labour and the Shortage of Capital'), RKYJ, no. 2 (1982), pp. 20–4.

Wang Xinrong, Chen Xiuying, 'Xiao chengzhen he nongcun jizhen de fazhan qianjing' ('Prospects for the Development of Small Cities and Towns, and Rural Market Towns'), JZXB, no. 4 (1983), pp. 35–8.

Xu Xueqiang, 'Shenghui chengshi renkou guimo de fazhan yu kongzhi' ('The Development and Control of the Population of Provincial Capitals'), CSGH, no. 4 (1982), pp. 41–5.

Xu Xueqiang, Hu Huaying, Zhang Jun, 'Wo guo chengzhen fenbu ji qi yanbian de jige tezheng' ('China's Urban Distribution and the Emergence of Certain Traits'), JJDL, no. 3 (1983), pp. 205–12.

Yang Chenggang, 'Tan nongye laodongli guosheng wenti' ('A discussion on the Question of the Surplus Rural Labour Force'), RKYJ, no. 5 (1983), pp. 22–6.

Yang Jingying, 'Guoli nongye laodongli de chulu hezai' ('What Path for the Surplus Agricultural Labour Force?'), RKYJJ, no. 4 (1982), pp. 13–16.

Zhao Lukuan, 'Zai lun laodong jiuye wenti' ('A Further Discussion on the

Employment Question'), RKYJ, no. 4 (1981), pp. 18–24.

Zhou Guangyang, 'Dui jiji fazhan xiao chengshi de renshi he jidian chu jian' ('Some Humble Opinions on the Question of Actively Developing Small Cities'), JZXB, no. 4 (1983), pp. 33–4/38.

Zhou Yixing, 'Lun wo guo chengzhenhua de diyu chayi' ('A Discussion on China's Regional Differentials in Urbanisation'), CSGH, no. 2 (1983), pp. 17–21/38.

Zhu Zhuo, 'Shilun wo guo renkou heli fenbu wenti' ('A Preliminary Discussion on the Rationality of China's Population Distribution'), RKYJ, no. 3 (1980), pp. 11–17.

Zuo Xiantang, 'Lun wo guo nongcun renkou wenti' ('A Discussion of China's Rural Population Question'), JWTS, no. 5 (1982), pp. 38–42.

Articles in Chinese Special Publication

Cai Yi, 'Zhongguo ruhe chengshihua' ('What Form of Urbanisation for China?'), in NDRZ, pp. 80–2.

Ding Jingxi, 'Guanyu wo guo chengshihua daolu wenti jiqi zai Jiangsu de tansuo' ('An Investigation into the Question of China's Road to Urbanisation, and the Situation in Jiangsu'), in NDRZ, pp. 72–9.

Sun Jingzhi, Li Muzhen, 'Zhongguo renkou yu guotu jingji kaifa' ('China's Population and the Opening-up of the Space-Economy'), in ZRKL, pp. 64–70.

Wei Jingsheng, 'Fazhan zhong guojia de dushihua' ('Urbanisation in Developing Countries'), in ZRKL, pp. 105–12.

Wu Youren, 'Guanyu wo guo shehuizhuyi chengshihua wenti' ('On the Question of China's Socialist Urbanisation'), in ZRKL, pp. 96–101.

Books and Articles in English

Aird, J. S., 'The Preliminary Results of China's 1982 Census', *China Quarterly*, no. 96 (December 1983), pp. 615–40.

——, 'Recent Provincial Population Figures', *China Quarterly*, no. 73 (1978), pp. 1–44.

Cell, C. P., 'De-Urbanization in China: The Urban-Rural Contradiction', *Bulletin, Concerned Asian Scholars*, vol. 11, no. 1 (1979), pp. 62–72.

Chang Sen-dou, 'The Changing System of Chinese Cities', *Annals of the Association of American Geographers*, vol. 66, no. 3 (September 1976), pp. 398–415.

Chao Kang, 'Industrialization and Urban Housing in Communist China', *Journal of Asian Studies*, vol. XXV, no. 3 (May 1966), pp. 381–95.

Chen Cheng-siang, 'Population Growth and Urbanization in China, 1953–1970', *Geographical Review*, vol. 63, no. 1 (January 1973), pp. 55–72.

DiMiao, A. J., Jr., *Soviet Urban Housing: Problems and Policies* (Praeger, New York, 1974).

Elvory, P., and Lavely, W. R., 'Rustication, Demographic Change and Development in Shanghai', *Asian Survey*, vol. XVII, no. 5 (May 1976), pp. 440–55.

Engels, F., *The Housing Question* (Progress Publishers, Moscow, 1954).

Farina, M. B., 'Urbanization, De-urbanization and Class Struggle in China 1949–79', *International Journal of Urban and Regional Research*, vol. IV

(December 1980), pp. 487–501.

Friedman, E., 'On Maoist Conceptualizations of the Capitalist World System', *China Quarterly*, no. 80 (December 1979), pp. 806–37.

Gayn, M., 'Mao Tse-Tung Reassessed', in F. Schurmann and O. Schell (eds.), *China Readings — 3: Communist China* (Penguin Books, Harmondsworth, 1968), pp. 91–107.

Gutnov, A., *The Ideal Communist City* (first published in Moscow, 1966; English edition: George Braziller, New York, 1970).

Howe, C., *China's Economy — A Basic Guide* (Elek, Granada Publishing, London, 1978).

———, 'The Supply and Administration of Urban Housing in Mainland China: The Case of Shanghai', *China Quarterly*, no. 33 (1968), pp. 73–97.

Kau Ying-mao, 'Urban and Rural Strategies in the Chinese Communist Revolution', in J. W. Lewis (ed.), *Peasant Rebellion and Communist Revolution in Asia* (Stanford University Press, Stanford, 1974), pp. 253–70.

Kueh, Y. Y., 'Economic Reform in China at "Xian" Level', *China Quarterly*, no. 96 (December 1983), pp. 665–88.

Lardy, N. R., *Economic Growth and Distribution in China* (Cambridge University Press, Cambridge, 1978).

Lin, C., 'Urbanization and Economic Development in Communist China', Independent Research Paper, MIT, 1971–2.

Lissitzky, E., *Russia — An Architecture for World Revolution* (first published in Vienna in 1930; English edition: Lund Humphries, London, 1970).

Ma, L. J. C., 'Anti-Urbanism in China', *Proceedings of the Association of American Geographers*, vol. 8 (1976), pp. 114–18.

Mao Tse-tung, 'On Coalition Government', in *Selected Works of Mao Tse-tung*, Volume III (Foreign Languages Press, Peking, 1965), pp. 205–26.

———, 'On the Ten Major Relationships', in *Selected Works of Mao Tse-tung*, Volume V (Foreign Languages Press, Peking, 1977), pp. 284–307.

———, 'Report on an Investigation of the Peasant Movement in Hunan', in *Selected Works of Mao Tse-tung*, Volume I (Foreign Languages Press, Peking, 1965), pp. 23–59.

———, 'Report to the Second Plenary Session of the Seventh Central Committee of the Communist Party of China', in *Selected Works of Mao Tse-tung*, Volume IV (Foreign Languages Press, Peking, 1961), pp. 365–71.

Marx, K., *Critique of the Gotha Programme* (Foreign Languages Press, Peking, 1972).

Marx, K., and Engels, F., 'Manifesto of the Communist Party', in *Karl Marx and Frederick Engels, Selected Works in Three Volumes* (Progress Publishers, Moscow, 1954), vol. 1, pp. 98–137.

Meisner, M., *Li Ta-chao and the Origins of Chinese Marxism* (Harvard University Press, Cambridge, Mass., 1967).

Murphey, R., 'Chinese urbanization under Mao', *Urbanization and Counter-Urbanization*, vol. 11 (1976), pp. 311–28.

———, 'The City as Centre of Change: Western Europe and China', *Annals of the Association of American Geographers*, vol. 44 (1954), pp. 349–62.

Onoye, E. T., 'Regional Distribution of Urban Population in China', *The Developing Economies*, no. 1 (1971), pp. 93–127.

Orleans, L., *Every Fifth Child: The Population of China* (Eyre Methuen, London,

1972).

———, 'The Recent Growth of China's Urban Population', *Geographical Review*, vol. 49 (1959), pp. 43–57.

Paine, S., 'Spatial Aspects of Chinese Development: Issues, Outcomes and Policies, 1949–1979', *Journal of Development Studies*, vol. 17 (January 1981), pp. 132–95.

Salter, C. L., 'Chinese Experiments in Urban Space: The Quest for an Agropolitan China', *Habitat*, vol. 1, no. 1 (1976), pp. 19–35.

Schram, S. R., *The Political Thought of Mao Tse-tung*, 6th edn (Praeger Publishers, New York, 1976).

Schurmann, F., *Ideology and Organization in Communist China*, 2nd edn (University of California Press, Berkeley, 1968).

Shabad, T., *China's Changing Map* (Praeger, New York, 1972).

Shen Bingyu, 'Urbanization in China: Policies and Population Redistribution', unpublished MA thesis, Brown University, Sociology Department, June 1981.

Stalin, J. V., *Economic Problems of Socialism in the USSR* (Foreign Languages Press, Peking, 1972).

State Statistical Bureau, Department of Population Statistics, *The 1982 Population Census of China (Major Figures)* (Economic Information and Agency, Hong Kong, 1982).

Tian Xueyuan, 'A Survey of Population Growth Since 1949', in Liu Zheng, Song Jian (eds,), *China's Population: Problems and Prospects* (New World Press, Beijing, 1981).

Tien, H. Y., 'The Demographic Significance of Organized Population Transfers in Communist China', *Demography*, vol. 1 (1864), pp. 220–6.

Ullman, M. B., 'Cities of Mainland China: 1953–1959' in Breese, G. (ed.), *The City in Newly Developing Countries* (Prentice Hall, London, 1972), pp. 81–103.

United Nations, *Demographic Indicators of Countries, Estimates and Projections as Assessed in 1980* (UN, Department of International Economic and Social Affairs, New York, 1982).

———, *Demographic Yearbook 1981* (UN, Department of International Economic and Social Affairs, Statistical Office, New York, 1983).

Vogel, E., *Canton Under Communism: Programs and Politics in a Provincial Capital, 1949–1968* (Harvard University Press, Cambridge, Mass., 1969).

Wakeman, F., Jr., *Strangers at the Gate: Social Disorder in South China, 1839–1861* (University of California Press, Berkeley, 1966).

White, L. T., III, 'The Chinese Model of Urbanization: Population and Capital Aspects', unpublished paper prepared for the Annual Meeting of the American Political Science Association, Chicago, September 1976.

World Bank, 'China: Socialist Economic Development', 9 vols. (World Bank internal publication, Washington, June 1981).

Xu Dixin *et al.*, *China's Search for Economic Growth: The Chinese Economy Since 1949* (New World Press, Beijing, 1982).

Ye Shunzan, 'Urbanization and Housing in China', *Asian Geographer*, vol. 1, no. 2 (1982), pp. 1–11.

INDEX